The Educational Spectrum

The Educational Spectrum

Orientations to Curriculum

John P. Miller

Longman

New York & London

375
M 648e

THE EDUCATIONAL SPECTRUM
Orientations to Curriculum

Longman Inc., 95 Church Street, White Plains, N.Y. 10601
Associated companies, branches, and representatives
throughout the world.

Developmental Editor: Nicole Benevento
Editorial and Production Supervisor: Ferne Y. Kawahara
Manufacturing Supervisor: Marion Hess

Library of Congress Cataloging in Publication Data
Miller, John P., 1943–
  The educational spectrum.
  Bibliography: p.
  Includes index.
  1. Teaching. 2. Education — Curriculum. I. Title.
LB1025.2.M477 1983   375   82-21642
ISBN 0–582–28385-X
Manufactured in the United States of America
9 8 7 6 5 4 3 2   91 90 89 88 87 86 85

To My Father

Contents

Preface

- The primary focus of schooling should be the transmittal of basic values.
- Schools should not try to do so much and simply concentrate on basic skills.
- Schools should teach children how to think and solve complex problems.
- It is impossible for the teacher to ignore the various needs of the whole child since these needs are interrelated.
- Education should help overcome the main problems that face society, such as racism, poverty, and economic decay.

Each of these statements reflects some basic stance toward education, or an orientation to curriculum. In this book I discuss seven orientations and their variations—behavioral, subject/disciplines, social, developmental, cognitive process, humanistic, and transpersonal. My aim is to provide a straightforward and thorough analysis of the various orientations so that teachers can clarify their own thinking about how they approach teaching and learning in the classroom.

Chapter 1 provides a brief overview of the orientations and how they can be applied. In the next seven chapters the orientations are discussed. Generally, these chapters contain three components. The first part of the chapter outlines the theoretical background to the orientation. Next, the programs and classroom strategies associated with the orientations are presented. In the final section of the chapter, the orientations are examined in terms of their contributions and limitations. The reader should be aware that I have written two books which reflect the humanistic and transpersonal orientations and that my own perspective on curriculum is rooted in these orientations. To some degree my analysis of the orientations reflects this perspective. However, the humanistic orientation has definite shortcomings, and I have not attempted to gloss over its weaknesses in Chapter 7.

In the last chapter I discuss various clusters or combinations of orientations. Since teachers do not usually adhere to just one orientation, their philosophy reflects some cluster of positions or a meta-orientation.

The teachers whom I work with in Northwestern Ontario have contributed a great deal to this book. In several courses and workshops I have had the opportunity to discuss these orientations and their relationship to the classroom. One teacher, Shirley Luft, has been instrumental in assisting me in examining the orientations and their implications for teaching.

I would also like to thank the Ontario Institute for Studies in Education, which provided the study leave so I could write this book. Finally, I would like to thank Margaret Iglinski, who has typed this manuscript with such care.

John P. Miller

Acknowledgments

Excerpts from Richard B. Smith, "Educational Objectives and the Systematic Improvement of Instruction," in *Four Psychologies Applied to Education: Freudian, Behavioral, Humanistic, Transpersonal*, edited by Thomas B. Roberts. Copyright © 1975 by Schenkman Publishing Co. Reprinted with permission of the publisher.

Excerpts and figure 1 from H. H. McAshan, *Competency-Based Education and Behavioral Objectives*. Copyright © 1979 by Educational Technology Publications. Reprinted with permission of the publisher.

Excerpts from the Biological Sciences Curriculum Study, *Biology Teachers' Handbook*. Copyright © 1978 by John Wiley & Sons. Reprinted with permission of the publisher.

"Inquiry into Inquiry," from Bernice Goldmark, "Critical Thinking: Deliberate Method," in *Social Education*, vol. 30 (May 1966). Reprinted with permission of the National Council for the Social Studies.

Excerpts from James P. Shaver and William Strong, *Facing Value Decisions: Rationale-Building for Teachers*. Copyright © 1976 by Wadsworth Publishing Company, Inc. Reprinted with permission of Wadsworth Publishing Company, Belmont, California.

Table 2 is from Donald W. Oliver and James P. Shaver, *Teaching Public Issues in the High School*. Logan, Utah: Utah State University Press 1974 (first printed by Houghton Mifflin Co., 1966). Reprinted with permission of the authors.

Excerpts from Carl Bereiter, "Games to Teach Thinking," first published by The Ontario Institute for Studies in Education in *Orbit* 11, vol. 3, no. 1, 1972. Reprinted with permission of *Orbit*.

Figure 2 is from Floyd G. Robinson, John Tickle, and David W. Brison, *Inquiry Training: Fusing Theory and Practice*. Copyright © 1972 by The Ontario Institute for Studies in Education. Reprinted with permission of OISE Publications.

Figure 2 is from Floyd G. Robinson, John Tickle, and David W. Brison, "Elementary School Thinking," first published by The Ontario Institute for Studies in Education in *Orbit* 32, vol. 7, no. 2, 1976. Reprinted with permission of *Orbit*.

Excerpts from Taba, Durkin, Fraenkel, and McNaughton, *Teacher's Handbook for Elementary Social Studies*. Copyright © 1971 by Addison-Wesley, Reading, Massachusetts. Pages 98, 99, 100, 103 reprinted with permission of the publisher.

Figure 4 is from George M. Gazda et al., *Human Relations Development: A Manual for Educators*. Copyright © 1973 by Allyn and Bacon, Inc. Reprinted with permission of the publisher.

Excerpts from *Education in the Primary and Junior Divisions* (1975) and *Science: Curriculum Guideline for the Intermediate Division* (1978) reprinted with permission of Ministry of Education, Ontario.

1

The Educational Spectrum

Each of us has his or her own distinct way of seeing things, or own world view. Our world view is a mixture of our values, attitudes, and perceptions and helps us organize what is happening around us. Our world view is our "map" of reality. This map, which is shaped by our background, experiences, and culture, will provide the context for how we see things.

Consider the following situation. Four psychologists are observing and interviewing a child. The child has been rather aggressive and each psychologist has an opportunity to interview the child and recommend the appropriate form of therapy. However, each of these psychologists has a different orientation to psychotherapy and thus sees the child in a different way. One psychologist comes to the interview with a Freudian background and sees the child's troubles in the context of early childhood experience. He recommends that past conflicts and identifications be examined and subjected to analysis. A second psychologist, however, comes to the interview with a social or family perspective. This psychologist chooses to view the child's problem within the context of the current family situation. She recommends treatment within the family so that the parents are included in the therapy sessions. A third psychologist is a humanist and after talking to the child recommends that therapy focus on the present concerns and feelings of the child. He suggests an accepting therapeutic atmosphere for discussion of these concerns with the child. Finally, the fourth psychologist is a behaviorist. She suggests that the child's environment be controlled in order to extinguish the negative behaviors and reinforce the positive behaviors.

Teachers, like psychologists, have orientations that influence the way they see children and how they work with students. This book

1

attempts to clarify these basic curriculum orientations so that we can see how we approach teaching and learning.

What is a curriculum orientation? It is a basic stance to teaching and learning. It encompasses a number of dimensions at both the theoretical and practical levels. Some of these dimensions include:

Educational aims. Each orientation has certain basic goals which provide an overall direction for the orientation.

Conception of the learner. The orientations have a view of the learner. Some orientations focus on the learner as an active agent; others view the student in a more responsive mode.

Conception of the learning process. The learning process can also vary with the respective orientations. For example, in the transpersonal orientation the emphasis is on the inner life of the students, while in other orientations learning is related to change in student behavior.

Conception of the instructional process. Each orientation has some conception of the steps the teacher should engage in to carry out instruction. These steps can be very specific or merely general guidelines.

Conception of the learning environment. Orientations also have some view of how the learning environment should be structured and what learning materials are appropriate. In some orientations the ideal environment is loosely structured; in other orientations the environment is highly structured.

The teacher's role. The role of the teacher also differs with the various orientations. In some orientations the teacher takes a strong directive role; in others the teacher's role is more nearly that of a facilitator of learning.

Conception of how learning should be evaluated. Evaluation procedures also vary with the different orientations. Some orientations rely on criterion-referenced tests; others use more experimental, open-ended techniques.

This book explores various orientations so teachers can clarify their approach to teaching and learning. This clarification process is ongoing as our curriculum orientation is constantly being refined by our experience. The orientations explored in this book include:

1. Behavioral
2. Subject/disciplines
3. Social
4. Developmental
5. Cognitive process

6. Humanistic
7. Transpersonal or holistic.

At one end of the educational spectrum are orientations which focus on the external person (e.g., student behavior). At the other end of the spectrum there is more stress on the inner person—his or her thoughts, feelings, and images. In the middle of the spectrum are the orientations which focus on the interaction between the inner and outer person. It should be noted this is not the only way of conceptualizing the relationships between the orientations. In the last chapter other relationships between the orientations are examined. However, the initial presentation of the orientation is along the inner–outer spectrum.

Outer person   Inner person

Behavioral Subject Social Developmental Cognitive Humanistic Transpersonal

A brief description of the orientations follows.

Behavioral Orientation

This orientation to curriculum is concerned with specific teaching methodologies that lead to specific behaviors. Thus, the teacher is concerned with shaping student behavior. The environment is structured so that the student is introduced to the appropriate stimuli. This orientation has been used in special education programs for the mentally retarded. In these programs learning tasks are often broken down into small components so that the child can succeed in small, definable activities. For example, tasks such as washing one's hands or tieing one's shoe are broken down into manageable steps so that the student can complete each component successfully. In all of these cases behavior is brought under environmental control. In the behavioral orientation it is important that teachers be able to describe student behavior in specific terms so that it can be observed and so that a structured program can be developed.

Competency-based education is also within the behavioral orientation. Through a structured sequence the students gain specific skills or competencies, which are usually evaluated through criterion-referenced tests.

B. F. Skinner has been one of the principal spokesmen for the behavioral orientation. Although some of his work has generated controversy, variations of the behavioral orientation have been adapted to many contexts and include programs in self-control, assertiveness training, and stress reduction. Educational technology and the use of computers are also associated with this orientation, since there is an emphasis on efficient instructional procedures.

Subject/Disciplines Orientation

The subject/disciplines orientation places primary emphasis on subject matter and the way that subject matter is developed and organized. In many respects this remains the primary orientation in most schools, particularly in secondary schools and universities, where various disciplines or subjects provide the basic organizing structure for the overall curriculum. Some individuals focus on traditional subjects and mastery of basic skills and thus are committed to a subject orientation. The back-to-basics movement is within this perspective.

Other individuals have focused on certain academic disciplines (e.g., science, math, language, etc.). These individuals argue that the academic disciplines have unique structures that allow for the development of new knowledge. The purpose of education, then, is to immerse the student in the structure of the various academic disciplines.

Sputnik gave this disciplines orientation a great deal of impetus in the late fifties and early sixties when many curriculum theorists focused on this orientation. Jerome Bruner was one of those theorists and he expounded on the disciplines orientation in his book, *The Process of Education*. It was also during this period that curriculum projects were developed and focused on such areas as math, physics, and biology. Specialists in these fields were recruited to help write new curriculum.

Social Orientation

This orientation places primary emphasis on social experience. This perspective sometimes focuses on cultural transmission, that is, the curriculum is seen as a socializing agent where the child is inculcated in the traditions and mores of society. This orientation in its purest form has occurred in totalitarian societies where the school is seen as a socializing agent. Here teachers inculcate the child in the philosophy of the state.

In a democratic society, however, the social orientation is conceptualized in a different manner. In the democratic process orientation, school is seen as a place where students can critically examine issues. Citizenship education is often developed within this orientation, as the school is seen as a place where children develop skills to participate in the democratic process. Thus the teacher focuses on developing critical thinking skills, group process skills, and other skills integral to participating in a democratic society.

Finally, there is a third social orientation, the social change position, which suggests the school should be at the forefront in dealing with social problems. For example, Fred Newmann has developed an approach that actively involves students in social change in the community. This model is described in his book, *Education for Citizen Action*.

Cognitive Process Orientation

This orientation has its roots in cognitive psychology and focuses on the development of cognitive skills. The process curriculum focuses on observation, analysis, synthesis, and evaluation as well as other intellectual skills. Unlike skills developed by the disciplines orientation, these skills are not necessarily developed in the context of a specific discipline but usually around specific tasks or problems. In fact, problem solving is a major focus within this orientation.

The development of intellectual autonomy is a major goal of this orientation. The process curriculum aims to develop skills so that the individual can examine problems, consider alternative solutions, evaluate those alternatives, choose an alternative, then implement and evaluate the solution.

David Ausubel and Carl Bereiter are names that we associate with this orientation. Ausubel, for example, has developed an advance organizer approach so that students can organize ideas and information around key concepts. This process is designed to facilitate the retention and conceptualization of data. Bereiter helped develop a conceptual skills program for preschool children in the sixties. Since then, Bereiter has argued that schools should focus on the development of cognitive skills and stay away from the development of personality and values education. Instead, he feels schools should concentrate on reasoning, analysis, and skill development.

Developmental Orientation

The developmental orientation is organized around the concept that children pass through distinct stages of ego, cognitive, and moral development. The focus of the orientation is not to accelerate development but to realize integration of the various aspects (e.g., ego, moral, cognitive, etc.) and to prevent stage retardation so that development is not arrested.

One of the main proponents of this orientation is Lawrence Kohlberg, whose work in moral development is well known and whose article, "Development as an Aim of Education," helped clarify the developmental orientation. Kohlberg argues that the developmental orientation is a direct descendant of the work of John Dewey.

Two other theorists with whom we associate this orientation are Erik Erikson and Jean Piaget. Although neither of these individuals is viewed as an educational theorist, their work has been applied to educational contexts. Piaget's work has had an impact on early childhood education and Erikson's ideas on adolescence have influenced some secondary school programs. Kohlberg has been more directly involved in education and has supported curriculum work in moral education.

Humanistic Orientation

The humanistic orientation has been influenced in part by humanistic psychology in general and the work of Carl Rogers and Abe Maslow in particular. Both of these individuals have focused on the importance of personal fulfillment. Maslow popularized the term "self-actualization," while Rogers developed his vision of the fully functioning person.

Self-actualization is the principal goal of many humanistic programs. In these programs the focus is on the present lives of the children, so that learning experiences are designed to involve the child both cognitively and emotionally. Skill learning, then, is integrated with affective development.

Values and purpose are important in the humanistic context. Focus on the technology of teaching is not enough for the humanist. Instead a prime concern is the exploration and development of personal and social values. Gerald Weinstein suggests five criteria for developing humanistic programs:

1. The needs of the individual are the central data source for decision making
2. Humanistic education increases the options of the learners
3. Personal knowledge gets at least as much priority as public knowledge
4. Each individual's development is not fostered at the expense of anyone else's development
5. All elements of the program contribute to a sense of significance, value, and worth of each person involved.[1]

Transpersonal or Holistic Orientation

Transpersonal education is similar to the humanistic perspective in that it recognizes the importance of individual fulfillment. However, it differs from humanism in certain major respects. While humanistic education focuses on the self or ego, transpersonal education focuses on the Higher Self or Center where the individual experiences a oneness or connectedness with other forms. Thus transpersonal education emphasizes self-transcendence as a stage beyond the humanistic goal of self-actualization. Various centering methods such as visualization, meditation, and movement are used to work toward self-transcendence.

Transpersonal education also stresses the importance of intuitive thought. Intuition is characterized by an immediate grasp of the whole.

In analytic thought there is a sequential process where each part is perceived. Transpersonal education seeks a balance and integration between intuitive and analytic thought. Transpersonal programs emphasize, then, the development of creativity, new approaches to problem solving, and the arts.

Finally, transpersonal education stresses the importance of spirituality or one's inner life. This inner awareness means a recognition of the importance of thought, images, and dreams. Again, visualization and meditation are often components in transpersonal programs to facilitate this inner awareness.

Applying the Orientations

These orientations can be useful in various ways. First, they can help a teacher clarify his or her own approach to teaching and learning. For example, as you immerse yourself in the orientations you can see which orientation or orientations most closely parallel your own perspective. Most individuals usually find that two or three orientations appeal to their way of thinking. It is appropriate, then, to speak of a cluster of orientations which form a meta-orientation. The transpersonal and humanistic orientations could be viewed in this manner as well as the discipline and cognitive process orientations. However, you should explore the implications of such clusters, as sometimes conflicts occur between the orientations which should be clarified or resolved.

The orientations are also helpful in clarifying the conceptual base of curriculum documents. For example, in examining a curriculum guideline the orientations help clarify the educational philosophy of the guideline; thus we can understand the basic approach of the guideline. Similarly, the orientations can be helpful in analyzing curriculum materials and whether they are appropriate to your learning context. If you are basically committed to a behavioral orientation, it is unlikely that materials from a humanistic orientation will work in your classroom. Thus the orientations provide conceptual lenses so that we can see where different learning approaches and teaching materials are grounded.

The orientations can be used as a vehicle for staff development. For example, a school staff seeking to develop an overall school philosophy may want to examine and work with the orientations. The staff may work toward a meta-orientation which encompasses two or three orientations that provide a basis for program development. By examining the various orientations the staff may also find support for their own programming in terms of philosophy, ideas, curriculum materials, and evaluation procedures that are associated with the orientations.

The orientations are also integral to the process of curriculum development, implementation, and evaluation:

Orientations → Aims → Development → Implementation → Evaluation.

The orientations provide a conceptual basis for curriculum development. Rooted in a conception of the person and derived from various foundation disciplines such as psychology, sociology, and philosophy, the orientations provide a guiding framework for curriculum planning. Once a curriculum committee has clarified its position concerning the orientations, it can develop some aims or goals for a program. The goals can be broken down into more specific objectives. The level of specificity, however, will often reflect the orientation. In the behavioral orientation the objectives are very specific, while in the transpersonal orientation the objectives tend to remain more general.

Teachers can then develop a program or set of learning experiences to achieve the stated aims. The program may be closely defined as in the subject orientation, or more open-ended or even emergent as in some humanistic programs. In fact, the curriculum cycle that is outlined here can vary with the orientations. Some programs in the humanistic and transpersonal orientations are emergent and thus do not follow a linear sequence.

If the program, or set of learning experiences, has been developed, it then needs to be implemented in the classroom. Implementation procedures need to be clearly planned or otherwise the curriculum can become a nonevent that never reaches the student.

Finally, the curriculum should be evaluated to see if it is meeting its expectations. Again, evaluation procedures can vary with the orientations being employed. In the subject orientation standardized achievement tests are sometimes employed. In a more open-ended curriculum, goal-free evaluation is sometimes used, since there are not clearly defined objectives.

The orientations, then, interact with curriculum and curriculum planning in a number of ways and along a number of dimensions. It is imperative that we understand these orientations, and more importantly that we clarify our own position on the educational spectrum.

Notes

1. Gerald Weinstein, "Humanistic Education: What It Is and What It Isn't," in Tim Timmerman and Jim Ballard, eds., *Humanistic Education Yearbook* (Amherst, Mass.: Mandala, 1976).

2

Behavioral Orientation

The behavioral orientation has exerted a strong influence on education for several decades, and it continues to be influential through the competency-based education movement. Competency-based education stresses behavioral objectives, criterion-referenced measurement, and other accountability measures. In this chapter three components of the behavioral orientation are examined: operant conditioning, counter conditioning, and competency-based education.

B. F. Skinner is recognized as the leading theorist in behavioral psychology. His theory of operant conditioning has also been applied extensively to school learning. In particular, he has advocated programmed learning and shaping student behavior through positive reinforcement.

Counter conditioning techniques have also been employed in behavioral therapy and in the classroom. Some of these programs have focused on stress management and assertive behavior.

Finally, competency-based education has its roots in the behavioral orientation. With its emphasis on behavioral objectives, criterion-referenced testing, and mastery learning techniques, this movement has affected teacher education programs and secondary and elementary education, as well as minimum competency requirements for graduation.

Operant Conditioning

For a generation, B. F. Skinner has exerted a strong influence on educational psychology. Skinner received his doctorate in 1931 from Harvard. In 1936 he joined the faculty of the University of Minnesota. While he was at Minnesota, he designed his "baby tender," a controlled environmental chamber for infants. His first daughter spent part of her infancy in the chamber. Skinner moved on to Indiana University and eventually to Harvard in 1948.

In 1968 Skinner published *The Technology of Teaching*. Although he does not consider himself an educational psychologist, he has written extensively on education. In the second chapter of this book, he asserts that "recent improvements in the conditions which control behavior in the field of learning are of two principal sorts."[1] The first is the law of effect, which allows us to shape "the behavior of an organism almost at will."[2] The second advance allows us to "maintain behavior in given states of strength for long periods of time."[3] In the second law, Skinner is referring to the use of reinforcers. Reinforcers are the central component of Skinner's theory of operant conditioning. An operant is a behavior that can be controlled through reinforcement. The basic law of operant conditioning involves reinforcement. "If the occurrence of an operant is followed by presentation of a reinforcing stimulus, the strength is increased."[4] In education, teaching is "the arrangement of contingencies of reinforcement under which students learn."[5] By arranging reinforcers the teacher can increase certain desired behaviors.

Skinner distinguishes between negative and positive reinforcers. Positive reinforcers, when added to a situation, will increase the behavior. A negative reinforcer will increase the frequency of behavior when it is removed. In general, Skinner supports the use of positive reinforcers. Aversive education, in Skinner's view, uses negative reinforcers and leads to "maladaptive or neurotic" behavior.

Punishment involves presenting a negative reinforcer or removing a positive reinforcer. Skinner does not favor punishment. Although punishment may appear successful at first, the effects are not permanent and the undesirable behavior can reoccur. The emotional side effects are also negative. "Replacing misbehavior with crying or anger is seldom a good solution."[6] Similar, punishment may produce side effects which are both unpredictable and unreliable.

Natural reinforcers occur in the environment. However, Skinner suggests that natural reinforcers are too slow to bring about change. In Skinner's opinion, if the teacher relies on the environment he or she actually abandons the role of teacher. Instead, the teacher must intervene to manipulate the environment. One technique that Skinner recommends is programmed learning.

Programmed instruction is primarily a scheme for making an effective use of reinforcers, not only in shaping new kinds of behavior but in maintaining behavior in strength. A program does not specify a particular kind of reinforcer (the student may work under aversive control or for money, food, prestige, or love), but it is designed to make weak reinforcers or small measures of strong ones effective.[7]

In starting a learning task, Skinner suggests that students be rewarded immediately. For example, in programmed learning steps should be small so that errors are minimized. Eventually, however, the student may become saturated. For example, if the student has been reinforced with chocolates, he or she may become tired of the reinforcer and the chocolates will lose their effect. Thus the ratio of reinforcers may have to be stretched. This is called intermittent reinforcement. If the reinforcers are administered only occasionally, then the desired behavior can be maintained by a small number of reinforcers. Thus the teacher attempts to increase the number of responses per reinforcement without losing student interest in the activity.

Skinner differentiates between ratio reinforcement and interval reinforcement. In ratio reinforcement the reinforcer is given after a certain number of responses. With interval reinforcement the reinforcers are administered at specific time intervals. Research suggests that ratio reinforcement is more effective than interval reinforcement. This seems logical in that interval reinforcement is not related to how the individual is responding while ratio reinforcement is.

Well-designed contingencies of reinforcement should keep a student busy at work. However, Skinner admits that it is difficult to design effective reinforcement schedules that deal with complex skills. For example, reading the Great Books is something that usually happens as a result of an unusual reinforcement schedule that is difficult to duplicate. Still, Skinner suggests that great artists are the products of variable ratio schedules.

A dedicated person is one who remains active for long periods of time without reinforcement. He does so because, either in the hands of a skillful teacher or by accident, he has been exposed to a gradually lengthening *variable-ratio* schedule. At first, what he did "paid off" quickly, but he then moved on to things less readily reinforced. It is perhaps presumptuous to compare a Faraday, Mozart, Rembrandt, or Tolstoy with a pigeon pecking a key or with a pathological gambler, but variable-ratio schedules are nevertheless conspicuous features of the biographies of scientists, composers, artists, and writers.[8]

If Skinner's argument about the artists seems to stretch the point, the application of operant conditioning to various special education programs has been effective. For example, Skinner describes the situation where a boy was born blind with cataracts. The boy's behavior became unmanageable. After an operation that removed the cataracts, he refused to wear glasses. If he did not wear the glasses, he would soon become permanently blind. His tantrums were uncontrollable and he was admitted to a hospital with a diagnosis of "child schizophrenia." In this case two principles of operant conditioning were used. The temper tantrums were extinguished by not rewarding them in any way, and the program of reinforcers was used to shape the desired

behavior of wearing glasses. Wearing empty frames was at first reinforced with food. After the boy began wearing the frames, the lenses
were inserted in the frames. Eventually he began to wear the glasses
about twelve hours per day.[9]

Skinner has advocated programmed learning. In programmed
learning there are sequences of questions with the student being reinforced by correct answers. Programmed learning usually proceeds from
the simple to more difficult questions. Below is an example of a program that focuses on a theme developed more fully in the second part of
this chapter—the development of behavioral objectives. The reader is
encouraged to complete the items, to not only get a feeling for programmed learning but to understand some of the concepts associated
with the behavioral orientation.

Keep the answer in the right-hand column covered until you have
filled in the blank in the left-hand column.

1-1. Educational objectives are statements of the goals that teachers have set for their students. The goals that teachers set for their students are called an/a _____ _____.	educational objective
1-2. When a teacher says that she wants her students to be able to write an anti-pollution petition, she has stated an/a _____ _____.	educational objective
1-3. A coach states that he wants his players to be able to make seventy-five percent of their free throws, he has formulated an/a _____ _____.	educational objective
1-4. If a music teacher states that she wants her students to enjoy all kinds of music, she has stated an/a _____ _____.	educational objective
1-5. The primary reason for formulating educational objectives is to facilitate the systematic improvement of instruction. Educational	a. systematic b. instruction

objectives make possible the a. _____
improvement of b. _____ .

1-6. If a teacher has not stated his
educational objectives or goals,   instruction
it is difficult for him to know
how effective his __ __ __ __ __
__ __ __ __ __ __ has been.

1-7. Is it likely that teachers will
design effective learning   No
experiences for their students if
they have no educational
objectives in mind? (Yes or No)

1-8. Is it likely that the evaluation
procedures of the teacher will   No
be valid if he has no educational
objectives in mind? (Yes or No)

Three Classifications of Educational Objectives

1-9. The educational objectives with
which teachers are concerned
can be divided into three
different classes or domains.   a. cognitive
Objectives concerned with   b. psychomotor
traditional verbal or numerical   c. affective
learning are in the *cognitive*   In any order
domain; objectives concerned
with the learning of physical
skills are in the *psychomotor*
domain, and objectives
concerned with emotional
learning are in the *affective*
domain. The three classes of
educational objectives with
which teachers are concerned
are a. _____,
b. _____ and
c. _____ objectives.

1-10. Educational objectives involving
the learning of verbal or
numerical material belong in the   cognitive domain
cognitive domain.
An economics teacher has as his
objective that his students be
able to recall the principle of

supply and demand. This
objective would be classified in
the _____ _____ .

1-11. If a teacher wants her students
to be able to define democracy,
this objective is concerned with
verbal learning and would be   cognitive
classified in the _____
domain.

1-12. An arithmetic teacher wants his
students to be able to recite the
multiplication tables through   cognitive domain
ten. This objective is in the

_____ _____ .

1-13. A second type of educational
objective with which teachers
are concerned involves the   motor skills
learning of motor skills.
Objectives involving the
learning of _____ _____
are classified as belonging to the
psychomotor domain.

1-14. A physical education teacher
has as an objective that his   a. motor skill
students be able to touch their   b. psychomotor
toes. This objective requires the
learning of an/a (a) _____
_____ , and would be
classified as belonging in the (b)
psy ___ ___ ___ m ___ t ___ ___
domain.

1-15. A home economics teacher
wants her students to be able to   a. motor skill
fold beaten egg whites into cake   b. psychomotor
batter. This objective requires
learning an/a (a) _____
_____ and would be
classified in the (b)
_____ domain.

1-16. The third classification of
educational objectives with
which teachers are concerned is
affective objectives. Educational

objectives involving the
learning of interests, attitudes,
appreciation and values belong
in the *affective domain*.
The _____ _____ contains   affective domain
educational objectives
concerned with student
interests, attitudes,
appreciations and values.

1-17. Objectives in the affective   emotional
domain are concerned with
e m _ _ _ _ _ _ _ learning.

1-18. When an English teacher says
that he wants his students to   affective domain
enjoy reading, he has specified
an educational objective that
belongs in the _____

_____.

1-19. When a social studies teacher
specifies that he wants his   affective domain
students to appreciate the
dignity and worth of the
individual, the objective is in
the _____ _____.

1-20. A mathematics teacher states
that he wants his students to   affective domain
like mathematics. This objective
would be classified in the

_____ _____.

1-21. *Information Frame*
It is important that you are able
to discriminate between   No response required
educational objectives in the
three domains. The following
frames are review frames. You
can use these frames to
determine if you can
discriminate between cognitive,
affective and psychomotor
objectives.

SOURCE: Richard B. Smith, "Educational Objectives and the Systematic Improvement of Instruction," in Thomas B. Roberts, ed., *Four Psychologies Applied to Education* (Cambridge, Mass.: Schenkman, 1975), pp. 215–19.

Other programs developed by Skinner focus on discrimination. Discrimination is learning to tell the differences among colors, shapes, patterns, different sounds, tempos, and so forth. Skinner has developed programs to be used in teaching machines that instruct preschool children in matching shapes, colors, and the rest. Teaching discrimination to a retarded person was done with operant conditioning. In this experiment a 40-year-old was said to have a mental age of about 18 months. Using chocolates as reinforcers, the experimenter taught the subject to discriminate among different types of shapes (e.g., circles, ellipses, etc.). The subject also learned to use a pencil appropriately in tracing letters.[10]

Skinner suggests that operant conditioning can be used in teaching writing. One method involves using paper that is treated chemically so that the pen writes in dark gray when a response is correct and yellow when it is incorrect. At first the student only completes a small part of the letter, but gradually he can compose the letter as a whole without the aid of the paper.

Skinner gives another example of programming to teach memorization skills. Here a short poem is projected on a screen. A few letters are omitted. The class then reads the poem out loud. Another slide is projected with more letters missing. Again the class reads the poem together. Eventually after five or six more slides (the blackboard can also be used as the teacher erases letters with each turn), the class can "read" the poem without any words showing.[11]

Skinner suggested that programmed learning be used with the teaching machine. The program would be set within the machine and if the student answered correctly he or she would turn a knob that moved the program along. Although programmed learning has had some impact on educational practice, the teaching machine never got off the ground. Generally, the teaching machine was relegated to the basement of the school along with out-of-date textbooks.

The trouble was that the devices—no matter how noble their aims—were, in the end, just somebody's old slide show, put together in a time remote from the pupil's, and whose basic lack of intelligence was only too swiftly exposed. To make matters worse they were almost always unreliable, being of such notoriously touchy components as tape recorders and slide projectors, and by the same token not cheap.[12]

Today we have the microcomputer, and its future looks different from the teaching machine. Although it is difficult to predict how microcomputers will be used in schools, it is clear that they are more appealing than teaching machines. First, the programs are more subtle and flexible and thus more stimulating for the student. It also appears that programs developed in such areas as mathematics and second languages are more reinforcing than programs developed for the teaching machines in the sixties. Even more important, the advanced student who develops some computer literacy can do his or her own programming. Simply put, the microcomputer has much greater potential for flexible interaction between the person and machine. Thus the microcomputer may fill the vision that Skinner outlined for his teaching machine.

Skinner has also developed a social vision that applies behavioral engineering to social change. These visions appeared in *Walden II* and *Beyond Freedom and Dignity*. In the latter book, Skinner attacks the concept of autonomous man. He argues that environmental control should replace individual freedom. Contingencies of reinforcement should be used to control such human attributes as aggression, industry, and attention. He argues that reinforcement should even replace the "last stronghold of autonomous man," which for Skinner is thinking. He suggests that what we call generalization and conception formation are merely contingencies of reinforcement that have produced a particular response. Skinner suggests that complex thinking skills can be controlled by an appropriate environment: "The culture promotes thinking by constructing special contingencies. It teaches a person to make fine discriminations by making differential reinforcement more precise. It teaches techniques to be used in solving problems."[13]

In Skinner's view, the concept of autonomy is used to explain what the science of behavior cannot explain. Skinner argues that we must give up the concept of the inner person if the culture is to survive. Instead of focusing on the inner person we must focus on cultural design. In other words, we need to develop contingencies of reinforcement that allow for society to prosper. Reinforcers should be developed that produce a society where there is less poverty and violence. For example, Skinner states that we need to design reinforcers that improve life in the city. Government, schools, and businesses should abandon the ideal of individual freedom and concentrate on more efficient means of control. Skinner believes the move to cultural design is part of an evolutionary process.

The designer of a culture is not an interloper or meddler. He does not step in to disturb a natural process, he is part of a natural process. The geneticist who changes the characteristics of a species by selective breeding or by changing genes may seem to be meddling in biological evolution, but he does so because his species has evolved to the point at which it has been able to develop a science of genetics and a culture which induces its members to take the future of the species into account.[14]

According to Skinner, if we do not use the means available to use, then western culture may be in serious trouble.

This could be a lethal cultural mutation. Our culture has produced the science and technology it needs to save itself. It has the wealth needed for effective action. It has, to a considerable extent, a concern for its own future. But if it continues to take freedom or dignity, rather than its own survival, as its principal value, then it is possible that some other culture will make a greater contribution to the future.[15]

Although Skinner is adamant in his vision, there is very little specificity. This is somewhat ironic for a behaviorist. For example, it is not clear exactly how we proceed to a state which will be controlled by benevolent behavioral scientists. How will these people be chosen and who will be chosen? A more specific vision is given in *Walden II* but this is a utopian vision. Criticisms of *Walden II* have been abundant: "A vision of the future in which man is controlled by science, made happy by technique, rendered well-adjusted by the manipulation of others. Emerson's vision? Only the hubris of science could take Thoreau's Walden, and dare to appropriate a word with such noble connotations, for such a vile vision."[16]

Problems develop with the behavioral orientation when Skinner and others in their zeal build their view of a new society on such a narrow theoretical base. It is one thing to develop a reinforcement program for a retarded child; quite another to talk about the radical restructuring of society based on the principle of operant conditioning. In Skinner's vision technique becomes ideology—and technology does not make for good theory.

Counter Conditioning

While operant conditioning stresses the role of reinforcement, counter conditioning substitutes one behavior for another. For example, if someone is attempting to give up smoking, he or she may substitute chewing gum.

Systematic Desensitization

Systematic desensitization is a counter conditioning technique developed by Joseph Wolpe to deal with anxiety. Generally, muscle relaxation and imagery are used as substitutes for anxiety. Muscle relaxation involves focused attention on the major voluntary muscle groups. The person usually starts the procedure by closing the eyes and relaxing. The individual will usually first tense and then relax a specific set of muscles. A session might begin with the following suggestion:

Now, I want you to be completely calm and relaxed, get a very pleasant relaxing scene in your mind, and let your body go completely limp. Breathe deeply and slowly and continue to relax. Now, I want you to focus your attention on your right hand. Make a fist with your right hand. That's it. Pull it tighter, tighter. Feel the tension across your fingers, arms, and wrist. Now, I want you to let your hand relax, let your muscles completely relax as your hand falls in the chair. Don't force it; just let the muscles go limp rather than forcing them to go limp. Feel the relaxing, feel the warmth; note how it is different from the tension. Now, let's do it again and notice the difference in relaxation and tension.[17]

Then the person will relax various parts of the body in some sort of sequence, for example, right hand/right arm, left hand/left arm, forehead, cheeks, jaw, neck and shoulders, left leg/right leg, chest, and, finally, the entire body.

Muscle relaxation is followed by the person imagining a scene that causes anxiety. The individual usually begins with the least threatening aspect. For example, people who are afraid of flying will gradually imagine themselves in situations leading up to takeoff. This might involve visualizing the airport, checking in, walking to the gate, waiting, walking into the plane, and buckling the seat belt. Wolpe suggests that a hierarchy of events from the least feared to the most feared be developed so that the individual can progress through the levels. Thus the person begins to experience the series of events with less anxiety.

Assertiveness Training

Another counter conditioning technique is assertiveness training. Assertiveness training attempts to improve the person's ability to express appropriate feelings. These feelings can be both positive and negative. Sometimes people who are shy can become entrapped by their inner feelings and have a difficult time expressing themselves. Thus the feelings can lead to rage or temper tantrums.

Assertive behavior can be distinguished from aggressive and nonassertive behavior. Individuals who are aggressive do not consider the feelings of others in making their own thoughts known. Nonassertive behavior is characterized by the inability to communicate one's own feelings. Thus the nonassertive person can develop feelings of incompetence. However, the assertive person is able to express his or her feelings in a manner that is mutually satisfying. Examples of these behaviors are outlined below:

Dining Out
Mr. and Mrs. A are at dinner in a moderately expensive restaurant. Mr. A has ordered a rare steak, but when the steak is served Mr. A finds it to be very well done, contrary to his order. His behavior is:

Nonassertive. Mr. A grumbles to his wife about the "burned" meat and observes that he won't patronize this restaurant in the future. He says nothing to the waitress, responding, "Fine!" to her inquiry, "Is everything all right?" His dinner and evening are highly unsatisfactory, and he feels guilty for having taken no action. Mr. A's estimate of himself and Mrs. A's estimate of him are both deflated by the experience.

Aggressive. Mr. A angrily summons the waitress to his table. He berates her loudly and unfairly for not complying with his order. His actions ridicule the waitress and embarrass Mrs. A. He demands and receives another steak, this one more to his liking. He feels in control of the situation, but Mrs. A's embarrassment creates friction between them, and spoils their evening. The waitress is humiliated and angry and loses her poise for the rest of the evening.

Assertive. Mr. A motions the waitress to his table. Noting that he had ordered a rare steak, he shows her the well-done meat, asking politely but firmly that it be returned to the kitchen and replaced with the rare-cooked steak he originally requested. The waitress apologizes for the error, and shortly returns with a rare steak. The A's enjoy dinner, tip accordingly, and Mr. A feels satisfaction with himself. The waitress is pleased with a satisfied customer and an adequate tip.[18]

Assertive behavior consists of verbal and nonverbal skills. For example, direct eye contact is considered an important nonverbal skill. Other behavioral skills include using the word "I," rather than "you" or "it." By using "I" the person accepts ownership of his or her feelings.

Assertiveness training is based on the assumption that new behavior can be substituted for old behavior. Assertiveness training, then, employs counter conditioning by substituting assertive behavior for aggressive or passive behavior. This approach views the person's self-concept as linked to behavior. As the individual learns assertive behavior, then the self-concept will also improve. Like other behaviorist approaches, assertiveness training assumes that past experience can be readily overcome with new learning.

The assertiveness approach usually consists of the following components:

1. Identifying target behaviors
2. Setting priorities for situations and behaviors
3. Role playing the instances
4. Reenactments
5. Transfer.[19]

In the first step the student identifies those behaviors that he or she would like to improve. For example, a situation might include difficulty in initiating a conversation with a person of the opposite sex.

After the situations have been identified, the student ranks all of them from the most difficult situation to the least difficult. After the situations have been chosen and ranked, the students attempt to role play the situations. Here the students may initially role play how they behave in the situation now, and then try new enactments where they role play a new, assertive behavior. The teacher can also do some modeling of assertive behavior. With the role play or enactment there is also discussion of how each behavior worked. The teacher and students can discuss how the different behaviors affect the other people in the situation. In the final phase, the students will transfer their learnings to real situations. After trying out the situation the person can discuss how assertiveness training is working in real life.

Competency-Based Education

Competency-based education has its roots in behavioral psychology. H. H. McAshan defines competency-based education where "the desired learning outcomes—usually referred to as competencies which represent the specific instructional intents of the program and the behavioral outcomes, sometimes referred to as assessment modes or evaluation indicators—are specified in advance in written form."[20] Competency-based education involves: (1) the selection of competency statements, (2) the specification of evaluation indicators to assess competency achievements, and (3) the development of an appropriate instructional system.

In his book *Competency-Based Education and Behavioral Objectives*, McAshan outlines the rationale for a competency-based approach. Some of these points include:

1. To avoid duplication of content. By stating the objectives of each course it is then possible for school personnel to examine courses at various grade levels and thus avoid duplication.
2. To improve individualization of instruction. By breaking down programs into small instructional modules, it is possible for students to master the various modules at their own pace. It is also possible to offer programs that contain different choices of modules and thus increase flexibility.
3. To improve methods of evaluating and reporting student achievement through more systematic methods. Competency-based education (CBE) attempts to clarify what is to be learned through clear objectives and thus provides a sound basis for evaluating student achievement. The emphasis in CBE is on assessing what the student has learned rather than comparing one student against another student.
4. To provide students with ongoing information regarding their personal progress. Programs in CBE are designed to provide immediate feedback to the students about how they are performing.
5. To prepare students to function at all levels of learning. Objectives

are broken into cognitive, psychomotor, and affective components
so that instructional programs can be built in these different areas.
6. To be better accountable to the general public. This is one of the
key elements in competency-based programs. By clearly stating
what is achieved and evaluating these objectives, the public can
be better informed about what educational institutions are
accomplishing.[21]

According to McAshan, CBE is based on behavioral learning
theory.

Learning theory indicates that learning begins when stimuli (either internal or
external) and their reinforcement cause an organism to react. Learning occurs
through this process, and the more complex cognitive, psychomotor, and affective motivational systems develop. Thus, all learning can be said to begin when
the learner is sensitized to the existence of stimuli. These stimuli may be
thought of as occurring from the result of teaching strategies (or enabling activities) that are part of the instructional delivery system in CBE programs.[22]

Competency statements, or learning outcomes, are the desired
ends of instructional activity and, according to McAshan, are the prime
purposes of education. All other components of CBE are means to
achieve instructional outcomes. Competency statements are broken
down into cognitive, affective, and psychomotor components.

Competency statements should be stated in specific terms.
McAshan asserts that "clarity and specificity are essential in well-stated
competencies." A competency statement should include (1) the identification of the learner, (2) the classification of the behavioral domain
(e.g. cognitive, psychomotor, and affective), (3) the specific content to
be learned, and (4) the statement of future time orientation. The classification of objectives should also be broken down into levels according to the various taxonomies developed by Bloom in his book, *Handbook I: The Cognitive Domain*.

The following is an example of a specific competency statement:

Cognitive

I. EDA 605 students should acquire *comprehension* of specific terms and related
concepts important in the development and understanding of systems and
in the use of the systems analysis process.
Communication Critique:
A. Accountable learner group—Students taking the course EDA 605.
B. Learning Task:
1. Domain—The word "comprehension" places the competency in the
Cognitive domain at classification level 2.00. This means that the
learning task is intended to help the students develop their skill or
ability to make translations, interpretations, and to extrapolate.
2. Specific content to be learned—"Specific terms and related concepts

important in the development and understanding of systems and in the use of the systems analysis process."

3. Future time orientation—The phrase "should acquire comprehension" indicates that proficiency in this competency is expected to occur at a later date.[23]

McAshan, unlike some competency-based educators, distinguishes competency statements from behavioral outcomes. Competency statements are the knowledge, skills, or abilities that a person achieves and that become part of the person's repertoire. They define the basic instructional intent of a program.

Behavioral outcomes are the specific responses which the learner performs as an indication of how he or she has achieved a competency. Behavioral objectives are used for assessment. Behavioral outcomes represent a sample response for the much more significant competencies that are the basis of the CBE programs.

McAshan argues that competency statements are more important than behavioral outcomes because they provide the guiding purpose for educational programs. Sometimes the more complex cognitive skills and aspects of the affective domain cannot be broken down into behavioral outcomes. Ideally, however, there should be congruence between behavioral outcomes and competency statements. Behavioral outcomes insure that competencies have become operational.

A behavioral outcome for the previous example is as follows:

EDA 605 students must:

A. Acquire comprehension of specific terms and related concepts important in the development and understanding of systems and the use of the systems analysis process. *Success will be evidenced by an eleven item written examination (consisting of terms to be defined, completion and true-false questions), on which they will achieve at least nine correct answers.*[24]

McAshan believes that competency statements and behavioral outcomes are both necessary for a sound competency-based program.

A competency or goal statement by itself lacks the behavioral outcome necessary for operationalization. An evaluation or behavioral outcome by itself lacks a purpose. By placing both components together as one statement, both shortcomings are eliminated.[25]

Developing Competency Statements and Behavioral Outcomes

In writing competency statements McAshan examines several possible approaches that have been associated with the behavioral objectives movement. These include:

Management by Objectives. This approach has been used in industry to establish personnel and program accountability. McAshan states that since management by objectives is not concerned with content, it is not appropriate to writing curriculum objectives.

Systems Analysis. This is a problem-solving approach that defines tasks that must be accomplished by individuals and organizations in order to achieve their goals. It is a comprehensive approach to organizational planning.

Task Analysis. In this approach activities are broken down into specific tasks or functions. For example, the school principal's activities can be analyzed into various functions that he or she performs.

Needs Assessment. This method involves identifying discrepancies between the present situation and the desired conditions.

Systematic Competency Analysis. In McAshan's view this is the most useful approach to developing competency statements. It is an adaptation of the systems analysis approach to determining educational programs. It involves answering the question "What are the major areas of content included within the content mission?" After answering this question the next step is to break down the content into subsystem components. Each subsystem then is broken down to a level of specificity where a competency statement can be developed. An example of this process is given in Figure 1. Systematic competency analysis begins with a mission goal such as "Ninth-grade math students will acquire an understanding of General Math." This general statement is broken into various content subsystems.

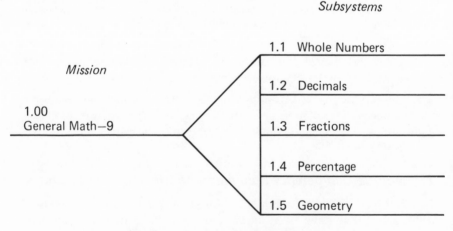

Figure 1. Breakdown of mission goal.

SOURCE: H. H. McAshan, *Competency-Based Education and Behavioral Objectives* (Englewood Cliffs, N.J.: Educational Technology Publishers, 1979), p. 121.

For each of the subsystems in Figure 1, competency statements are developed. For example, the geometry unit would contain the following competency statements.

1.5.3.1 Ninth grade general math students will acquire an understanding of the formula for area of a parallelogram, $a = bh$.

1.5.3.2 Ninth grade general math students will acquire an understanding of the formula for area of a rectangle, $a = lw$.

1.5.3.3 Ninth grade general math students will acquire an understanding of the formula for area of a triangle, $a = \frac{1}{2}bh$.

1.5.3.4 Ninth grade general math students will acquire an understanding of the formula for area of a trapezoid, $a = \frac{1}{2}h\,(a + b)$.

1.5.3.5 Ninth grade general math students will acquire an understanding of the formula for area of a circle, $a = \pi r^2$.[26]

These competency statements are then used to develop behavioral outcomes and learning tasks.

Criterion-Referenced Objectives

As mentioned earlier, behavioral outcomes should be developed that are congruent with the original competency statement. Behavioral outcomes should also identify appropriate situations to observe measurable performance and the criteria to establish a standard level of success. These behavioral outcomes are also referred to as criterion-referenced behavioral objectives. A criterion-referenced objective consists of "a goal, which is the competency purpose, or desired end that is sought; a measurable behavioral performance; and criteria for determining the minimum level at which the behavioral activity will be considered acceptable."[27]

Below are two examples of criterion-referenced behavioral objectives:

Environmental studies students will acquire an understanding of the land use categories commonly accepted and used by urban planners, so that when given a written 20-item short-answer test that presents descriptions of urban land uses, students will be able to correctly name the proper category designation for at least 75 percent of the items.

Home economics students will develop an understanding of how to distinguish between a nap fabric and a fabric without nap, so that when given ten fabric swatches to be identified through either visual or tactile discrimination, the students will orally identify at least nine correctly.[28]

Behaviorists such as McAshan and James Popham argue that criterion-referenced measures are superior to standardized tests, which are norm-referenced. Norm-referenced measures are used to compare students, while criterion-referenced tests are used to assess student competencies.

Behaviorists such as James Popham argue that criterion-type tests should drive instruction. Popham has worked with the Detroit public schools to develop a program where "properly fashioned tests can and should become the force that drives curriculum."[29] These tests are criterion-referenced. In Detroit teachers are urged to teach to the test "not in the sense of a particular set of test items, but in the sense that the test represents defensible competencies which students should acquire.[30] In Popham's view criterion-referenced tests should serve as "curricular magnets" and not as "curricular mirrors." Popham's view differs from McAshan's. For McAshan, competency goals should drive instruction and criterion-referenced tests should mirror the competency goals. In many cases these competency goals and behavioral outcomes are interchangeable. However, McAshan would disagree with Popham that criterion-referenced tests should be the driving force in curriculum.

Mastery Learning

Mastery learning has also been associated with the behavioral objectives movement. In mastery learning the student completes a certain segment of learning and then after achieving a certain level of competency he or she moves on to the next segment. Mastery learning is based on the notion that units of learning can be mastered by almost all students.

Benjamin Bloom has become a proponent of mastery learning. He argues that mastery learning is based on the construct that most students become similar with regard to learning ability and motivation when provided with favorable learning conditions. According to Bloom, the research demonstrates that when students are working under unfavorable learning conditions, they tend to become more dissimilar in how they perform. If students are given enough time and the appropriate learning conditions, they can master a learning task. Bloom's system contains the following characteristics:

1. Mastery of any subject is defined in terms of sets of major objectives which represent the purposes of the course or unit.
2. The substance is then divided into a larger set of relatively small learning units, each one accompanied by its own objectives, which are parts of the larger ones or thought essential to their mastery.
3. Learning materials are then identified and the instructional strategy selected.
4. Each unit is accompanied by brief diagnostic tests to measure the student's developing progress (the formative evaluation) and identify the particular problems each student is having.
5. The data obtained from administering the tests are used to provide supplementary instruction to the student to help him overcome his problems.[31]

With this system students of lesser ability may need more time to accomplish learning tasks, but in Bloom's view, the mastery learning system will support success rather than failure. Instruction within a mastery format is usually individualized. The student remains with a learning task until he or she reaches a desired level of proficiency. The level of proficiency is then assessed by criterion-referenced tests.

Summary and Appraisal

Operant Conditioning

Aims.   To shape desirable behavior and reduce undesirable behavior.

Conception of Learning.   Learning consists of acquiring new behaviors. Teacher manipulates contingencies of reinforcement to shape behavior.

Conception of Learner.   The learner is viewed in relation to environmental control. Although the emphasis is on the learner as passive respondent to reinforcers, it is also possible for the learner to engage in self-control and counter control.

Conception of the Instructional Process.   The teacher manipulates reinforcers to shape student behavior. Skinner endorses positive reinforcement and does not advocate punishment with its negative side effects. In positive reinforcement the desirable behaviors are increased with reinforcers.

Learning Environment.   The learning environment is highly structured. The focus is on control of student behavior with appropriate reinforcers.

Teacher's Role.   The teacher devises reinforcement schedules. It is possible, however, that the teacher can negotiate with students about what types of reinforcers are used.

Evaluation.   Students are tested to see if they have acquired the specific behavior. This may involve observation of behavior or pencil-and-paper tests.

Competency-Based Education

Aims.   Student acquisition of specific competencies in cognitive, affective, and psychomotor domains.

Conception of Learning.   Learning consists of reacting to stimuli so that the student acquires the desired competency. Competencies are defined specifically so that it is clear that the student has achieved a certain level of proficiency.

Conception of the Learner. The learner is viewed as someone who can succeed in acquiring various competencies. In some approaches such as mastery learning it is expected that almost all students will achieve the desired level of proficiency.

Conception of the Instructional Process

1. Identification of desired competencies and behavioral outcomes.
2. Designing of instructional delivery program to achieve objectives.
3. Evaluation through criterion-referenced tests to see whether the person has achieved the competencies.

Learning Environment. The learning environment tends to be structured and in many cases individualized. The environment is designed to encourage competency development. Programs are often broken down into specific learning modules.

Teacher's Role. The teacher defines the competency and develops an instructional program so students achieve the desired level of competency. The teacher attempts to build programs so students can become proficient in various competencies.

Evaluation. Criterion-referenced tests are used. Teachers develop criterion-referenced items in relation to competencies. Some individuals such as Popham argue that tests should drive instructional programs.

The behavioral orientation has focused on a central issue: the advantages and disadvantages of behavioral objectives. Individuals advocating competency-based education suggest that behavioral objectives should be used for the following reasons:[32]

1. Communication is enhanced. By being as specific as possible, the use of behavioral objectives increases clarity of communication.
2. Behavioral objectives help in planning curriculum. These objectives assist the teacher in knowing what is expected and in designing programs that achieve the stated objectives. Popham states, "Precise objectives stated in terms of measurable learner behavior make it definitely easier for the teacher to engage in curricular decisions. The clarity of precisely stated goals permits the teacher to make more judicious choices regarding what ought to be included in the curriculum."[33]
3. The use of behavioral objectives helps the schools become more efficient. Since objectives are well defined, there is less wasted effort and students are more certain about where programs are going.

4. Behavioral objectives assist with individualizing instruction. Mastery learning uses behavioral objectives to clarify competency levels and to promote individualized instruction.
5. Finally, objectives stated behaviorally improve evaluation procedures. If objectives are too vague or too general, evaluation becomes more difficult. Consider the comments of Lessinger:

General objectives, goals, or purposes serve a useful purpose, but American education suffers no shortage of them. On the other hand, we need more performance criteria that clearly specify the student competency to be displayed, the methods for displaying it, and the standards for judging whether it is sufficient. For example, we can specify that 90 percent of all students should score 90 percent or higher on a given test of reading based on certain materials. Auditors and local officials will discuss, in advance, which tests to use and what numbers are acceptable, but performance criteria, however they are phrased, must always be specific.[34]

However, there are disadvantages to developing curriculum solely on the basis of behavioral objectives.

1. The complexity of human activity makes it difficult to reduce all worthwhile activities to specific behavioral terms. For example, complex thinking skills as well as some affective objectives cannot be stated in specific observable terms. Thus the behavioral orientation can force educators into an inappropriate reductionism.
2. Another objection arises from the fact that we can lose sight of fundamental human goals. Because of their complexity, goals of developing creativity, divergent thinking, and moral autonomy are seldom included in lists of behavioral objectives. Does this mean these goals should be excluded from school programs? Even James Popham has stated, "However, there are more important goals which we have for our children which are currently unassessable. To the extent that such goals are extremely meritorious they are worth the risk of our pursuing them even if we cannot reliably discern whether they have been accomplished."[35]
3. Although behavioral objectives can help clarify the direction of programs, they can also hinder teachers' flexibility and creativity. Sometimes it is important that teachers "move" with student interests in such a way that it takes the teacher beyond stated objectives. If competency-based programs are stated in terms too rigid, then the teacher may feel that he or she is working within a straitjacket.
4. "Instruction based on the performance paradigm largely destroys the opportunities for student and teacher to engage in choice making, in probing alternative courses of action, in risk-taking activities, in testing out intuitive hunches, and cooperatively selecting and

planning activities that are meaningful and significant—in short in engaging in the sheer joy of just 'growing up' or being oneself."[36] Behavioral objectives remove the chance for children to explore randomly or to perform other activity that is the source of creativity.

5. Lists of behavioral objectives can be cumbersome. Specific competencies listed for each part of the curriculum can add up to an extremely long list of objectives. Some programs with behavioral objectives can be so long that the teachers cannot develop a curriculum given their limited time and resources.

Behavioral objectives can have a place in the overall curriculum. However, it makes more sense that their place be limited to those portions of curriculum where they are appropriate, rather than reducing all aspects of the curriculum to behavioral terms. For example, they can be used in those areas where we have some evidence that behavioral techniques devised by Skinner and others work. These might include conditioning programs for retarded students and counter conditioning programs that deal with stress.

As mentioned previously, problems develop in this orientation when it is used as encompassing educational philosophy. Carl Rogers in a debate with B. F. Skinner pointed out some of the difficulties with the behavioral social vision.

With these several points of basic and important agreement, are there then any issues that remain on which there are differences? I believe there are. They can be stated very briefly: Who will be controlled? Who will exercise control? What type of control will be exercised? Most important of all, toward what end or what purpose, or in the pursuit of what value, will control be exercised?[37]

Rogers raises the importance of values and what he calls prior subjective choice. For example, we can use reinforcers to improve instruction in the three Rs and in problem solving. But Rogers argues there is the question of whether we should spend more time on problem solving in the schools than on the three Rs.

Now, if I wish to determine whether problem-solving ability is "better" than knowledge of the three Rs, then scientific method can also study those two values but *only*—and this is very important—in terms of some other value which I have subjectively chosen. I may value college success. Then I can determine whether problem-solving ability or knowledge of the three Rs is most closely associated with that value. I may value personal integration or vocational success or responsible citizenship. I can determine whether problem-solving ability or knowledge of the three Rs is "better" for achieving any one of these values. But the value or purpose that gives meaning to a particular scientific endeavor must always lie outside of that endeavor.[38]

In defining an educational and social vision we have to agree on the ends or purposes of the vision. Many find Skinner's vision of happy, well-behaved people in a controlled society unacceptable and thus reject his vision. Behaviorism may help us to achieve some of our goals but it does not provide much help in defining the direction we should go.

Notes

1. B. F. Skinner, *The Technology of Teaching* (New York: Appleton Century Crofts, 1968), p. 10.
2. Ibid.
3. Ibid.
4. B. F. Skinner, *The Behavior of Organisms: An Experimental Analysis* (New York: Appleton Century Crofts, 1938), p. 21.
5. Skinner, *The Technology of Teaching*, p. 64.
6. Quoted in Winfred Hill, *Learning: A Survey of Psychological Interpretation* (New York: Thomas Y. Crowell, 1971), p. 64.
7. Skinner, *The Technology of Teaching*, p. 156.
8. Ibid., p. 165.
9. Ibid., p. 67.
10. Ibid., p. 76–78.
11. Ibid., pp. 81–82.
12. Christopher Evans, *The Micro Millennium* (New York: Viking, 1979), p. 117.
13. B. F. Skinner, *Beyond Freedom and Dignity* (New York: Alfred A. Knopf, 1971), p. 194.
14. Ibid., p. 180.
15. Ibid., p. 181.
16. Ernest Becker, *Beyond Alienation* (New York: George Braziller, 1967). pp. 243–44.
17. Henry Adams, *Abnormal Psychology* (Dubuque, Ia.: Wm. C. Brown, 1981), p. 174.
18. Robert Alberti and Michael Emmons, *Your Perfect Right: A Guide to Assertive Behavior* (San Luis Obispo, Calif.: Impact Publishers, 1978).
19. Bruce Joyce and Marsha Weil, *Models of Teaching* (Englewood Cliffs, N.J.: Prentice-Hall, 1980), p. 420.
20. H. H. McAshan, *Competency-Based Education and Behavioral Objectives* (Englewood Cliffs, N.J.: Educational Technology Publishers, 1979), p. 30.
21. Ibid., pp. 31–35.
22. Ibid., p. 51.
23. Ibid., p. 60.
24. Ibid., p. 82.
25. Ibid., p. 89.
26. Ibid., p. 121.
27. Ibid., p. 131.
28. Ibid., p. 133.
29. W. James Popham, "Crumbling Conceptions of Educational Testing," in *Educational Evaluation: Recent Progress, Future Needs* (Minneapolis: Minnesota Research and Evaluation Center, 1981), p. 32.
30. Ibid.
31. Joyce and Weil, *Models of Teaching*, p. 447.
32. J. Galen Saylor and William M. Alexander, *Planning Curriculum for Schools* (New York: Holt, Rinehart & Winston, 1974), pp. 172–77.

33. W. James Popham, "Objectives and Instruction," in Robert Stake, ed., *Instructional Objectives* (Chicago: Rand McNally, 1969), p. 40.

34. Leon Lessinger, *Every Kid a Winner: Accountability in Education* (New York: Simon & Shuster, 1979), p. 86.

35. W. James Popham, "Must All Objectives Be Behavioral?" *Educational Leadership*, 29 (April 1972), 608.

36. Saylor and Alexander, p. 177.

37. Carl R. Rogers and B. F. Skinner, "Some Issues Concerning the Control of Human Behavior," in Roger Ulich et al., eds., *Control of Human Behavior* (Glenview, Ill.: Scott Foresman, 1966), p. 307.

38. Ibid., p. 310.

3

Subject/Disciplines Orientation

The most traditional form of curriculum organization has centered on subjects and academic disciplines. In the elementary school this has meant a focus on the three Rs and in the secondary school it usually has included subjects such as science, math, English, history, and a language. Today this orientation is reflected in the back-to-basics movement.

In this chapter two approaches are examined. One approach is the subject orientation, which centers on subjects traditionally offered in elementary and secondary schools. In the other approach, the disciplines orientation, the emphasis is on the academic disciplines and particularly the procedures that a scholar uses within a discipline. In the disciplines orientation, the student attempts to carry out inquiry as a biologist or historian would.

Subject Orientation

The subject orientation is the oldest form of curriculum organization, whose use can be traced back to ancient Rome and Greece. For example, in Greece the Seven Liberal Arts were taught, and they consisted of two divisions: the trivium (grammar, rhetoric, and logic) and the quadrivium (arithmetic, geometry, astronomy, and music).

In the subject orientation, the curriculum is organized according to how knowledge has been developed in the various subject areas. Since specializations in the various fields have become so numerous, some subject areas can become extremely complex. English, for example, involves grammar, literature, creative writing, oral expression, linguistics, reading, spelling, and so forth.

Another common feature of the subject curriculum is the emphasis on direct instructional techniques such as lecture and recitation.[1] Lectures are used to explain the subject in a logical fashion. Usually lectures proceed from simple to complex ideas. In chemistry, for example, an explanation will usually begin with basic elements and then proceed to more complex organizations. Sometimes exposition of the material will be chronological in form, as in history. Besides lectures, other teaching procedures usually involve discussion, written exercises, oral reports, debates, and the like. Experiential techniques such as role playing, simulation games, and movement activities exercises are rarely used.

Another standard feature of the subject curriculum is that certain subjects will be required and others will be elective.[2] The required subjects are sometimes referred to as the "core" subjects in the curriculum. In the late sixties and early seventies, there was a trend toward more electives and fewer requirements in the secondary schools and in the universities. Today there is a general return to more required subjects and fewer electives. An emphasis on required core subjects does not necessarily mean that all students are exposed to the same learning experiences. Even in required subjects there is usually a portion of the course that allows for teacher choice in what he or she will emphasize. Even the core part of the course can be taught with different methodologies.

The subject curriculum also involves planning what courses will be required at different levels. Prerequisites must be decided in accordance with the sequence of course offerings. In other words, the organizers of the curriculum must decide what learning experiences are necessary at the different grade levels.[3]

Proponents of the subject curriculum suggest that there are allowances for individual differences. Electives are provided to suit different interests, and instructors with required courses can make some accommodation to different student needs. Guidance programs and special education programs are also provided to meet individual needs within the subject matter orientation. Extracurricular activities that are run after school or during breaks are also developed to present opportunities for students to pursue their individual interests.[4]

To teach in the subject-oriented curriculum, teachers are often trained in a particular subject field.[5] Teachers, then, usually attain a level of mastery in one subject area. Thus to teach science in secondary school the teacher often will have majored in science in university. Although the teacher cannot be expected to be a scholar in his or her field, the teacher should have a broad knowledge of the field so that it can be clearly articulated to secondary school students.

The length of the class period is also organized around the

subject.[6] At the university level, the classes have traditionally been organized so that lectures can be delivered. In certain subjects such as science, laboratory periods are somewhat longer.

One of the strongest spokesmen for the subject curriculum was Henry Morrison (1871–1945). Morrison was state superintendent of public instruction in New Hampshire and later he joined the College of Education of the University of Chicago.

Morrison argued that literacy skills were essential in the elementary school curriculum.[7] Thus he thought that the elementary school should focus on the three Rs. Morrison felt that reading was the basis for the school curriculum since it allows access to the rest of the curriculum. The next important element in the curriculum, for Morrison, was the development of computational skills. Morrison indicated that the main task of mathematics education was to acquire elementary concepts of number and the ability to deal with basic mathematical relationships.

Handwriting is the next essential aspect of the curriculum. Morrison felt that writing encourages the student to organize his or her ideas in a clear and concise manner.

Morrison also saw the school as transmitting cultural values. Morrison's views are a good example of how the subject orientation and cultural transmission position often combine to form a meta-orientation. Morrison stated that students should learn to get along with others and to accept the teacher's authority in the classroom.[8]

At the secondary level Morrison thought that the school should focus on developing student interest in one subject area. However, a variety of courses should be offered. According to Morrison, secondary education should also be developed so that the student eventually becomes "self-dependent." Morrison felt that one of the most basic goals of education should be self-discipline and the ability to make judgments without reference to the teacher.[9]

Morrison developed the unit approach to learning. He argued that material should be organized into units which the student must master if he or she is to progress to the next level. His concept of mastery is similar to the current concept of mastery learning.

The use of Morrison's mastery formula involves the teacher and the learner in well-defined stages of systematic instruction. Morrison's formula involves the following sequential steps: (1) pretest; (2) teaching; (3) testing the result of instruction; (4) adapting the instruction procedure; (5) teaching and testing again until the unit has been completely mastered by the student.[10]

Today the subject orientation is reflected in the back-to-basics movement. This movement has arisen from what some people believe was a relaxation of academic standards during the sixties and seventies. People calling for a return to basics include some parent groups, individuals in the media, religious fundamentalists, and university academics. They have expressed a concern about too many electives, automatic promotion, and grade inflation. Since 1975, "devoting more attention to teaching the basics" has been ranked from first to third in the Gallup poll. In response to this trend most states have developed some sort of minimum competency standards for elementary and secondary students.

In many respects the back-to-basics movement is a continuation of the position articulated by Morrison, Arthur Bestor, and others:

Although the back-to-basics movement means different things to different people, it usually connotes an Essentialist curriculum with heavy emphasis on reading, writing, and mathematics. Solid subjects—English, history, science, mathematics—are taught in all grades. History means U.S. and European history and perhaps Asian and African history, but not Afro-American history or ethnic studies. English means traditional grammar, not linguistics or nonstandard English; it means Shakespeare and Wordsworth, not Catcher in the Rye or Lolita. Creative writing is frowned upon. Science means biology, chemistry, and physics—not ecology. Mathematics means old math, not new math. Furthermore, these subjects are required. Proponents of the basics consider elective courses in such areas as scuba diving, transcendental meditation, and hiking as nonsense. Some even consider humanities or integrated social science courses too "soft." They may grudgingly admit music and art into the program —but only for half credit.[11]

Some critics of the back-to-basics movement have attempted to refute some of the movement's claims. They suggest that higher student/teacher ratios and fewer students who drop out of secondary school have contributed to lower test scores. Critics also suggest that the back-to-basics movement will stifle creativity and independent thinking. Finally, they also suggest that the back-to-basics movement focuses on skills which may become irrelevant very soon with advanced technology. The strengths and weaknesses of the subject orientation will be analyzed more completely at the end of this chapter.

Disciplines Orientation

The disciplines orientation differs from the subject orientation by distinguishing the criteria that constitute an academic discipline. While the subject orientation does not distinguish the principles that clearly identify what constitutes a subject, the disciplines orientation has focused on what makes an academic discipline unique. For example, King and Brownell state that a discipline is a community of discourse that is characterized by "a community of persons, an expression of human imagination, a domain, a tradition, a mode of inquiry, a conceptual structure, a specialized language or other system of symbols, a heritage of literature and a network of communications, a valuative and affective stance and an instructive community."[13] Other definitions of a discipline have been less inclusive, but even this one limits the idea of a discipline to academic areas (e.g., math, physics, history, language) and excludes such subjects as home economics, shop, and accounting.

During the fifties Arthur Bestor was recognized as one of the leading spokesmen for the disciplines orientation. Trained as a historian, Bestor was president of the Council for Basic Education from 1956 to 1957. He wrote two books—*The Restoration of Learning* and *Educational Wastelands*—that were critical of progressive education and argued for a curriculum based on the intellectual disciplines.

Bestor stated the main activities in elementary schools should be reading, writing, and arithmetic with some emphasis on science, geography, and history. In junior high school, study should become more rigorous, with work in algebra, biology, and history. In high school, mathematics should include advanced algebra, plane geometry, trigonometry, analytical geometry, and calculus. Science, according to Bestor, should consist of chemistry, physics, and biology. The other essentials in secondary school should be history, English, and a second language.[14] For Bestor, training in the intellectual disciplines was a prerequisite for a college education and even vocational education. Thus Bestor argued that all secondary students should be exposed to the intellectual disciplines. Bestor felt that even slow learners should be exposed to this curriculum. He also suggested that students be advanced according to their mastery of a particular subject rather than according to age.

Bestor felt that school curriculum should be developed by scholars in the disciplines. Teacher training should focus mostly on an academic area rather than on courses in education. Bestor did not support an interdisciplinary approach, and thus he was critical of social studies and language arts programs.[15] In Canada Helen Neatby articulated the disciplines position in her book *So Little for the Mind*.

The position articulated by Bestor and Neatby became dominant after the launching of Sputnik in 1957. A year after Sputnik was launched a conference of scientists, mathematicians, psychologists, and educators was held at Woods Hole in Massachusetts. It was convened by the National Academy of Sciences and assisted by agencies such as the National Science Foundation, the U.S. Air Force, the RAND Corporation, the U.S. Office of Education, the American Association for the Advancement of Science, and the Carnegie Corporation. The conference provided an impetus to curriculum development for the next decade.

The Process of Education

The conference chairman, Jerome Bruner, wrote a book entitled *The Process of Education* that became a curriculum manifesto for the disciplines orientation. On page 2, Bruner outlines the objective of the disciplines orientation: "The main objective of this work has been to present subject matter effectively—that is with due regard not only for coverage but also for structure."[16] Bruner acknowledges that in the past leading scholars have not been involved in developing curriculum for the schools and argues that this must change. He notes that with the Woods Hole conference the trend is being reversed. He also asserts that psychologists should become involved in curriculum by focusing on the structure of subject matter and the transfer of learning.

What does Bruner mean by the structure of a subject? In the first chapter he refers to some examples:

Much more briefly, to take an example from mathematics, algebra is a way of arranging knowns and unknowns in equations so that the unknowns are made knowable. The three fundamentals involved in working with these equations are commutation, distribution, and association. Once a student grasps the ideas embodied by these three fundamentals, he is in a position to recognize wherein "new" equations to be solved are not new at all, but variants on a familiar theme. Whether the student knows the formal names of these operations is less important for transfer than whether he is able to use them.[17]

Bruner's idea of structure, then, is a general one. It is concerned with applying principles of a particular discipline to various contexts. Learning, in this orientation, involves recognizing the applicability of an idea, and these "ideas" are the fundamental principles of a discipline. In order that the principles become central to the school curriculum, Bruner, like Bestor, suggested that leading scholars in each discipline should be involved in developing curricula for schools. This was exactly the procedure that was used in the Physical Science Study Committee (PSSC) and the Biological Sciences Curriculum Study (BSCS).

Bruner noted, however, that fundamental principles should not just be presented to the student. Instead, learning situations should be structured so that the student discovers these ideas. Although Bruner suggests that the student should not be expected to discover all the principles of a discipline, there should at least be a balance between exposition and what came to be known as "the discovery method." Bruner gives an example of the discovery technique:

A sixth-grade class, having been through a conventional unit on the social and economic geography of the Southeastern states, was introduced to the North Central region by being asked to locate the major cities of the area on a map containing physical features and natural resources, but no place names. The resulting class discussion very rapidly produced a variety of plausible theories concerning the requirements of a city—a water transportation theory that placed Chicago at the junction of the three lakes, a mineral resources theory that placed it near the Mesabi range, a food-supply theory that put a great city on the rich soil of Iowa, and so on.[18]

The disciplines orientation differs in part from the subject matter position in that the process of learning is emphasized. Bruner presents four basic reasons for using the disciplines orientation.[19] First, he suggests that understanding fundamental principles makes a subject more comprehensible. Once the student has gained some understanding of a principle, such as a nation must trade in order to live, then the student can more readily understand the triangular trade of the American colonies with England and the Caribbean before the American Revolution.

Another rationale is that learning is retained more readily if placed within a structured pattern. If learning is accomplished within the structure of a discipline and built around fundamental principles of a discipline, more learning is retained over a longer period of time.

A third rationale that Bruner presents is that learning fundamental principles is the basis for transfer of training. In other words, ideas can be transferred to other contexts more readily if they are learned in the context of broad fundamental principles.

A final claim for the disciplines orientation, according to Bruner, is that one can narrow the gap between "advanced knowledge" and "elementary knowledge." The fundamental principles provide a mechanism for making sure that what is presented in schools is up-to-date and centered around key ideas in the discipline.

Readiness for Learning

Central to the disciplines orientation, as presented by Bruner, was the notion that "any subject can be taught in some effectively honest form to any child at any stage of development."[20] Bruner argued that students are able to understand the fundamental principles of a discipline at almost any age. He cites the statement of a mathematics teacher to support his case: "In teaching from kindergarten to graduate school, I have been amazed at the intellectual similarity of human beings at all ages."[21] Bruner and his colleagues viewed the child as a miniature scholar. At almost any age, in Bruner's view, the child can understand the operations of a discipline. At the Woods Hole conference, the curriculum specialists focused on the idea that the cognitive processes of the child differ only in degree, not in kind, from the cognitive processes of an adult. Bruner even cites Piaget and Inhelder to support his case.[22] Of course, developmentalists have generally made the opposite point in that they suggest that the curriculum must be altered to each stage of development. In the developmentalists' view, the thinking processes of early childhood, for example, differ in kind not in degree from adulthood. Bruner ignored the fact that children up to about age 11 are incapable of abstract thinking. Abstract thought, of course, is essential to study of most disciplines.

The bending of Piaget to support Bruner's case is a classic example of how one's orientation to curriculum will shape one's use of data. This example supports the general theme of this book, that an individual's orientation to curriculum shapes his or her view of how children learn.

Bruner's view that the child is a miniature scholar is also seen in how he thinks material should be selected for the classroom. He suggests that the main criterion for selecting a subject to be taught in elementary school is whether an adult should know the subject.

Related to Bruner's view of the child is his idea of the "spiral curriculum." Although in Bruner's view the child is able to understand basic principles at any age, the curriculum should present subject matter in a gradually more comprehensive and complex manner. For Bruner, if the material is not worth knowing to an adult, then the material should not clutter the curriculum.[23]

It is clear that, in Bruner's view, students must accommodate themselves to the subject matter, not vice versa. This view of the child and the curriculum is also seen in the last section of *The Process of Education*, which deals with learning aids and programmed learning. Bruner indicates that teaching machines, automatizing devices as he called them, are an extension of the art of teaching. He suggests that programmed learning can take some of the load off the teacher's shoulders. As Tanner and Tanner point out, Bruner really does not explore the relationship between programmed learning and his concept of discovery learning outlined earlier in the book. Discovery learning, according to Tanner and Tanner, is an emergent process, while programmed learning is a convergent process.

The failure of Bruner and the members of the Woods Hole Conference to recognize the essential conflict between the inquiry-discovery rationale and the operant-conditioning rationale of programmed instruction remains a mystery. Although the early progress reports of some of the national curriculum-reform projects indicated that consideration was being given to developing programmed materials, it became evident to the scholars working on these projects that programmed instruction is not compatible with the processes of scientific investigation. Consequently, efforts to develop programmed instructional materials for the leading curriculum-reform projects were abandoned in favor of textbooks supplemented by a variety of resource materials, such as laboratory units, cartridge films, slides, teachers' resource books, and paperbacks.[24]

One of the most interesting chapters in *The Process of Education* is entitled "Intuitive and Analytic Thinking." Here Bruner explains how thinking in the disciplines is sometimes intuitive in nature. Bruner suggests that an individual will sometimes arrive at a solution with a leap of intuition rather than through step-by-step analysis. However, the intuitive solution can be checked through analytic methods.

Indeed, the intuitive thinker may even invent or discover problems that the analyst would not. . . . Unfortunately, the formalism of school learning has somehow devalued intuition. It is the very strong conviction of men who have been designing curricula, in mathematics and the sciences particularly, over the last several years that much more work is needed to discover how we may develop the intuitive gifts of our students from the earliest grades onward.[25]

Bruner's comments on intuitive thinking sound like many transpersonal educators who today are calling for an emphasis on intuitive thinking in the classroom. This, then, is a tentative link between the disciplines orientation and the transpersonal orientation. Bruner suggested that intuition is often crucial to the development of hunches or hypotheses that can be subjected to more formal analysis.

Eleven years after *The Process of Education* was published, Bruner acknowledged some of the weaknesses of the disciplines orientation. He called for a movement away from academic formalism to a focus on social problems. In the midst of Vietnam and urban decay he suggested:

I believe I would be quite satisfied to declare, if not a moratorium, then something of a de-emphasis on matters that have to do with the structure of history, the structure of physics, the nature of mathematical consistency, and deal with curriculum rather in the context of the problems that face us. We might better concern ourselves with how these problems can be solved, not just by practical action, but by putting knowledge, wherever we find it and in whatever form we find it, to work in these massive tasks. . . . The issue is one of man's capacity for creating a culture, society, and technology that not only feed him but keep him caring and belonging.[26]

Conceptual Structure and Syntactical Structure

Another proponent of the disciplines approach has been Joseph Schwab. He has written several articles and books articulating his position and has argued that the disciplines have a twofold importance to education.

In brief, the structures of the disciplines are twice important to education. First, they are necessary to teachers and educators: they must be taken into account as we plan curriculum and prepare our teaching materials; otherwise, our plans are likely to miscarry and our materials, to misteach. Second, they are necessary in some part and degree within the curriculum, as elements of what we teach. Otherwise, there will be failure of learning or gross mislearning by our students.[27]

Schwab's concept of a discipline is different from Bruner's. For Schwab disciplines center mainly around what he calls conceptual and syntactical structures. Schwab states that the conceptual structures include the general conceptions that guide inquiry in a discipline. These general conceptions determine what will be studied in a discipline. Unlike Bruner, Schwab does not stress the broad application of these conceptions. In fact, pursuing these conceptions will clearly limit what is to be studied.

The general conceptions of a discipline can also change. An example of how the conceptual structure of a discipline changes can be found in physics in the early part of this century. Classical physics based on a Newtonian world view gave way to the new physics with a relativistic view of space and time. The new physics changed the way in which scientists approached problems.

The emphasis on general conception leads in Schwab's view to emphasis on the study of patterns and process rather than cataloguing information.

This shift from catalogues to patterns in the disciplines means, in turn, that teaching and learning take on a new dimension. Instead of focusing on one thing or idea at a time, clarifying each and going on to the next, teaching becomes a process of focusing on points of contact and connection among things and ideas, of clarifying the effect of each thing on the others, of conveying the way in which each connection modifies the participants in the connection—in brief, the task of portraying phenomena and ideas not as things in themselves but as fulfillments of a pattern.[28]

Schwab suggests that this interconnectedness within a discipline increases its complexity. It is more difficult to study light, for example, as separate from electricity and magnetism. Instead, the interdependence of light, electricity, and magnetism must be acknowledged.

Besides the guiding principles of a discipline (the conceptual structure), Schwab refers to what he calls the syntactical structure, which focuses on the "operations that distinguish the true, the verified, and the warranted in that discipline from the unverified and unwarranted.[29] Each discipline has its own syntactical structure. The methods of verification in history differ from those in biology, and those in biology differ from those in physics.

Schwab's conception of a discipline then leads to a variety of disciplines with few interconnections between them. Schwab's narrow conception of a discipline seems to preclude interdisciplinary activity. Some scientists disagree with this narrow conception of a discipline.

Moreover, many leading scientists do not agree with Schwab's contention that even within the field of science the conceptual schemes are so widely different that it is fruitless to find any unity of knowledge. The Nobel laureate Albert Szent-Gyorgi observed that the "unification of knowledge is the greatest achievement of science," and he went on to propose that "What I would like to see taught in school is this new subject—nature, not physics and chemistry."[30]

Schwab, like Bruner, moved away from this narrow conception and toward an acknowledgment of the relationships among disciplines. Schwab began to talk about the importance of what he called the "practical" or second mode beside the disciplinary mode. The practical aims "to discover the relations which exist or which can be induced among various subject areas—the arts which make possible recognition and repair of divorces." Schwab even argues that eclecticism must be accepted.

A curriculum grounded in but one or a few subsubjects of the social sciences is indefensible; contributions from all are required. There is no foreseeable hope of a unified theory in the immediate or middle future, nor of a metatheory which will tell us how to put those subsubjects together or order them in a fixed hierarchy of importance to the problems of curriculum. What remains as a viable alternative is the unsystematic, uneasy, pragmatic, and uncertain unions and connections which can be effected in an eclectic. And I must add, anticipating our discussion of the practical, that *changing* connections and *differing* orderings at different times of these separate theories, will characterize a sound eclectic.[31]

Analytic Simplification, Synthesis, and Dynamism

Phillip Phenix has also been a proponent of the disciplines orientation. For example, he argued that "all curriculum content should be drawn from the disciplines, or, to put it another way, that only knowledge contained in the disciplines is appropriate to the curriculum."[32] For Phenix, knowledge in the disciplines is distinctive because it is instructive, while knowledge outside the academic disciplines is not suited to teaching. Phenix suggests that knowledge in the disciplines is instructive because it is characterized by analytic simplification, synthetic coordination, and dynamism.

Analytic simplification is common to disciplines because they involve abstraction or drawing out key elements for the purposes of generalization. Phenix states the function of abstraction is to simplify and to reduce complexity through analysis. According to Phenix, a discipline not only simplifies understanding but also reveals significant patterns and relationships. Work in the disciplines can allow the student to see patterns in the disciplines and coordinate elements into coherent structures. A second characteristic, then, is synthesis.

The third characteristic of a discipline, according to Phenix, is dynamism. For Phenix, "disciplines do not merely simplify and coordinate; they also invite further analysis and synthesis. A discipline contains a lure to discovery."[33]

Like Bruner and Schwab, Phenix later modified his position on the disciplines. He acknowledges that "disciplinary studies alone tend toward fragmentation and sense of irrelevance" and suggests an interdisciplinary approach with a focus on personal and social issues. Some of his later writing can be included in the humanistic and transpersonal orientations.

Curriculum Projects

The disciplines orientation found its realization in several curriculum projects. Many began in the early sixties and several are still in use today. In the next section I will outline some projects conducted in science and the social studies.

Science. The Biological Sciences Curriculum Study (BSCS) was designed to teach students skills similar to those biologists use in the laboratory. One of the main emphases in the courses developed by the BSCS was on scientific investigation and methods of inquiry in biology[34]. Schwab was a supervisor in the BSCS, and his name is associated with one of the teacher's handbooks. In the handbook the emphasis is on how biologists carry out their investigations. The BSCS was critical of many texts in biology which focused solely on exposition of scientific conclusions. The BSCS argued that these texts gave students the impression that science consists of unalterable, fixed truths and that science is complete. Thus the student was not made aware that generalizations change and science is dynamic, as Phenix had suggested. The BSCS attempted to show students how knowledge is developed and how it is formed from raw data. Most texts had ignored the scientific process and also the fact that scientists do much of their work by trial and error. The BSCS felt the focus of study should be on inquiry.

The essence, then, of a teaching of science as inquiry, would be to show some of the conclusions of science in the framework of the way they arise and are tested. This would mean to tell the student about the ideas posed, and the experiments performed, to indicate the data thus found, and to follow the interpretation by which these data were converted into scientific knowledge.[35]

The BSCS course indicates the tentative nature of science. In place of conclusions it uses what is called "a narrative of inquiry." Here ideas in biology are related to a course of inquiry. The laboratory aspect of the BSCS course stimulates students to deal with problems that biologists might deal with. Thus there are no easily identifiable solutions to these projects; instead, the activities push the student to the "frontiers of knowledge."

Part of the curriculum is called "Invitations to Inquiry," and Schwab has also been associated with this material. These units encourage the student to become involved directly in scientific investigation. Some of the subjects in the "Invitations" series include the cell nucleus, seed germination, plant physiology, plant nutrition, population growth, environment, and disease. In these units the students learn about interpretation of simple and complex data, systematic and random error, construction of hypotheses, and sampling.

Below is an example of a lesson from the seed germination unit.

INVITATION 3
(Subject: Seed Germination)
(Topic: Misinterpretation of Data)

(It is one thing to take a calculated risk in interpreting data. It is another thing to propose an interpretation for which there is no evidence— whether based on misreading of the available data or indifference to evidence. The material in this Invitation is intended to illustrate one of the most obvious misinterpretations. It also introduces the role of a clearly formulated *problem* in controlling interpretation of the data from experiments to which the problem leads.)

To the student: (a) An investigator was interested in the conditions under which seeds would best germinate. He placed several grains of corn on moist blotting paper in each of two glass dishes. He then placed one of these dishes in a room from which light was excluded. The other was placed in a well-lighted room. Both rooms were kept at the same temperature. After four days the investigator examined the grains. He found that all the seeds in both dishes had germinated.

What interpretation would you make of the data from this experiment? Do not include facts that you may have obtained elsewhere, but restrict your interpretation to those from *this experiment alone.*

(Of course, the experiment is designed to test the light factor. The Invitation is intended, however, to give the inadequately logical students a chance to say that the experiment suggests that moisture is necessary for the sprouting of grains. Others may say it shows that a warm temperature is necessary. If such suggestions do not arise, introduce one as a possibility. Do so with an attitude that will encourage the expression of unwarranted interpretation, if such exists among the students.)

(If such an interpretation is forthcoming, you can suggest its weakness by asking the students if the data suggest that corn grains require a glass dish in order to germinate. Probably none of your students will accept this. You should have little difficulty in showing them that the data some of them thought were evidence for the necessity of moisture or warmth are no different from the data available about glass dishes. In neither case are the data evidence for such a conclusion.)

To the student: (b) What factor was clearly *different* in the surroundings of the two dishes? In view of your answer, remembering that this was a deliberately planned experiment, state as precisely as you can the specific problem that led to this particular plan of experiment.

(If it has not come out long before this, it should be apparent now that the experiment was designed to test the necessity of light as a factor in germination. As to the statement of the problem, the Invitation began with a very general question: "Under what conditions do seeds germinate best?" This is not the most useful way to state a problem for scientific inquiry, because it does not indicate where and how to look for an answer. Only when the "question" is made specific enough to suggest what data are needed to answer it does it become an immediately useful scientific problem. For example, "Will seeds germinate better with or without light?" is a question pointing clearly to what data are required. A comparison of germination in the light with germination in the dark is needed. So we can say that a general "wonderment" is converted into an immediately useful problem when the question is made sufficiently specific to suggest an experiment to be performed or specific data to be sought. We do not mean to suggest that general "wonderments" are bad. On the contrary, they are indispensable. The point is only that they must lead to something else—a solvable problem.)

To the student: (c) In view of the problem you have stated, look at the data again. What interpretation are we led to?

(It should now be clear that the evidence indicates that light is *not* necessary for the germination of *some* seeds. You may wish to point out that light is necessary for some other seeds [for example, Grand Rapids Lettuce] and may inhibit the germination of others [for example, some varieties of onion].)

(N.B.: This invitation continues to deal with the ideas of data, evidence and interpretation. It also touches on the new point dealt with under paragraph (b), the idea of a *problem*. It exemplifies the fact that general curiosity must be converted into a specific problem.)

(It also indicates that the problem posed in an inquiry has more than one function. First, it leads to the design of the experiment. It converts a wonder into a plan of attack. It also guides us in interpreting data. This is indicated in (c), where it is so much easier to make a sound interpretation than it is in (a), where we are proceeding without a clear idea of what problem led to the particular body of data being dealt with.)

(If your students have found this Invitation easy or especially stimulating, you may wish to carry the discussion further and anticipate to some extent the topic of Invitation 6 [planning an experiment]. The following additions are designed for such use.)[36]

Other "Invitation to Inquiry" materials encourage the student to move from "wonderments" to solvable problems. Part of the learning process for the student is to define the problem and then carry out an investigation.

The Physical Science Study Committee (PSSC) was started in 1956. MIT physicist Jerrold Zacharias was the principal figure in this project, which was sponsored by the National Science Foundation. By 1960 the

PSSC had introduced a textbook along with supplementary materials. Initially the focus of the PSSC was development of a two-year course in physics and chemistry. However, the committee eventually moved away from this objective toward the development of a one-year course in physics.

The PSSC emphasized an approach similar to the Schwabian concept of structure. The focus was on the "central ideas of physics." The PSSC stressed that students should pursue inquiry as a physicist would. Although there was an emphasis in the rationale of the PSSC on how the course would apply to the general student, the thrust of the course was on complex principles and procedures. The PSSC and BSCS will be analyzed at the end of this chapter.

Social Studies. Although science and mathematics courses were at the forefront of the disciplines movement, projects were also conducted in languages and the social studies. In social studies, Edwin Fenton was one of the leaders of this thrust. He outlined his position in two books: *The New Social Studies* and *Teaching the New Social Studies in Secondary Schools.* Fenton stated that there are three basic objectives in the new social studies: the development of inquiry skills, the development of attitudes and values, and the acquisition of knowledge. Fenton directed a project at Carnegie Tech and the major focus of this particular project was on inquiry. This focus reflects the influence of Schwab.

Teachers in every field share responsibility for teaching the skills of inquiry. Physicists, historians, and teachers of literature should all challenge their students to develop and test hypotheses—tentative explanations adopted provisionally to explain certain facts and guide the investigation of others—and to learn the rules of logic which govern the process. Each discipline has its own peculiar elements. Historians cannot set up an experiment to determine the cause of the Civil War any more than physicists could determine whether or not the first atomic bomb would work by poking through dusty records in a library. Hence, although the responsibility to teach skills falls on every teacher, each discipline must work at the problem within its own framework, a framework determined largely by the structure of the discipline itself.[37]

Fenton cites Schwab's definition of conceptual and syntactical structures as a basic definition of structure. However, he translates Schwab's definition into his own language: "Structure consists of a method of inquiry made of two parts: the formation of a hypothesis and the process of proof."[38] For Fenton, Schwab's "body of imposed conceptions" in social studies provide the basis of inquiry in social studies. Fenton suggests that concepts can be used in this manner. Such concepts might include class, status, role, and norm. Fenton suggests that these concepts can be used in the classroom to help guide the student's search for information. For example, in studying Russian society before 1900 these concepts can provide a framework for examining social issues. With these concepts the student can examine what classes existed and what social roles existed. The student can also look at norms, or patterns of behavior, that existed in the society.

Concepts such as leadership can also be used to explore issues in the social studies. Like the concepts of role, class, and norm, the concept of leadership can be used to frame questions and develop hypotheses. Concepts like leadership and class provide the "imposed conceptions" of the social studies that shape inquiry. Fenton also outlines what he calls the process of proof. This process involves the following steps: identifying a problem, formulating hypotheses, recognizing implications of hypotheses, gathering data, analyzing the data, and evaluating the hypotheses in light of the data.[39]

Fenton argues that the modes of inquiry should allow students to cope with the knowledge explosion. By learning inquiry skills, Fenton argues that the student will have the tools to examine the appropriateness of the information that he or she encounters.

How does the inquiry method work in the classroom? Fenton presents an example of the inquiry method. This method was used to examine statements about life in the Soviet Union.

Inquiry into Inquiry

Inquiry into Method: What Did We Do?
How Did We Do It?

TEACHER: Let's stop to summarize. We saw that communism and democracy are based on different definitions of man, different goals for man, and different ways of achieving the separate goals. When we looked at these two paragraphs about Soviet communism, how did we analyze them?

PUPIL: First we tried to find out just what the author's argument was.

TEACHER: How did we organize this finding out?

PUPIL: We looked for categories to see what topics he was talking about and if he left some out that biased his thinking.

PUPIL: Then we looked to see what he said in each category, all the related sentences in his argument.

PUPIL: Then we examined the words he used to see if we could understand them, and if they were used in a special way.

PUPIL: Also to see if they were used to convince us of the argument.

TEACHER: Do you think you could build an argument using language as a tool to convince someone of your point of view? We'll try it later and compare the categories and the words each one selects. What did we do after we analyzed what was said and how it was said?

PUPIL: We predicted what would happen if we believed each author.

TEACHER: We said, "If we believe author A, then ..."; "If we believe author B, then ..." What were we doing when we said this?

PUPIL: It looks like hypotheses.

TEACHER: Why did we make these hypotheses?

PUPIL: So that we could make a prediction about the ends-means and methods of each one.

TEACHER: After we predicted these, what did we then do?

PUPIL: We looked for the reasons why each author might believe what he does.

PUPIL: Then we looked at what he might be assuming when he held this view.

TEACHER: What did we find?

PUPIL: They each had different assumptions and, therefore, different conclusions. Our whole world might be different depending upon which one we believed.

PUPIL: I think they had different attitudes about communism and about war.

PUPIL: Then we decided we could pose a new alternative with new assumptions.

Inquiry into Criteria for Method

TEACHER: Why do you suppose we spent so much time talking about these articles?

PUPIL: So we would see that people had different points of view and were trying to convince us of them.

PUPIL: So we wouldn't just believe everything we read.

TEACHER: But if someone presents the fact, shouldn't we believe them?

PUPIL: But, the facts look different to different people. These authors probably both know the same facts about the Soviet Union, but they mean something different to each one.

TEACHER: Why do they look different to different people?

PUPIL: I guess because they start out assuming different things.

PUPIL: And they value different things also.

TEACHER: How would you make a judgment about this subject, once you had done all this studying?

PUPIL: I'd see which conclusions I liked better, which I valued most.

Alternative Judgment-Making Methods

TEACHER: Are there other ways in which judgments can be made?

PUPIL: I guess we could believe what we want to believe without even looking at the consequences.

PUPIL: Or, we could believe what someone tells us to believe. But then it would be hard to choose which authority to believe.

Criteria for Inquiry Method

TEACHER: What advantages does this method have?

PUPIL: We can bring everyone's ideas out in public and see what their bias is.

PUPIL: We can examine the consequences and see what we value most.

PUPIL: We have to learn to defend our arguments, and tell why we believe them.

TEACHER: Are there times when we wouldn't want to use the inquiry method?

PUPIL: Maybe if we were at war, this would be dangerous.

PUPIL: Or, if a jury were deciding a case, we shouldn't try to influence them.

PUPIL: Maybe if the FBI is investigating someone, we shouldn't bring everything out in the open.

PUPIL: Maybe sometimes we just have to follow an authority and are not allowed to question and argue.

Assumptions of the Method

TEACHER: If we use this method of inquiring, then what are we valuing?

PUPIL: Questioning, discussing, changing points of view.

TEACHER: If we value this, what are we assuming?

PUPIL: I guess we assume that we *can* change people's points of view by discussing if we show them the consequences of their views.[40]

Fenton also cites the Amherst history project as an example of the new social studies. In this project students pursued inquiry like historians as they examined historical sources such as "letters, diaries, public documents, speeches, tables of statistics," and so forth, which have been organized around a particular historical event.

During the seventies Fenton was influenced by Kohlberg and the developmentalist orientation. His work at Carnegie Tech in the social studies reflected this change as he developed materials designed to facilitate moral development.

Summary and Appraisal

Subject Orientation

Educational Aims.   Mastery of basic skills (e.g., literacy and computation skills) in elementary school and traditional subject areas (e.g., English, science, math, history, and a language) in secondary school.

Conception of Learning.   Learning focuses on mastery of skills and retention of knowledge.

Conception of the Learner.   The learner is conceived as someone who must adapt himself or herself to learning the subject. In this orientation there is generally not much emphasis on the needs and interests of the learner; instead, the course is presented according to its own internal logic.

The Instructional Process.   Instruction involves exposition through lectures, drill, and discussion.

Learning Environment.   The teacher is in control of the environment, which is usually highly structured.

Teacher's Role. The teacher is the central authority and directs the learning activities. The teacher, particularly at the secondary level, is expected to have a thorough knowledge of one particular subject area.

Evaluation. Evaluation focuses on how the student has mastered the subject matter. In many subject areas the tests involve recall of information and mastery of some basic skills.

Disciplines Orientation

Educational Aims. Student mastery of the conceptual framework and methods of inquiry of academic disciplines.

Conception of Learning. The conception can vary with the specific discipline. However, there is a general emphasis on discovery learning, where the student discovers basic principles of the discipline and applies them to other contexts.

Conception of the Learner. The learner is viewed in a more active manner than in the subject orientation. Often the student is viewed as mini-scholar who carries out inquiry in the particular discipline.

Conception of the Instructional Process. The teacher assists the learner in the discovery process. The teacher will present an initial situation where the student can develop a hypothesis, examine the hypothesis in relation to the data, and then generate conclusions based on the investigation.

Learning Environment. The environment contains learning materials associated with a particular discipline. For example, in history original sources are used so that the student conducts an inquiry as a historian would carry out an investigation.

Teacher's Role. The teacher supplies resources and acts as a support to the inquiry process. The teacher should have expertise in the discipline and be prepared to model the inquiry process within the discipline. The teacher does not dominate but stimulates inquiry and discovery.

Evaluation. Evaluation focuses on how the student has mastered basic principles and modes of inquiry of a discipline. There is also an emphasis on how the student can apply the concepts and inquiry skills to different contexts.

In a time when we hear the call of "back-to-basics" it is appropriate to review the strengths and weaknesses associated with the subject orientation.[41]

One argument used to support the subject orientation is that it organizes the curriculum in a systematic way. It is argued that economy and efficiency are main advantages to using the subject matter orientation in organizing curriculum in the schools. It has been suggested that this type of approach to curriculum is easy to administer. Scheduling can be easily built around subjects and the time slots for classes are uniform (e.g., 40 to 50 minutes).

Another argument is based on the power of tradition. Since high schools and colleges have long been designed around subject matter, it allows the teacher to continue to work within a familiar framework. Since many teachers are comfortable with this framework, it continues as the principal organizing framework in most secondary schools. Parents are also familiar with this orientation and they resist changes to it.

Textbooks and learning materials are also organized around the different subjects. Thus most curriculum materials support the subject orientation, as few learning materials have been developed to support an interdisciplinary or integrated approach to learning.

Tradition provides a large part of the case for the subject matter orientation. Although it is possible to refute tradition on logical and empirical grounds, the power of tradition has been acknowledged by those who have been studying the problems of implementing innovations in the classroom. Seymour Sarason, in his book *The Culture of School and the Problem of Change*, suggests the subject matter orientation is one of the "programmatic regularities" that dominate the life at school.

Despite the argument that subject matter can assist the logical organization of the curriculum, evidence presented by learning theorists suggests that the structure of subject matter does not correlate with how children learn and develop. For example, much subject matter is presented in an abstract manner that is contrary to what we know about how children learn. In elementary school it is clear most children need concrete experiences to assist learning and development.

The breakdown of subject matter into separate subjects also makes it difficult to relate ideas and concepts between subjects. Thus the subject matter orientation establishes arbitrary distinctions that make it difficult to explore relationships outside of a particular subject.

There is also the danger that this orientation can become divorced from social concerns. Thus subject matter specialists can lose themselves in an area of study and ignore problems of poverty, racism, and economic decay. Smith et al. state:

The products of the subject curriculum know more about the crusades than they know about the management of modern industry; more about the structure of the earthworm than about their own bodies and the status of public provisions for their health; more about the exploits of Napoleon than about the nature and workings of their own economic and political systems . . . [42]

Although certain subject areas may help us deal with some problems, organizing the curriculum around a subject is not particularly helpful in relating subject matter to deeper social concerns. It also is not appropriate for relating subject matter to the needs and interests of students. Although in secondary schools electives are developed to meet this concern, there is no guarantee that even within electives teachers will gear the subject to the needs and interests of students. Thus in a history course the teacher may cover the material chronologically without exploring specific issues or problems that are of interest to students. In English, literature is sometimes used which is well beyond the capabilities of some students. Zais comments:

The importance of beginning instruction on the *student's* own psychological ground is a well-established pedagogical principle. When, as is commonly the case in the subject design, students are coerced through marks, promotions, and other external forces to learn subject matter in a form that is alien to their experience, they usually *also* learn to despise the school, the subject, and the people who teach it to them. Though unintended, this is indeed a sad fate for so noble an institution, so great a cultural heritage, and so honorable a profession.[43]

Another criticism is that traditionally the subject matter orientation has been related to lower levels of learning, that is, the focus has been on information recall and basic skills with little opportunity to develop high-order analytic and conceptual skills. Similarly, the affective domain has often been ignored as well. Other orientations have been developed in response to this difficulty, particularly the humanistic and developmental orientations. The humanistic orientation gained strength in the late sixties and focused on developing curriculum in harmony with student interests, while the developmental position focused on constructing programs in accordance with the appropriate student level of development.

Many of the arguments supporting the subject matter orientation have also been used in support of the disciplines position, in that the disciplines conform to present school structures and allow for an economical and efficient presentation of material. It has also been argued that the disciplines position is in keeping with the western intellectual tradition. The academic disciplines reflect the highest intellectual achievements of the culture, and the disciplines orientation most closely reflects these achievements. Bruner also argued that the disciplines taught around fundamental principles allow for ready transfer and application of learning.

One of the key differences between the subject matter position and the disciplines orientation is the emphasis in the latter on inquiry and discovery learning. It attempted to engage the student more actively in the learning process. The stress on intuitive thinking by Bruner was in line with the discovery approach.

Despite this emphasis, however, the disciplines orientation suffers from many of the same weaknesses as the subject curriculum. Many of these weaknesses became apparent in the late sixties, and the proponents of the disciplines orientation moved away from the narrow conception of learning that they had originally articulated. Schwab, for example, talked about the "practical" and the acceptance of eclecticism in order to deal with social problems.

It has also been argued that many of the programs designed on this orientation such as the BSCS courses and the PSSC courses are only applicable to the college-bound student. These programs were designed for an elite group of students and were not appropriate to large numbers of students who were not bound toward liberal arts study at the university level. Related to this notion is the assumption that the student should behave like a scholar in the various disciplines. How realistic is it to expect students who are not going to be specialists in science or math to actually pursue study as if they were scholars in those fields?

There is some evidence that programs such as those developed by the PSSC did not produce the desired effects. Tests comparing students who took the PSSC course with students who took conventional courses did not reveal significant differences. Tanner and Tanner also suggest that the PSSC physics course contributed to a decline in the number of students majoring in physics in college. During the sixties the proportion of National Merit finalists in the United States majoring in physics declined from one out of five to only one out of ten. Tanner and Tanner acknowledge that some of this decline reflects the cultural emphasis of the sixties, but they state that "many knowledgeable observers attributed the enrollment declines to the curriculum reforms as exemplified by the PSSC Physics."[44] Other studies indicate that much of the money put into teacher upgrading in specific subjects such as physics was wasted. The report of Harvard Project Physics indicated "teacher personality and student attitudes and interests are much more potent predictors of pupil achievement than the extent of the teachers' specialized study of physics."[45]

Despite these difficulties, both the subject and disciplines orientations have enjoyed a revival in the eighties. Neil Postman, who at one time argued from a humanistic orientation, has suggested that the school curriculum should be an alternative to the "curriculum" of television. He argues that the school curriculum should center on a historical perspective that reflects the "ascent of humanity."

In any event, the virtues of adopting the ascent of humanity as a scaffolding on which to build a curriculum are many and various, especially in our present situation. For one thing, with a few exceptions which I shall note, it does not require that we invent new subjects or discard old ones. The structure of the subject-matter curriculum which presently exists in most schools is entirely usable....But best of all, the theme of the ascent of humanity provides us with a non-technical, noncommercial definition of education....You will note that such a definition is not child-centered, not training-centered, not skill-centered, not even problem-centered. It is idea-centered and coherence-centered. It is also otherworldly, in the sense that it does not assume that what one learns in school must be directly and urgently related to a problem of today. In other words, it is an education that stresses history, the scientific mode of thinking, the disciplined use of language, a wide-ranging knowledge of the arts and religion, and the continuity of human enterprise.[46]

Postman, then, calls for intellectual rigor in the school curriculum, like a number of other academics. Postman feels that schools should maintain a traditional emphasis on subjects and academic disciplines, and not try to educate the whole child.

Notes

1. B. Othanel Smith, William O. Stanley, and J. Harlan Shores, *Fundamentals of Curriculum Development* (New York: Harcourt Brace and World, 1957), p. 231.
2. Ibid., p. 234.
3. Ibid., p. 236.
4. Ibid., p. 237.
5. Ibid., p. 239.
6. Ibid., p. 249.
7. Gerald Lee Gutek, *Philosophical Alternatives in Education* (Columbus, Ohio: Charles Merrill, 1974), p. 89.
8. Ibid.
9. Ibid., p. 90
10. Ibid.
11. Allan C. Ornstein, "Curriculum Contrasts: A Historical Overview," *The Phi Delta Kappan*, 63(6) (February 1982), 405.
12. Ibid.
13. Cited in Robert Zais, *Curriculum Principles and Foundations* (New York: Harper and Row, 1976), p. 404.
14. As described by Gutek, *Philosophical Alternatives in Education*, pp. 91–92.
15. Ibid., p. 93.
16. Jerome Bruner, *The Process of Education* (Cambridge, Mass.: Harvard University, 1960), p. 2.
17. Ibid., pp. 7–8.
18. Ibid., p. 21.
19. Ibid., pp. 23–26.
20. Ibid., p. 33.

21. Ibid., pp. 39–40.

22. Ibid., pp. 33–46.

23. Ibid., p. 52.

24. Daniel Tanner and Laurel Tanner, *Curriculum Development: Theory into Practice* (New York: Macmillan, 1975), pp. 433–44.

25. Bruner, *The Process of Education*, pp. 58–59.

26. Jerome Bruner, "The Process of Education Reconsidered," in Robert Leeper, ed., *Dare to Care/Dare to Act* (Washington, D.C.: Association for Supervision and Curriculum Development, 1971), pp. 29–30.

27. Joseph Schwab, "The Concept of the Structure of a Discipline," in Elliot Eisner and Elizabeth Vallance, eds., *Conflicting Conceptions of Curriculum* (Berkeley, Calif.: McCutchan, 1974), p. 163.

28. Ibid., p. 169.

29. Ibid., p. 173.

30. Tanner and Tanner, *Curriculum Development*, pp. 411–12.

31. Joseph Schwab, "The Practical: A Language for Curriculum," in David Purpel and Maurice Belanger, eds., *Curriculum and the Cultural Revolution* (Berkeley, Calif.: McCutchan, 1972), p. 87.

32. Phillip Phenix, "The Uses of the Disciplines as Curriculum Content," in Donald E. Orlosky and B. Othanel Smith, eds., *Curriculum Development Issues and Insights* (Chicago: Rand McNally, 1978), p. 83.

33. Ibid., p. 87.

34. Tanner and Tanner, *Curriculum Development*, pp. 413–14.

35. Biological Sciences Curriculum Study, *Biology Teachers' Handbook* (Joseph J. Schwab, ed.) (New York: John Wiley & Sons, 1965), p. 40.

36. Ibid., pp. 57–58.

37. Edwin Fenton, *The New Social Studies* (New York: Holt, Rinehart & Winston, 1967), p. 11.

38. Ibid., p. 12.

39. Ibid., pp. 16–17.

40. Bernice Goldmark, "Critical Thinking: Deliberate Method," *Social Education* 30 (May 1966), 332. Reprinted in Fenton, *New Social Studies*, pp. 45–47.

41. Zais, *Curriculum*, pp. 400–401.

42. Smith et al., *Fundamentals of Curriculum Development*, p. 248.

43. Zais, *Curriculum*, pp. 402–403.

44. Tanner and Tanner, *Curriculum Development*, pp. 440–41.

45. Ibid.

46. Neil Postman, *Teaching as Conserving Activity* (New York: Delacorte Press, 1979), pp. 135–36.

4

Social Orientation

This orientation stresses social experience. It views the person within a social context and attempts to develop programs within that context. However, within this orientation there are different perspectives on the role of the school.

One variation emphasizes cultural transmission. Within this framework the school inculcates the student in the values, traditions, and mores of the society. Sociologists such as Talcott Parsons have articulated this position. Parsons suggests that in school students learn the appropriate roles that exist within society. The student learns what role behaviors are expected and how to meet various role expectations.

Another position within this orientation is the democratic citizenship position. Here the school does not merely transmit values but expects the student to exercise autonomous thinking. Curriculum theorists such as James Shaver have emphasized how the school can assist the student in developing skills to analyze value conflicts and make decisions within a democratic context.

A third position within this orientation focuses more on social change. This orientation acknowledges the deficiencies in society and suggests that the school can help overcome these problems. Educators such as Alfred Alschuler and Fred Newmann have developed approaches that let teachers and students not only examine issues but become involved in social change in the school and in the community.

Cultural Transmission

This approach to curriculum is one of the oldest orientations and calls for the school to inculcate the student into the ways of society. Some sociologists have argued that the function of school is to introduce students to the culture and the roles that they should play in that culture. Emile Durkheim, the French sociologist, viewed education as a process for internalizing what he called the "social facts" or "social being" rather than stressing personal growth or what he called "individual being." Durkheim stated:

[The social being] is a system of ideas, sentiments, and practices which express in us, not our personality, but the group or different groups of which we are part; these are religious beliefs, moral beliefs, and practices, national or occupational traditions, collective opinions, of every kind. Their totality forms the social being. To constitute this being in each of us is the end of education.[1]

Schools are responsible for transmitting the social being to each student. When the social being is internalized, it constitutes the moral authority within the individual.

Talcott Parsons has viewed education as cultural transmission. He suggests that schools have a dual role as an agency of socialization and manpower allocation. As a socializing agency, the school commits the student to internalize society's values and eventually to learn adult roles in society. Thus the school works with students in learning their roles and meeting other people's expectations in interpersonal behavior. The school also distributes human resources within society and thus acts as an agency of manpower allocation.[2]

Other sociologists in the functionalist school have made analyses similar to that of Parsons. For example, Yehudi Cohen, a cultural anthropologist, shows how schools affect students. First Cohen distinguishes between socialization and education. Socialization involves inculcation of various behaviors through interaction with parents, relatives, and other members of the community. By being with and observing the behavior of others, the individual adopts basic attitudes, values, and skills that predominate in society. Education, on the other hand, inculcates values and skills through more standardized and stereotyped procedures. In Cohen's view, education differs from socialization in that it is more planned and controlled. Education, then, tends to occur at regular intervals, while socialization occurs more spontaneously.

Socialization consists of such daily events in the life of a child as a parent expostulating "No!" when the child does something undesirable, or receiving a reward after having done something well. The interaction between the parent and child might be predictable—as when a child tortures a cat or a younger sibling—but it is not stereotyped and standardized in the sense that the interaction occurs at regular times, in predictable ways, and at set places.[3]

Cohen suggests that in modern times schools are intertwined with the rise of the national state. Schools emphasize the universal values of the state. The procedures for inculcating these values are standardized in the schools. Cohen argues schools promote loyalty to the state beyond local ties. The state requires the individual's loyalty and often seeks this loyalty through commitment to a nationalist ideology. Flags, pictures of national leaders, and the singing of national anthems are used in schools to promote this loyalty.

Of what relevance is the ubiquitous portrait of Washington, Mao, or Lenin to the teaching of grammar and the use of a slide rule in an American, Chinese, or Soviet classroom? Of what relevance is a cross in a religiously sponsored school to the learning of geography, history, literature, and the like? The relevance is this: As part of the state bureaucracy, schools are generally maintained under the sponsorship of the state organization that controls and supports them in one way or other. Just as courts are part of the state bureaucracy and display the material symbols of the state organization of which they are a part, so do schools. The relevance is also this: Learning is a rewarding experience for most children. Hence—as every variety of behavioristic psychology has demonstrated repeatedly—it is hardly a startling insight to suggest that, whether anyone is consciously aware of it or not, the child comes to associate everything he learns with the state's symbols that face or envelop him while he is learning. These symbols become as much a part of his mind as the alphabet and the concept of zero. School is not only the place to learn arithmetic; it is also the place to learn zealotry.[4]

Cohen suggests that in some cases the schools are devoted to free inquiry. However, this is rare, because the state could not be expected to finance institutions that are counter to its aims of social stability and control. Schools, in Cohen's view, emphasize one mode of behavior rather than several modes. Examinations are used to support an emphasis on one response. Students are required to provide the one "right answer," and this emphasis promotes a general uniformity of behavior.

Schools in Cohen's view also stress impersonal authority. Teachers change from year to year so that the students do not build strong identifications with a particular individual. Since the stress in schools is on universal loyalty, the school is structured so that the student's loyalty to specific teachers does not override the general ethic of universal conformity.

Recently it has become more popular to argue that schools should socialize the child. For example, Neil Postman has suggested that schools should more actively pursue their socializing function. Postman outlines his position in his book, *Teaching as Conserving Activity*:

It is also why the school ought properly to be a place for what we might call "manners education": The adults in school ought to be concerned with teaching youth a standard of civilized interaction . . . . It [school] is a social situation requiring the subordination of one's own impulses and interests to those of the group. In a word, manners.[5]

Postman reverses an earlier position he had taken in the late sixties, when he suggested in *Teaching as Subversive Activity* that schools were generally oppressive and stifled individual growth.

In terms of specific educational programs, it has been suggested that such programs as vocational education, career education, and work-study programs as well as behavioristic programs fit into the cultural transmission mode. This may or may not be the case. It probably is the case, however, if there is little opportunity for the student formally to reflect on his or her experience. If the focus is solely on how the student must meet the role expectations of the employer without any broader analysis or critical perspective, then these programs can be viewed as cultural transmission.

Democratic Citizenship

The focus in democratic citizenship is on developing knowledge of the democratic process and certain cognitive skills such as critical thinking, values analysis, and group process skills so that the individual can participate in a democracy.

One of the chief proponents of this view has been James Shaver. Working originally with Don Oliver and Fred Newmann, Shaver developed the jurisprudential approach to social studies education in the sixties. Since then, he has continued to be a spokesman for teaching students how to make decisions within a democratic context.

With William Strong, Shaver has written a book entitled *Facing Values Decisions: Rationale Building for Teachers*, which outlines an approach to social decision making based on a thorough understanding of democracy.[6] Implicit in Shaver's view of democracy are such basic values as individual dignity, self-determination, intelligence, pluralism, and community. At the base of this value structure is respect for individual dignity. This means each person has intrinsic worth and must be treated with respect.

Another key value in this framework is self-determination. People in a democracy have the right to make choices, particularly decisions that affect their own lives. Faith in the intelligence of the individual is also important to democracy. Citizenship education places an emphasis on developing rational capabilities so that the person can deal with conflicts that arise in a democracy. Decision making is based on an examination of the facts while taking into account various value positions.

Another value inherent in this view of democracy is pluralism. In fact, democracy is based on a variety of values and life styles that are inherently pluralistic. Sometimes these values and life styles conflict and the individual must make critical choices.

The general values of individual dignity, rationality, and pluralism are translated into more specific values such as freedom of speech and assembly and equality of opportunity. These values form the "American creed," which is expressed in the Constitution and particularly in the first ten amendments, known as the Bill of Rights. The American creed provides the legal and ethical framework of this orientation. However, the values of freedom and equality of opportunity can come into conflict. For example, these values can conflict in affirmative action plans. Citizenship education teaches students to work through such value conflicts in a rational manner.

The teacher's role is transmitting democratic values in a manner that enhances the rationality of the students. In the words of Scheffler:

> To teach, in the standard sense, is at some points, at least, to submit oneself to the understanding and independent judgment of the pupil, to his demand for reasons, to his sense of what constitutes an adequate explanation. To teach someone that such-and-such is the case is not merely to try to get him to believe it. . . . Teaching involves further that . . . we try also to get him to believe it for reasons that within the limits of his capacity to grasp, are our reasons. Teaching, in this way, requires us to reveal our reasons to the student, and, by so doing, to submit them to his evaluation and criticism . . .[7]

One aspect of the democratic citizenship process is analyzing value conflicts within the context of the American creed. Students are taught to relate their concepts to the underlying precepts of democratic government. Shaver calls this process "label generalization." For example, consider the idea of fairness, which children develop in their play. In the classroom the teacher, using Shaver's framework, would relate this idea of fairness to the political and legal concept of equal treatment before the law.

Label generalization is important because it helps students become fluent in the language of democracy. In Shaver's words:

> Helping students to begin to use labels with basic value meanings serves several related instructional and societal functions: (1) It provides a basis for value identification and clarification. (2) It gives students a more powerful conceptual scheme as they relate their own untutored commitments to the basic values of the society. (3) It gives students a more powerful value language for analysis, discussion, and persuasion. And (4) it helps to insure a nationwide values vocabulary at the basic value level among people who, unlike news commentators, politicians, and lawyers, frequently would not otherwise use such terms in their thinking and disputes. In short, the process of label generalization is important because it relates the student's own developing value vocabulary and conceptual schema to the broader and more powerful basic values of a democratic society.[8]

Shaver then gives an example of how label generalization can be used in the classroom:

Problem. *Focus on the value of "fairness" as you read this section.*

A news item I read to my ninth-grade homeroom said that a white college student had been denied admission to law school because the institution had a "quota" system—a system that gave preferential admissions to minority students. The white student was suing the school because his qualifying entrance scores were higher than those of blacks who had gained admission.

"What's your reaction?" I asked.

Dick Simmons was grinning from ear to ear. "That white dude, he knows what it's like now! About time, too!"

"What do you mean?"

"Oh, you know, man! Step to the back of the bus and all that jive? So let the honky sweat it out—be good for him! Like maybe it'll build his *character*, you know?" Dick's voice was drawling and sarcastic.

I glanced around the room. Joanie Anderson's face was pink with anger. Her hand stabbed into the tense quiet Dick had created.

"Well, I don't think it's *fair*," she blurted out. "I mean . . ."

"*Fair!*" Dick interrupted in a half-shout. He swung round in his desk. "You gonna talk about *fair* to me? Huh? You think Whitey was talking *fairness* and all that honky crap when they sent the slave ships over? You think working blacks on the plantations was *fair*? Or breaking up the families? Or white masters screwing the black women? You think being denied the right to vote was *fair*? Or segregated housing and restaurants and schools?" Dick let the questions hang and then drove in his point. "Hey, baby—you *owe* us—and you better get used to payin' up!"

Joe Sheridan didn't even bother to raise his hand. "Dick, you're full of it. Joanie don't owe you *nothing*. And neither do I. Nobody owes nobody—that's what I think."

Dick's sneer was cool and stylized. "Four hundred years, dig? That's what you owing blacks in this country!" His fist went up in the clenched symbol of black power. "Ain't no way you gonna turn back the clock!"

The challenge was unmistakable in Dick's voice. "That's true," I said. "Whites can't turn back the clock and neither can blacks. That's the terrible thing about our history. But it's also the great thing, too, because it shows us how far we've really come in the past few years."

"Blacks ain't been nowhere 'cept down the river," Dick said.

"I don't know," I shrugged. "I mean, look at this news clipping we've been discussing. Why, ten or fifteen years ago we couldn't have had this kind of talk."

Dick's eyes snapped with anger. "And you know why? 'Cause niggers hadn't learned how to play with matches yet!"

"You could have a point," I conceded. "Maybe that's what convinced *some* white politicians. But what about everyday people like Joanie and Joe? What about me? Do you think that burning down our places would encourage us to support the black movement?"

Dick fell silent as he chewed over my question for a moment. "Let's talk over this value of fairness," I added. "Maybe this kind of discussion can help us work things out for ourselves in the future."

Follow-up. *Dick and the other students who entered into the discussion seem to have different meanings for the value of "fairness." Can you identify the various definitions—such as justice, equality of opportunity, retribution—and whom they fit? Which are basic democratic values?*

How would you work with this class to help them identify and clarify their commitments and relate them to basic value labels?[9]

Citizenship education in a democracy deals, to large extent, with analysis of value conflicts. For example, the Harvard Public Issues Project had this focus as case studies were developed to deal with various ethical, legal, and social dilemmas. Most of these dilemmas focus on public policy issues. Public policy involves a choice for action by citizens or officials in the community. For example, Should capital punishment be abolished? is a public policy question. Other issues in the project center on the choices for personal action: Should I write the legislature to support human rights legislation? Should I support a political candidate even though I don't agree with all of his or her platform? Some of the issues of the Harvard Project are oulined in Table 1. The sample topic areas in the project are listed with corresponding conflicting values.

Table 1. Identification of General Problem Areas

Problem Areas	Sample Unit Topics	Conflicting Values[a]
Racial and ethnic conflict	School desegregation	Equal protection
	Civil rights for nonwhites and ethnic minorities	Due process
		Brotherhood of man
	Housing for nonwhites and ethnic minorities	vs.
		Peace and order
	Job opportunities for nonwhites and ethnic minorities	Property and contract rights
		Personal privacy and
	Immigration policy	association
Religious and ideological conflict	Rights of the Communist party in America	Freedom of speech and conscience
	Religion and public education	vs.
		Equal protection
	Control of "dangerous" or "immoral" literature	Safety and security of democratic institutions
	Religion and national security: oaths, conscientious objectors	
	Taxation of religious property	
Security of the individual	Crime and delinquency	Standards of freedom
		Due process
		vs.

Table 1. (*continued*)

Problem Areas	Sample Unit Topics	Conflicting Values[a]
Conflict among economic groups	Organized labor Business competition and monopoly "Overproduction" of farm goods Conservation of natural resources	Peace and order Community welfare Equal or fair bargaining power and competition General welfare and progress of the community vs. Property and contract rights
Health, education, and welfare	Adequate medical care: for the aged, for the poor Adequate educational opportunity Old-age security Job and income security	Equal opportunity Brotherhood of man vs. Property and contract rights
Security of the nation	Federal loyalty-security programs [Foreign policy]	Freedom of speech, conscience, and association Due process Personal privacy vs. Safety and security of democratic institutions

[a] The "vs." in the listing of values suggest that the top values conflict with the bottom values. While this is generally true, there are, of course, many exceptions. One can argue, for example, that a minimum wage law was a violation of property and contract rights and that it also was against the general welfare.

SOURCE: Donald W. Oliver and James P. Shaver, *Teaching Public Issues in the High School* (New York: Houghton Mifflin, 1966; Logan: Utah State University Press, 1974), pp. 142–43.

In Canada, John Eisenberg and his associates have also focused on a case study approach. However, the conceptual framework for the Canadian Critical Issues Project differs from the Shaver approach. Reflecting differences in the two societies, the Canadian project is not built around a specific set of values (e.g., the American creed). Instead, the project has two main goals: (1) development of social understanding, which is related to various concerns and conflicts in Canada, and (2) the development of discussion and decision-making skills that are necessary to deal with ethical dilemmas.

In effect, students discussing the materials in our program would:

• Read and discuss a case with sensitivity and open-mindedness toward the various positions taken

- Take a stand, if only tentatively, on the issue under consideration
- Defend their positions by giving reasons, invoking principles, and presenting evidence
- Argue against opposing views in the same open and rational manner
- Modify their positions in light of their dialogue with others.[10]

Some of the units in the Canadian Critical Issues Series include:

Crisis in Quebec
Don't Teach That!
Foreign Ownership
Issues in Cultural Diversity
Native Survival
Problems of Urbanization (Winter 1979)
On Strike!
Rights of Youth
The Law and the Police
The Right to Live and Die
Women in Canadian Society[11]

Social Change

This orientation suggests that education can play a role in restructuring society. In this section three approaches to social change are examined: Reconstructionism, Social Literacy Training, and Social Action.

Social Reconstructionism

In this century one of the strongest spokesmen for the school as an agent of social change was George Counts. Counts believed that teachers should be actively involved in social change and even run for political office. He prodded progressive educators to take this stand in his book, *Dare the Schools Build a New Social Order?* which was published in 1932. Counts argued that educators should collaborate with other groups to effect social change. Counts also felt that schools cannot be morally neutral. In Counts's view, educators should clarify their assumptions and values and make them explicit. Counts was particularly critical of progressive educators who espoused a position of value neutrality:

If Progressive Education is to be genuinely progressive, it must emancipate itself from the influence of this class, face squarely and courageously every social issue, come to grips with life in all of its stark reality, establish an organic relation with the community, develop a realistic and comprehensive theory of welfare, fashion a compelling and challenging vision of human destiny, and become less frightened than it is today at bogies of *imposition* and *indoctrination*.[12]

Today Counts's position has been taken up by the Social Reconstructionists. Theodore Brameld, for example, has called for educators to take a stronger position in promoting social change. Brameld refers to Saul Alinsky and Ralph Nader as examples of how teachers should become involved in overcoming injustice and inequities in society. Social Reconstructionism, then, encourages schools and teachers to be at the forefront of social change.

Social Literacy Training

Paulo Freire has exerted a strong influence on the position that education should effect social change. His first book, *The Pedagogy of the Oppressed*, outlines his approach to teaching illiterate peasants in Brazil. He developed a method for teaching basic literacy skills to Brazilian students which was based on raising their social consciousness. Freire's work was initially supported by the Brazilian government and the U.S. Agency for International Development. However, the government changed in Brazil and Freire was forced into exile.

Freire's approach defines oppression: "An act is oppressive when it prevents individuals from becoming more fully human."[13] In Freire's view, becoming fully human requires psychological and economic growth. When people are prevented from being fully human, there is oppression or exploitation. Exploitation occurs when one group blocks the development of other groups. For example, practices that encourage discrimination are oppressive. Schools where educators control the resources (e.g., grades, punishment, etc.) that keep students dependent could also be viewed as oppressive.

Freire's analysis focuses on the social order. It is the "unjust order that engenders violence in the oppressors, which in turn dehumanizes the oppressed."[14] Thus in schools Alfred Alschuler states, "discipline conflicts are initiated by teachers who oppress, who exploit, who fail to recognize students as persons."[15]

Freire also describes how individuals can move through different stages so that they overcome oppression. In the first stage, the magical conforming level, people are passive and do not see their situations as oppressive. In the next stage, naive reforming, the focus is on the individual and it is assumed problems can be solved without reference to larger social structures. At the third level—the critical transforming stage—people begin to analyze their culture and become active participants in changing their status.

Alschuler suggests that each of these stages can be applied to schools. The magical conforming way of looking at problems is to view things as static and unchangeable. For example, statements such as "There will always be a group of bad kids" reflect this position.

Teachers see their situation as fixed with little opportunity to change it. At this stage, teachers are often characterized by a sense of resignation and helplessness. In Alschuler's words, this "inaction is a form of passive collusion, though unconscious and unintentional, to maintain oppressive conflict-laden situations."[16]

In the next stage, naive reforming, Alschuler suggests that the focus is on the individual rather than the system. "He can't cope with things" is an example of this stage. At the naive reforming stage, the individual will try to improve himself or herself. The system is accepted so the onus for change lies with the individual.

In the critical transforming stage, people now critically examine the structure in which they are working. The responsibility for change is no longer on the individual, but instead rests on people who work collaboratively to ask questions and to deal with problems. According to Freire, this type of questioning is

characterized by depth in the interpretation of problems; by the substitution of causal principles for magical explanations; by the testing of one's "findings" and by openness to revision; by the attempt to avoid distortion when perceiving problems and to avoid preconceived notions when analyzing them; by refusing to transfer responsibility; by soundness of argumentation; by the practice of dialogue rather than polemics; by receptivity to the new for reasons beyond mere novelty and by the good sense not to reject the old just because it is old—by accepting what is valid in both old and new.[17]

Education, then, in the Freirian sense involves movement toward the critical transforming stage. When he worked in Brazil, Freire developed a literacy program for adults based on this overall objective:

We wished to design a project in which we would attempt to move from naivete to a critical attitude at the same time we taught reading. We wanted a literacy program which would be an introduction to the democratization of culture, a program with people as its subjects rather than as patient recipients, a program which would be an act of creation, capable of releasing other creative arts, one in which students would develop the impatience and vivacity which characterize search and invention.[18]

To move toward the critical transforming stage, Freire developed a procedure with the following three steps.

1. Name the important conflicts in the situation. In Brazil a team of teachers, social workers, and psychologists would enter a community and interview the people in that community. Through these discussions the team would develop a list of key words. These words are chosen to represent conflict situations in the society. For example, a key word might be "slum." The teachers would introduce this word to encourage analysis of the concept. For example,

they might ask the students, What are the causes of poverty? Why is housing inadequate in the slums? By generating interest in these key words, literacy is enhanced.

2. Analyze the systemic causes of conflict. Here the discussion goes beyond the immediate list of key words to analyze the system that produces conflict. This analysis often focuses on various social, political, and economic factors that promote social inequality.

3. Encourage collaborative action to resolve conflicts.

In this last step, Freire encourages individuals to work together to solve various social problems. The students, then, collaborate to overcome oppression.

Alschuler has applied this model to what he calls Social Literacy Training. Social Literacy Training involves working with people in schools to name, analyze, and solve social problems, particularly discipline problems. Some of the strategies of this approach will now be examined.

According to Alschuler, Social Literacy Training can start in school with a small group of teachers. A Social Literacy group composed of four or five teachers names the "essential systemic causes of widespread problems." After examining causes, the group looks at alternative solutions and proposes some form of action. In one school system that Alschuler worked in for several years, a Social Literacy group came up with the following solutions:

- One group wanted to reduce referrals to the office. Instead of sending students to the vice-principal, the teachers in one social literacy group made a "mutual aid agreement." Disruptive incidents were defused by sending the student to another teacher's class or having one of the teachers in the Social Literacy group come into another teacher's class to help deal with the problem. Referrals in this school were reduced by 75 percent.

- Three teachers in one Social Literacy group identified the teaching of geography as a problem. They were then able to meet regularly to develop more relevant curriculum in this subject area.

- Some teachers were concerned about new legislation that meant special education students were to be "mainstreamed" into regular classrooms. This Social Literacy group worked with special education teachers to develop an inservice program for the regular classroom teacher. During this process, they focused on developing new methods for individualizing instruction.

- In one junior high school the students moved from class to class as one group. The Social Literacy group in that school felt that the scheduling tended to limit student options and "fix them into a narrow social role." The teachers approached a university professor to help them install flexible scheduling with assistance of a computer.

- A Social Literacy group identified the use of the intercom as a problem in the school. Its use was leading to long disruptions in the classroom. The teachers met with the principal, who agreed to limit the use of the intercom.
- Teachers set up a "care" room in the school. Teachers who participated in this project were entitled to send students to the room, where there was a teacher for special help. The room also provided a cooling-down period for students.
- Women in one school formed a consciousness-raising group to deal with the problem of sexism in the school.[19]

Alschuler comments on these examples:

These examples illustrate several unique characteristics of socially literate methods of reducing the discipline problem: (1) Socially Literate solutions do not blame individuals. Individuals cooperate to change the rules and roles of the system. (2) Social Literacy leads to multileveled solutions that win peace in interpersonal, classroom, and schoolwide war games. (3) Socially Literate solutions yield a broad range of outcomes related to better discipline—fewer classroom conflicts, more learning of the subject matter discipline, greater disciple-ship and increased personal discipline.[20]

Several techniques are used in Socially Literate groups. One of the techniques is called the Nuclear Problem-Solving Process. Again, this process is best done in a small face-to-face work group of five or six teachers. There are four steps to this problem-solving method.

The first step is naming the problematic incident. At the beginning, one teacher poses a problem. The teacher has five minutes to do this. The problem can vary from a discipline problem to an interpersonal difficulty. In explaining the problem, the teacher should focus on who was involved and what happened. Next, the teacher should identify what led up to this incident. Finally, the teacher should outline the consequences of the event. In other words, how did the people feel after the incident and what events occurred as a result of the incident?

The second step is identifying patterns of conflict. According to Alschuler, Social Literacy groups focus on patterns rather than specific incidents. Successful solutions do not deal with isolated problems, but instead they center on the underlying patterns. To seek out patterns teachers can ask questions such as

How does this incident illustrate a pattern? Has this incident occurred before? Have you reacted in this way before? Has the other person? Has the type of incident occurred with other people involved? Is this pattern for the class? For other teachers? For the whole school?

If this pattern were described as a game, what would the title be? How would you "make points"? How would the other person "make points"? If you were to write a rule book so that another teacher could play this game exactly as you did, what would those rules be? What would be the rules for the other person(s)?

Please complete each of the following three sentences as many times as you can.

What I really wanted in this situation was . . .
What the other person(s) really wanted in this situation was . . .
The basic conflict was . . .[21]

One teacher was having discipline problems in his classroom. As a result, he videotaped his classroom. By videotaping he was able to identify an underlying pattern to the discipline problem—outside interruptions.

The third step is brainstorming alternative solutions. Here the group examines the "rules and roles that govern people's behavior." Alschuler provides an example from one middle school. In this school there were a number of discipline problems. Instead of starting a schoolwide crackdown, the teachers examined the rules and found that they were inconsistent. The Social Literacy group developed a new student handbook based on suggestions from students, teachers, and support staff.

In finding a solution, the brainstorming technique is used. In this technique the group tries to develop as many solutions as possible. There is no limit on the number of alternatives and the group does not evaluate the alternatives as they are being proposed. The group should encourage unusual, creative solutions.

The fourth and final step develops democratic plans for implementing one solution. Here the teacher who posed the problem in the first step chooses the alternative to be proposed. The teacher chooses one of the solutions and discusses an action plan to implement that solution. The group should then agree on a follow-up method to check out how the solution is working.

Alschuler has developed a method for evaluating the nuclear problem-solving process. The process is more effective if

- The problem is identified as a pattern of behavior
- The analysis focuses on rules and roles rather than individuals
- The brainstorming generates a large number of alternatives
- People affected by the change in the rules are involved in providing a solution
- The solution is developed by a consensus approach that is mutually satisfying to those involved
- The solution provides a permanent solution to the problem.[22]

Social Action

Another approach to social change is Fred Newmann's Social Action Model. In some ways this model is closest to the ideal of social change, since it encourages the student to become involved in social action in the community. Unlike work-study programs, this model does not just support participation in a community activity but attempts to effect change through social and political action.

To counter student passivity the Newmann approach does not emphasize activity per se; instead, the basic aim is *environmental competence*. Environmental competence stresses action that will have specific consequences for the environment. Newmann feels that civic education has focused mostly on self-oriented projects (i.e., clarifying personal values) rather than the development of competence.

Theory

Why pursue environmental competence? Newmann brings up several points in support of a program in citizen action. These points include morality, psychological development, and consent of the governed.

Morality. Newmann suggests a direct relationship between the ability to exert influence on the environment and the degree to which persons can consider themselves moral agents. Newmann defines a moral agent as "someone who deliberates upon what he or she ought to do in situations that involve possible conflicts between self-interests and the interests of others, or between the rights of parties in conflict."[23] Unfortunately, many young people do not feel they can affect the environment and thus are not interested in moral questions.

Students may perceive injustice regarding the environment, civil rights, and economic exploitation. Because they feel they cannot influence these areas, however, they do not see them as relevant to their lives. If moral issues are to have meaning, the individual must feel that he or she can affect the problem in some manner. A sense of environmental competence is integral to the development of moral sensibility.

Psychological Development. Not only is the ability to influence the environment important if one wishes to be a moral agent but it is essential to one's psychological development. Newmann refers to the work of Robert White, whose research supports the notion that much of human behavior is explainable by the need to feel competent. (This contrasts with the belief that most human activity is an attempt to cope with basic instinctual drives.) The ability to gain a sense of competence is integral to the development of ego strength or "the ability to overcome anxiety associated with perceived 'dangers' or 'threats' because of the accrued confidence that one can act upon, rather than be a victim of, the environment."[24]

Consent of the Governed. The consent of the governed requires that each "citizen has an equal opportunity to affect the use of power; through periodic selection of leaders and through direct participation to affect the outcome of specific issues."[25] The consent of the governed attempts to insure that equal rights are not violated and that ideas and policies are tested in the public arena. Low levels of citizen participation endanger this principle. When general participation is low, special-interest groups can control or manipulate the political process. The Newmann program is based on the premise that developing social action skills can improve the democratic process by facilitating the consent of the governed. "Social action" is not meant to imply militant forms of protest but is construed more generally to take in all behavior directed toward exerting an influence in public affairs. Social action can thus include

telephone conversations, letter writing, participation in meetings, research and study, testifying before public bodies, door-to-door canvassing, fund-raising media production, bargaining and negotiation; and also publicly visible activity associated with the more militant forms. Social action can take place in or out of school and, if out of school, not necessarily in the streets, but in homes, offices, and workplaces. It might involve movement among several locations or concentration at one.[26]

To qualify as social action, however, the above activities must be part of a strategy to influence public policy in a particular direction. Issues can vary: "Students may wish to work for better bicycle trails, improved low-income housing, a 'freer' school, the opening of a drug counseling center, the election of a particular official. They might wish to oppose a curfew ordinance, high-rise apartments, credit practices of a particular firm, or a school's dress code."[27]

Newmann suggests that environmental competence should be an important aim of the school, but other competencies should not be ignored. Nonetheless, he makes a strong case for citizen action as the priority that should not be sacrificed or subordinated to other objectives.

The first step in implementing Newmann's model is to formulate policy goals based on moral deliberation and social policy research. Having formulated goals (e.g., the repeal of antiabortion laws), the citizen gathers support to implement the goals. This requires knowledge of the political process, advocacy skills, group-process skills, and management skills. Involvement in citizen action may also bring to the surface definite psychophilosophic concerns that must be dealt with. The results of the overall process are the actual policy outcomes.

Formulating Policy Goals

There are two basic components of the task of formulating policy goals: moral deliberation and social policy research.

In moral deliberation, Newmann suggests that individuals must be prepared to engage in reasoned, open debate concerning their policies and principles. Rational argument should be combined with substantive values to bring about effective moral deliberation. In short, Newmann rejects ethical relativism and adopts the position that some values or principles (e.g., the right to life) should hold priority over others (e.g., the right to property). Newmann recognizes that values compete with one another and that only through rational argument and commitment to substantive values can the moral deliberation process lead to ethically justifiable goals.

Social policy research attempts to ascertain the consequences of certain policies. The student examines the possible effects of different social action alternatives (e.g., the effects of interracial busing on pupil achievement). Such research sometimes produces tentative and conflicting findings because the individual often has to make conclusions based on limited information.

Working for Support of One's Goals

After someone has developed a position through moral deliberation and social policy research, he or she must engage in a number of activities to achieve the desired goals. The social activist must become familiar with the rules of the game. This involves knowing how a bill becomes law, how decisions can be appealed, and so forth. Equally important is knowing about informal, less public channels of influence; for example, key individuals who are potential allies or groups that have resources in people, money, and bargaining power.

Equally important in working for support are advocacy skills. These skills are related to one's ability to plead a cause in a systematic and rational manner. Advocacy skills also mean arguing the case so that people can identify with the message and respond emotionally and cognitively to the position.

As an individual begins to work for support, group-process knowledge and skills are also important. The person must decide whether to join an existing organization or form a new group. If a new group is formed, such issues as membership, internal authority, and division of responsibility must be considered. Knowledge of interpersonal behavior in groups is also a consideration. This means learning what helps and what hinders group functioning, as well as how to integrate this knowledge into interpersonal behavior. For example, instruction could be offered in listening skills, seeking clarification of other group members' ideas and feelings, summarizing individual contributions to form a group position, and giving and receiving feedback in an honest and open group.

Finally, organization-management skills are necessary. For example:

When is the right time for door-to-door canvassing? Would a mail or phone campaign be more effective? How soon should we contact the press and what should we tell them? Could we raise more funds through a bake sale or by soliciting special donations? Should we accept the man's word or press him to sign a statement?[28]

Practice

Newmann has implemented his approach in a secondary school course, the Community Issues Program, in Madison, Wisconsin. Newmann suggests the following course sequence:

First semester: Political-legal process course
                 Communications course
                 Community service internship

Second semester: Citizen action project
                 Action in literature project
                 Public message[29]

The competencies to be developed in these courses include:

1. Communicate effectively in spoken and written language.
2. Collect and logically interpret information on problems of public concern.
3. Describe political-legal decision-making processes.
4. Rationally justify personal decisions on controversial public issues and strategies for action with reference to principles of justice and constitutional democracy.
5. Work cooperatively with others.
6. Discuss concrete personal experiences of self and others in ways that contribute to resolution of personal dilemmas encountered in civic action and that relate these experiences to more general human issues.
7. Use selected technical skills as they are required for exercise of influence on specific issues.[30]

The curriculum includes a year-long program in which students would spend almost their entire time (e.g., 9:30 A.M. to 2:00 P.M.). They would earn two credits in English and two credits in social studies and would have time to take an additional course in math, science, or a foreign language. Newmann and his associates also recommend that the program be open to about sixty students and run by two full-time teachers. The courses in the program are described in the following paragraphs.

1. *Political-legal process course*, three mornings a week, for fourteen weeks during the first semester. Here the student would learn the "realities" of the political system. There would be an examination of the formal structure of the system, as well as of informal processes like lobbying and bargaining. Students would also have firsthand opportunities to observe these processes in action through field experiences. These experiences could include attending meetings and conducting interviews. The course could also focus on developing skills in data gathering and drawing valid conclusions. Moral deliberation skills would also be dealt with in this part of the program, and the student would have the opportunity to develop position papers on controversial issues.

2. *Communications course*, four afternoons a week, for sixteen weeks during the first semester. Here the student would develop skills in written, spoken, and nonverbal communications. Skills would be applied to four contexts: intrapersonal, interpersonal, group, and the public. For example, the student could work on interpersonal helping skills such as empathy and regard, as well as group skills such as problem identification and clarification. Emphasis would also be given to building trust and group cohesion so that the student could work with others.

3. *Community service internship*, two mornings a week, for fourteen weeks during the first semester. Students would perform volunteer work in social agencies, government bodies, and public interest groups.

The intern might work in an understudy relationship to one adult for the entire period (e.g., as an aide to a TV news reporter), might have short tours of duty among different groups (e.g., helping in several different departments in an environmental protection agency), might be involved in special projects (e.g., gathering data for a neighborhood organization), might offer direct social services to "clients" (e.g., tutoring young children or assisting the elderly). The placement should expose the student to the daily functioning of the agency, should provide opportunities for the student to communicate actively with agency people (rather than passively observe them), and should require that the student make a contribution to the agency's mission.[31]

As the students become involved in internship, they could analyze institutional processes of the agency in the political-legal process course and work on relevant language skills in the communications course. One afternoon per week, students could "share their volunteer experiences, discuss common problems, and begin to explore issues that might develop into the citizen action project for the second semester."[32]

4. *Citizen action project*, four mornings a week, for ten weeks during

the second semester. In this part of the program the students would work to affect public policy.

Project could include working for political candidates, establishing special youth institutions, revising administrative regulations, lobbying for legislation, and so forth. The issues could concern national, state, or local agencies, including the schools; for example, student rights within a school, zoning provisions to protect the environment, consumer protection, interracial cooperation, improved social services for youth in trouble.[33]

The project could develop from the first semester's work. During the project the students could also take "skill clinics" on such matters as canvassing techniques, negotiation skills, fund raising, and how to run a meeting. "Project counseling sessions" would also be offered to deal with various issues that arise during the project and would provide psychological support to the students.

5. *Action in literature project*, two afternoons a week, for ten weeks during the second semester. This course has a more general focus than the others and deals with such issues as What is meaningful social change? Can an individual make a difference? and How should humans govern themselves? These questions can be pursued through fiction, biography, poetry, and drama. For example, students might read a biography of Gandhi, Thoreau on civil disobedience, a novel such as *All the King's Men*, and the work of James Baldwin.

6. *Public message*. Each citizen action group would develop a final "message" on their activities to be shared with their peers and the public at large. Students would study the various media and prepare a report on their activities for one of them. The emphasis would be on what had been accomplished in the project and would aim to interpret the students' experience to the public.

Newmann recommends the overall program be open to students in grades eleven and twelve. Although social action programs should rate a high priority, it is suggested that actual course work not be required for all students because this would constitute an unjustified restriction on students' freedom. Newmann also indicates that not enough research has been done to be certain about program outcomes. Finally, it is also recommended that student self-selection be used in choosing students for the program. The main objective—environmental competence—should be strongly publicized so that students are aware of the purpose of the course.

Student Projects. Three community involvement projects are identified for the program. "In exploratory research students investigate the community, gathering information through field trips, interviews, guest speakers, informal observation in community institutions, and other means."[34] Volunteer service places the student in a direct helping relationship to others. For example, students work in homes for the elderly, day-care centers, tutoring programs, and neighborhood clean-up campaigns. Social action projects ask the student to take an advocate position and attempt to effect change congruent with that position. Newmann suggests that a developmental relationship might exist with the three projects. Exploratory research is more self-oriented as the individual goes into the community to gather relevant information. Volunteer service requires more participation as the individual may help or care for others. Finally, in the advocacy role, students emerge as autonomous agents who engage in concerns that relate to a broader social context.

Although the advocacy role is seen as the most congruent with the aim of environmental competence, the other projects are legitimate components of a social action program. Newmann recommends that a tangible product be developed during the activity.

The creation of the product encourages a more systematic approach to the project than merely "having an experience." The products also assist in the evaluation process.

Evaluation of the program focuses on four areas: (1) proficiency, or the mastery of knowledge and skills related to citizen action; (2) productivity, which emphasizes the importance of completing the project; (3) persistence, which refers to taking the project seriously and becoming fully engaged in the activity; and (4) pleasurability, or the amount of enjoyment the student gets from the program. The staff and students should not expect that all criteria will apply all the time, but they should come to some mutually agreed-upon priorities with respect to program criteria. Evaluation of the four Ps is difficult. Newmann recommends that staff not focus on individual proficiency as a sole criterion; rather, they should try to retain a perspective on the total project. Newmann is opposed to giving grades but does feel students' work should be evaluated according to completion of definite levels of work, giving private feedback to enhance learning, and ample documenting of student activities.

Summary and Appraisal

Cultural Transmission

Educational Aims.   Inculcation of values and roles that are essential to the culture.

Conception of Learning.   Learning is seen as a process where students adapt themselves to the expectations of school and society. Students learn what is expected of them so that they can function in society.

Conception of the Learner. The learner is conceived as acting in a passive manner as the student absorbs the information and values that are passed on.

Conception of the Instructional Process. The teacher is in control of the instructional process. Basic teaching methods include didactic instruction, drill, and other direct instructional approaches. In values education the basic emphasis is on modeling behavior and exhortation.

Learning Environment. The environment is structured as the teacher remains in firm control of the situation.

Teacher's Role. The teacher is the central authority in the teaching/learning process and is responsible for transmitting knowledge, values, and role expectations to students. It is also important that the teacher be an appropriate role model for the student. He or she should represent what society wants the student to become.

Evaluation. Evaluation is used to determine whether knowledge and skills are being transmitted. Tests should reflect knowledge and skills that students must master so that they can function in society.

Democratic Citizenship

Educational Aims. Respect for democratic values, skills analyzing values conflicts, dialogue skills, role-taking skills, and knowledge of the democratic process.

Conception of Learning. Learning involves an interactive process between learner and environment. Learning is enhanced by immersion in public policy dilemmas and conflicts. These public policy dilemmas reflect various values that exist in a pluralistic democratic society. Ideally, the classroom should be a microcosm of pluralism and allow for open examination of issues and debate on public policy.

Conception of the Learner. Learner is viewed as someone capable of exercising rational intelligence in approaching public policy issues.

Conception of the Instructional Process

1. Teachers present case study or public policy dilemma.
2. Value conflicts are clarified and factual data are outlined. Basic dilemma is highlighted.
3. Student takes a position on the dilemma.
4. Teacher explores student position through Socratic dialogue. Analogies are used by the teacher to encourage students to reflect on and in some cases modify their positions.

5. Students reexamine positions in the context of discussion and Socratic dialogue. Students may develop new positions.

Learning Environment. Materials (case studies, films, newspapers) which focus on public policies are necessary. Discussion can be highly charged as students and teacher explore controversial issues.

Teacher's Role. The teacher must play several roles in this orientation. Specifically, the teacher must first create a supportive emotional climate where students will want to participate. This is partially achieved by effective listening and encouraging student participation. After the supportive climate has been developed, the teacher must be prepared to probe the student's position with analogies and questions. Some teachers in this orientation become masters of the Socratic dialogue. The teacher should have a sound grasp of public policy and issues that arise with each dilemma. The teacher should be prepared to deal in depth with various issues that arise from analyzing a particular case study.

Evaluation. Evaluation centers on skills necessary to analyze public policy conflicts and skills needed to participate in policy debates. Evaluation focuses on how well the student presents his argument in both oral and written forms.

Social Change

Educational Aims. Student involvement in social issues and development of skills in effecting social change.

Conception of Learning. Learning is related to direct contact with social problems. The student learns through analyzing a social problem and then trying to effect social change. Learning not only involves interaction with the social environment but follows from the student's attempt to improve that environment.

Conception of the Learner. The learner is seen as someone who can actively become involved in social change. The learner is viewed as a change agent.

Conception of the Instructional Process

1. Student identifies a problem
2. Student examines alternative courses of action
3. Alternatives are examined in relation to their ethical, legal, and social implications
4. One alternative is selected

5. Student becomes involved in implementing solution in the school or community
6. Student analyzes project to assess its effectiveness and what he or she learned from the activity.

Teacher's Role. First, the teacher helps to clarify the direction of the student activity and helps to provide necessary resources. The teacher should also be prepared to participate in social action. Finally, the teacher provides the key link between school and community.

Evaluation. Evaluation can occur along a number of dimensions. The teacher can assess written materials produced by the student. Knowledge of a particular issue can also be assessed. Finally, evaluation can also include observation of the student in his or her work to see how he or she works with others in a group setting.

In examining these three orientations let us first examine their basic emphases. It is clear that the democratic citizenship and social change positions are most compatible with a democratic society. The cultural transmission position holds an essentially passive view of the student, who must learn to fit into the social fabric. In its most pure form the transmission orientation is most appropriate to totalitarian societies, where the state is monolithic. However, it should be noted that even in the most free societies, some socialization and inculcation are inevitable. No program can be value-neutral, and it is important to clarify the assumptions of school programs. The key element in moving to the democratic citizenship position is the opportunity for students to reflect and analyze for themselves. By encouraging the student to conduct his or her own analysis of a problem, the student's basic autonomy is upheld.

Although the democratic citizenship and social change orientations are congruent with a democratic society, their respective views on student learning are different. The democratic citizenship orientation emphasizes cognitive skills and verbal exchange. It is confined to the classroom. The social change orientation goes beyond verbal exchange and emphasizes student involvement in school and community. Although there are classroom activities that deal with analysis of policy, the basic thrust of the social change orientation is to effect either a change in the immediate environment of the school (Social Literacy) or in the community (Social Action).

Although the positions within the social change orientation have been well articulated, their impact has been very limited. It is clear that having student and teacher involved in social change is beyond the expectations of most school systems. Although we espouse the value of participation in the democratic process, the potential of disruption is too much for many administrators and teachers. In some schools it is difficult for students to even obtain hall passes, and the idea of letting students pursue projects outside the school is viewed as a major administrative problem. Thus the cultural transmission perspectives and social change position can come into direct conflict. There is pressure in most school systems for principals to "run a tight ship," and this pressure can conflict with programs oriented to social change.

There are also limitations to the democratic citizenship position. It is interesting to note the differing careers of Don Oliver and Fred Newmann, who originally worked with James Shaver in the Public Issues project. Both Oliver and Newmann saw the limitations of programs that attempt to develop a democratic perspective based only on verbal analysis. Recognizing these limitations, Oliver has become more involved in community education and holistic education. Newmann, of course, developed the social action model outlined in this chapter.

Although the democratic citizenship position would seem to represent an acceptable middle ground between cultural transmission and social action, we should recognize the limitations of programs that focus solely on cognitive analysis. Students can clearly differentiate when they are "playing school" and when they are dealing directly with real social problems. Although schools will always contain a degree of artificiality in order to have a society in which there is personal and social integration, it is apparent that we should move toward orientations where boundaries between school and community are removed.

Notes

1. Emile Durkheim, *Education and Society* (Glencoe, Ill.: Free Press, 1956), p. 124.

2. Talcott Parsons, *Social Structure and Personality* (New York: Free Press of Glencoe, 1964), pp. 129–54.

3. Yehudi Cohen, "The Shaping of Men's Minds: Adaptations to the Imperatives of Culture," in Murray Wax, Stanley Diamond, and Fred Gearing, eds., *Anthropological Perspective on Education* (New York: Basic Books, 1971), p. 22.

4. Ibid., pp. 41–42.

5. Neil Postman, *Teaching as Conserving Activity* (New York: Delacorte Press, 1979), p. 209.

6. James Shaver and William Strong, *Facing Value Decisions: Rationale Building for Teachers* (Belmont, Calif.: Wadsworth, 1976).

7. Israel Scheffler, *The Language of Education* (Springfield, Ill.: Charles Thomas, 1960), pp. 57–58.

8. Shaver and Strong, *Facing Value Decisions*, pp. 101–102.

9. Ibid., pp. 112–13.

10. Paula Bourne and John Eisenberg, *Social Issues in the Curriculum* (Toronto: Ontario Institute for Studies in Education, 1978), p. 12.

11. Ibid.

12. George Counts, *Dare the School Build a New Social Order?* (New York: Day, 1932), pp. 9–10.

13. Paulo Freire, *The Pedagogy of the Oppressed* (New York: Herder and Herder, 1972), p. 42.

14. Ibid., p. 28.

15. Alfred Alschuler, *School Discipline: A Socially Literate Solution* (New York: McGraw-Hill, 1980), p. 13.

16. Ibid., p. 14.

17. Paulo Freire, *Education for Critical Consciousness* (New York: Seabury Press, 1973), p. 43.

18. Ibid.

19. Alschuler, *School Discipline*, pp. 40–41.

20. Ibid., p. 42.

21. Ibid., pp. 110–11.

22. Ibid., pp. 115–17.

23. Fred W. Newmann, *Education for Citizen Action: Challenge for Secondary Curriculum* (Berkeley, Calif.: McCutchan, 1975), p. 29.

24. Ibid., p. 35.

25. Ibid., p. 47.

26. Ibid., pp. 54–55.

27. Ibid., p. 55.

28. Ibid., p. 91.

29. Fred Newmann, Thomas Bertocci, and Ruthanne M. Landsness, *Skills in Citizen Action: An English–Social Studies Program for Secondary Schools* (Skokie, Ill.: National Textbook, 1977), pp. 9–10.

30. Ibid., p. 6.

31. Ibid., pp. 48–49.

32. Ibid., p. 10.

33. Ibid.

34. Newmann, *Education for Citizen Action*, p. 143.

5

Developmental Orientation

Developmental psychologists have had a strong impact on education over the past two decades. Increasingly, educators have turned to the work of developmental psychologists such as Piaget, Kohlberg, and Erikson to provide guidelines for the school curriculum. These guidelines have formed an orientation to curriculum.

A central concept of this orientation is that each individual passes through definite stages of development and curriculum planning and instructional strategies should be designed to facilitate this development. In particular, learning environments should be designed so that development is not arrested or retarded at any stage. Also, developmentalists have focused on integration, so that cognitive, moral, and ego development are interrelated and one aspect of development (e.g., cognitive) does not outstrip the other aspects.

Three researchers who have been central in defining the developmental perspective are Jean Piaget, Erik Erikson, and Lawrence Kohlberg.

Jean Piaget, the Swiss psychologist, who died in 1980, is noted for his work in cognitive development. Originally a zoologist, his work in cognitive growth reflected his interest in natural science. His curiosity about how children develop and learn began when he was associated with the Binet laboratory in Paris, where he did intelligence testing on French schoolchildren. He became interested in the children's responses, particularly the wrong responses, because they indicated something to Piaget about basic mental processes. To continue his observations of how children develop and learn he took detailed notes on his own children, Jacqueline, Lucerne, and Laurent, which he presented in scores of articles and books.

Erik Erikson was born in Europe and immigrated to the United States during the thirties. The young Erikson was an artist who developed a reputation for portraits, particularly of young children. The father of one of the children he painted was Sigmund Freud. After being introduced to Freud, Erikson began a series of discussions with the psychoanalyst that led to Erikson's being invited to join the Psychoanalytic Institute of Vienna for the study of child analysis. Although Erikson has worked within a psychoanalytic perspective, he has gone beyond Freud to present a more optimistic view of personal development.

Lawrence Kohlberg developed his view of moral development while completing his doctoral studies at the University of Chicago. Working from a Piagetian or cognitive developmental framework, Kohlberg has concentrated on how individuals reason about moral dilemmas. Kohlberg has spent a great deal of time listening to children and adults and classifying their reasoning within a developmental framework. The results of this work present an intriguing perspective on moral growth.

The developmental continuums portrayed by these three psychologists complement each other and offer related views on the developing child. The psychologists themselves, for example, have commented on the complementary nature of their work on several occasions. Kohlberg, for example, has referred to research on adolescents which indicates a relationship between the development of identity (Erikson) and more adequate forms of moral reasoning (Kohlberg).[1] Erikson has also suggested that the attainment of the Piagetian stage of formal operations allows the adolescent to think more clearly about personal and occupational commitments, which allows more readily for the development of identity. At a round-table discussion in Geneva, Piaget and Erikson acknowledged the mutual compatibility of their work.[2]

It should be noted, however, that significant differences exist between Erikson's psychosocial perspective and the cognitive developmental framework of Piaget and Kohlberg. For example, Piaget and Kohlberg have focused on the structure of reasoning, while Erikson has dealt with specific psychosocial concerns that confront the individual at various stages. Piaget and Kohlberg suggest that most individuals do not reach the highest stages of development, while Erikson identifies eight stages that most humans experience.

Piaget, Erikson, and Kohlberg are not the only individuals who have made contributions in this area. Kohlberg's associate, Robert Selman, has developed stages of social perspective taking; James Fowler has outlined stages of faith development; and Jane Loevinger has constructed hierarchical stages of ego development. All these theorists present an overall conception of the individual who develops through specific stages which are also interrelated. Table 2 outlines the developmental continuums of Erikson, Piaget, and Kohlberg.

Table 2. Comparison of the Theories of Erikson, Piaget, and Kohlberg

Age (Year)	Erikson	Piaget	Kohlberg
0			
1	Basic trust vs. mistrust	Sensorimotor operations	
2	–	–	
3	Autonomy vs. shame	Preconceptual stage	
4	–	–	–
5	Initiative vs. guilt	Intuitive thought	Punishment-reward orientation
6			
7	–	–	
8			
9	Industry vs. inferiority	Concrete operations	Instrumental-relativist orientation
10			
11	–	–	–
12			
13			Interpersonal orientation
14			
15	Identity vs. identity diffusion	Formal operations	Social system orientation
16			
17			
18			
19			

Table 2. (*continued*)

Age (Year)	Erikson	Piaget	Kohlberg
Young adulthood	Intimacy vs. isolation		Social contract orientation
Adulthood	Generativity vs. self-absorption		Universal ethical principle orientation
Old age	Integrity vs. despair		

The next portion of this section outlines these stages in terms of infancy, early childhood, childhood, adolescence, and adulthood. A significant part of this chapter is devoted to the description of these stages since they are so central to the theory.

Infancy

Infancy is a period characterized by children's immediate sensory experience and the need for maternal affection.

Cognitive Development

Piaget calls this the sensorimotor stage, as the learning that occurs within this stage of development occurs within a physical orientation. One of the principle learnings is *visual projection*, or following the path of a moving object. For example, if you drop a ball in front of a 4-month-old baby, the infant will continue to look at the hand which held the ball. However, at the end of the sensorimotor period, the child is able to follow the ball to the ground. The infant also gains an understanding of *object permanence*, or the recognition that when an object disappears from view it still exists. If you hold a ball in front of an 18-month-old child and then place it behind your back, you will usually find that the infant will go behind you to find the ball because he or she knows that the object is not gone. In short, memory is beginning to develop. However, its development is contingent on the experience of seeing things appear and disappear and a stimulating environment.

Between 12 and 18 months the infant engages in *directed groping* as it begins to experiment to see what will happen when it plays with objects. Piaget describes his son Laurent breaking off a piece of bread and dropping it to see where it would fall. Many parents would be disturbed by the "mess" Laurent made, but Piaget watched and noted the child's absorption. "Like a serious young Galileo, the little boy dropped the bread from various positions and watched it land in different places on the floor."[3]

Emotional Development

As the infant is learning to deal with objects, in terms of emotional development, Erikson states children gain feelings of trust or mistrust. The baby's experience with her mother will determine how the child develops. If physical contact during feeding periods, bathing, and cuddling is warm and affectionate, the child will develop a sense of trust. However, if the mother is tense when she interacts with the child, then the infant will develop a sense of mistrust about himself or herself and the surrounding environment. Physical sensory experience is the key to the baby's emotional development just as it is important to cognitive development.

Although Erikson states that it is important for the child to come away with feelings of trust, some portion of the balancing emotion is also necessary. By developing some mistrust, the child gains a sense of readiness for danger and anticipation of discomfort, which is necessary for survival in a rapidly changing society.

Early Childhood

During early childhood children's main preoccupations are language development, the realization of autonomy and initiative, and making moral decisions on the basis of their physical consequences.

Cognitive Development

One of the principal preoccupations during this period is language development, as the child can symbolically represent experience. There is a rapid increase in vocabulary as the average 2-year-old understands about 250 words; the average 5-year-old understands about 2,000 words. As the child uses *language*, however, Piaget noticed that words can take on a special power. For example, a child might start crying for being called "dumb" because he feels that the tag of "dumb" actually makes him stupid. At the beginning of early childhood, Piaget argued, children do not really have conversations but engage in "collective monologues," where speech serves as a mutual call to action rather than as a means for exchange of ideas. Language is also a vehicle for play. Words themselves become part of this spontaneous process, as "bathroom language" often leads to hysterical outbursts by preschool children.

Toward the end of early childhood, elementary reasoning appears. This reasoning is based on appearance, however. If the child is presented with two rows of five coins and one row is longer, he will usually identify the longer row as having more coins. Judgments are based on appearance, as the child cannot retain his original perspective if appearances are changed.

Related to this is the fact that the children cannot relate individual parts to the whole. They can focus on one element at a time but cannot master relationships between the elements. An example of this phenomenon is when a toy car finishes a race first; it is called the fastest car, even if it traveled a shorter distance than the other cars in the race. It is only during middle childhood that a more complete understanding of relationships develops.

Emotional Development

In terms of emotional development middle childhood is characterized by increasing autonomy and initiative. Erikson calls the period from 18 months to 3 years the period of autonomy and shame. The child breaks away from maternal dependence toward greater personal autonomy. This autonomy is physical; that is, the child begins to walk, run, and dress himself. Perhaps the period can be characterized by the young child's phrase "do myself." One example of an activity that the 3-year-old may want to do himself is the opening and closing of doors. This may be difficult for the parent to accept, particularly if the mother is in a hurry. But if children are not given an opportunity to try these activities they will not develop a sense of personal effectiveness.

Erikson also identifies certain biological functions with the different stages of development. In infancy the feeding relationship is important and during the autonomy period the focus shifts to elimination of bodily wastes. Autonomy, then, is linked to toilet training, which should not be too punitive or too permissive. If parents are too demanding about toilet training or on the other hand leave everything to the child, then the child could be overwhelmed by shame. This balance in parental attitudes must apply to other activities as well. According to Erikson, if the child is not given freedom to explore the home and neighborhood, this will also lessen the chance for autonomy. On the other hand, if the child is allowed to roam totally unsupervised, shame can also develop. The mother who is too restrictive or protective is guilty of "Momism," or in other words, the mother feels that everything is her responsibility and that the children cannot assume any responsibility for themselves. This attitude is similar to the teacher who constantly corrects students and often puts them down.[4]

Erikson calls the next period of development initiative versus guilt. Identification with an adult model becomes a key concern at this time, as young boys will often compete with the father for the mother's attention or the young girl will rival the mother for the father's affection. If the father has been away on a trip, he may come home to find that his son is not eager to see him. In fact, the son may be happy to see his father leave again. A young girl may also express her wish to marry Daddy when she grows up.

Imagination and play are integral to the development of initiative. Children need time to be alone and to daydream and thus "play out" some of their fantasies. In group situations with other children the children can also act out some of their collective concerns. Erikson cites a passage from *Tom Sawyer* to make this relationship between play and ego development explicit.

He took up his brush and went tranquilly to work. Ben Rogers hove in sight presently—the very boy, of all boys, whose ridicule he had been dreading. Ben's gait was the hop-skip-and-jump—proof enough that his heart was light and his anticipations high. He was eating an apple, and giving a long, melodious whoop, at intervals, followed by a deep-toned ding-dong-dong, ding-dong-dong, for he was personating a steamboat. As he drew near, he slackened speed, took the middle of the street, leaned far over to starboard and rounded to ponderously and with laborious pomp and circumstance—for he was personating the *Big Missouri*, and considered himself to be drawing nine feet of water. He was boat and captain and enginebells combined, so he had to imagine himself standing on his own hurricane-deck giving the orders and executing them.

Erikson then comments:

One "meaning" of Ben's play could be that it affords his ego a temporary victory over his gangling body and self by making a well-functioning whole out of brain (captain), the nerves and muscles of will (signal system and engine), and the whole bulk of the body (boat). It permits him to be an entity within which he is his own boss, because he obeys himself.[5]

Early childhood in terms of emotional development finds children expanding their ability to control their behavior in wider spheres, as the earlier sense of autonomy now applies to the children's interaction with pets, friends, schoolmates, and siblings as well as parents.

Moral Development

Toward the end of early childhood children begin to exhibit moral reasoning. Up to the age of 6 or so the children usually do not exhibit any moral reasoning; instead, children's actions become their judgments. Good is what they like and want and bad is what they do not like or do not want.

Around the age of 6 or 7, however, children begin moral reasoning. They usually think in terms of the automatic physical consequences of an act. Children reason that behaviors are bad if they lead to punishment and good if they lead to rewards. Children will assert that it is not good to steal because they will have to go to jail if they are caught, or they might say that cleaning up their room is good because they get a chocolate for doing it. The value of life is also seen in terms of physical objects.

The child at this period is not able to recognize the interests of others and is unable to relate differing viewpoints. Children will also confuse the perspective of authority with their own perspective.

Middle Childhood

During middle childhood the child gains an understanding of relationships, develops feelings of competence, and makes moral judgments based on his own needs.

Cognitive Development

Piaget refers to this period as "concrete operations," which means the ability to understand and conduct various operations on concrete materials. One example of an operation is conservation. This means that the child is no longer fooled by appearances but sees that quantities do not change even if their form changes. For example, the child at the concrete operations stage will not be fooled by the length of the rows of coins. If one row is longer but there is an equal number of coins in each row, he or she will be able to conserve number and realize that each row contains the same number of coins.

Children in this period also learn to conserve volume. For example, if water is poured from a low, wide beaker into a tall, narrow beaker, they will assert that each beaker contains an equal amount of water. During early childhood, children usually think that the tall beaker holds more water. Children during middle childhood are also able to reverse operations. In other words, if the children are unsure about the water–beaker problem, they will pour the water back and forth between the beakers to return the problem to its starting point. The stage is called *concrete* operations because children prefer to work with concrete materials. In dealing with the coin or beaker problem they rely on the physical presence of the coins and the beakers to solve the problem. If the problem is given verbally, they will not be able to solve it.

Children can also begin to relate individual parts to the whole and vice versa. For example, if the child is given a box of 16 brown wooden beads and 5 white wooden beads, he or she can understand the relationship of the color of the beads to the class of wooden beads. Children understand that there are altogether more wooden beads than in either the subclass of white or brown.

Concrete operations develop in certain stages. With regard to spatial qualities, children appraise size in terms of length, then width, and finally volume. The spread of operational thinking is gradual. Children may hold to egocentric thinking or beliefs in other areas during much of middle childhood. If threatened, for example, children may return to the intuitive thinking of early childhood.

Although children begin to abandon magical thinking and imaginary "friends," they rely almost too closely on initial perceptions of reality. Thus they cannot distinguish between hypothesis and fact:

In one study, seven- to ten-year-old children were presented with a number of reasons why Stonehenge (a prehistoric site in England) was a fort rather than a religious center. When the rival hypothesis was presented, with new facts, they refused to change their minds. This indicated that they confused facts and theories. The concept of a theory was beyond their mental organization or system and thus their responses were limited to the fact as presented initially. "Just gimme the facts," a child might say.[6]

Children during middle childhood are also very literal in their interpretation of jokes and commands.

One researcher illustrates this juvenile sophistry with the following story (again a favorite at this age): An eight-year-old boy comes to the table with his hands dripping wet. When his mother asks him why he didn't dry his hands, he replies, "But you told me not to wipe my hands on the clean towels." His mother throws up her hands and replies, "I said not to wipe your dirty hands on the towels."[7]

Play, which was becoming more structured toward the end of early childhood, becomes very rule oriented. Rules become more universal in that they are used repeatedly and apply to larger groups of participants.

Emotional Development

In terms of emotional development, the children's autonomy and initiative expand to larger spheres. This period, industry versus inferiority, refers to the child's interaction in a larger arena—school, the neighborhood, or the gang. Since children no longer have "collective monologues" but exchange ideas, they can form new groupings based on common interests. The groups are usually made up of all girls or all boys. Not only are groups decided according to categories, but other activities and decisions are made on a yes-or-no basis. This is congruent with the period of concrete operations, where the ability to classify is often carried to an extreme.

The prime characteristic of the period, however, is the drive to mastery. In school, children begin to read, to write, and to compute. If these activities are not "pressured" on children, they will usually enjoy developing their abilities in these areas. Not only does school provide an area for mastery but many other activities are open to children—for instance, swimming, baseball, football, hockey, sewing, cooking, skating, and a variety of other games.[8]

Moral Development

With regard to moral development, right action for most children at this stage consists of what satisfies one's own needs, and occasionally the needs of others. At this point in development, children also begin to identify the interests of others. Deals or agreements can be made on an equal-exchange basis. This exchange morality is sometimes summarized by the saying "You scratch my back and I'll scratch yours!" Children see things from the perspective of isolated individuals who value things subjectively.

This perspective differs from the previous stage, since earlier the child was not aware of various individual perspectives but had a single perspective defined in terms of automatic, physical responses. The perspective of middle childhood can lead to relativism, since all values are subjectively defined.

Some individuals never go beyond this stage. For example, the "Playboy Philosophy" is an example of this morality in operation. Many chronic criminal offenders also function at this moral stage.

The value of human life is also seen in terms of this hedonistic perspective. The following question, "Should the doctor 'mercy kill' a fatally ill woman requesting death because of pain," is answered by someone operating at stage two by the following statement: "Maybe it would be good to put her out of her pain, she'd be better off that way. But the husband wouldn't like it, it's not like an animal. If a pet dies you can get along without it—it isn't something you really need. Well, you can get a new wife, but it's not really the same."[9]

Adolescence

During adolescence the person is capable of logical thought, the development of identity, and conventional moral reasoning based on what others (the family, the group, or the institution) expect.

Cognitive Development

Piaget refers to this period as "formal operations." By this he means that individuals can conduct operations (i.e., conservation) without reference to concrete materials. The adolescent enters the world of ideas and contemplation. The person also begins to hypothesize about relationships. He or she can consider "If-then" statements and any number of possibilities in relation to a particular problem. In brief, the individual takes a logical, systematic approach to problem solving. This systematic approach is seen in the following example.

An example of the shift from concrete to formal operations may be taken from the work of E. A. Peel. Peel asked children what they thought about the following event: "Only brave pilots are allowed to fly over high mountains. A fighter pilot flying over the Alps collided with an aerial cableway, and cut a main cable causing some cars to fall to the glacier below. Several people were killed." A child at the concrete-operational level answered: "I think that the pilot was not very good at flying." A formal-operational child responded: "He was either not informed of the mountain railway on his route or he was flying too low, also his flying compass may have been affected by something before or after take-off, thus setting him off course causing collision with the cable."

The concrete-operational child assumes that if there was a collision the pilot was a bad pilot; the formal-operational child considers all the possibilities that might have caused the collision. The concrete-operational child adopts the hypothesis that seems most probable or likely to him. The formal-operational child constructs all possibilities and checks them out one by one.[10]

Compared with how they analyzed events at the concrete operations stage, individuals are no longer satisfied with observation of specific events but see these events as a point of departure for conceptualizing and hypothesizing. An example of an actual experiment can clarify these differences. In this situation a balance scale was set up with varying weights to be placed on differing points on the crossbar. The scale was presented to children of differing ages with equal weights on each arm but placed so that the crossbar was out of balance. The children were asked to balance the arms. The youngest children did so by pressing down on the arm. When asked to make the scale balance without the use of his hands, one four-and-a-half-year-old replied: "You can't."[11]

Older children began to experiment with adding weights to each side, but the idea of reversibility, of subtracting weight to reach balance, did not occur until around age 7. At the formal operations level, however, the individual not only brings the scale to equilibrium but can formulate a law of equilibrium: "The heavier it is, the closer to the middle." Thus he can speculate and theorize on the concrete operation of balancing.

Sam (13:8) discovers immediately that the horizontal distance is inversely related to weight. "How do you explain that? *You need more force to raise weights placed at the extremes than when it's closer to the centre ... because it has to cover a greater distance.* How do you know? *If one weight on the balance is three times the other, you put it a third of the way out because the distance* [upward] *it goes is three times less.* But once you referred to the distance [horizontal gesture] and once to the path covered? *Oh, that depends on whether you have to calculate it on whether you really understand it. If you want to calculate, it's best to consider it horizontally; if you want to understand it, vertically is better. For the light one* [at the extremity] *it changes more quickly, for the heavy one less quickly.*"[12]

At the formal operations level the individual can apply his speculations to social problems: he can hypothesize or imagine the consequences or possible solutions to various problems. This is important to personal and moral development. For example, in examining moral dilemmas at the advanced stages it is important that the individual understand how others see issues and imagine the consequences and implications of several perspectives.

Like concrete operations, there is a gradual development through formal operations. The substage of formal operations is described below.

Substage 1. Formation of the inverse of the reciprocal. Capacity to form negative classes (for example, the class of all not-crows) and to see relations as simultaneously reciprocal (for example, to understand that liquid in a U-shaped tube holds an equal level because of counterbalanced pressures).

Substage 2. Capacity to order triads of propositions or relations (for example, to understand that if Bob is taller than Joe and Joe is shorter than Dick, then Joe is the shortest of the three).

Substage 3. True formal thought. Construction of all possible combinations of relations, systematic isolation of variables, and deductive hypothesis testing.[13]

Emotional Development

Erikson's stage of identity versus identity diffusion is well known and focuses on self-definition. If the individual gains a coherent sense of where he or she is going in life, then an identity results. If there is excessive confusion about present commitments and values, then identity diffusion occurs. Sometimes there may also be *premature* closure, where the adolescent takes on a social identity without experimentation with different roles, for example, jobs, clothes, sexual roles. The other extreme, identity diffusion, is trying out a number of roles and not synthesizing them into coherent self-definition.

The danger of this stage is identity diffusion; as Biff puts it in Arthur Miller's *Death of a Salesman*, "I just can't take hold, Mom. I can't take hold of some kind of life." ... Youth after youth, bewildered by some assumed role, a role forced on him by the inexorable standardization of American adolescence, runs away in one form or another; leaving schools and jobs, staying out all night, or withdrawing into bizarre and inaccessible moods.[14]

It is not easy to attain a sense of identity because of the long periods of training needed for so many jobs in a technological society. Some professions require study until individuals are in their late twenties or early thirties. Because of this long dependent status as a student, it is difficult for an identity to emerge; the individual sees himself or herself as a marginal person and not really part of society. In some societies there are definite rituals to confirm the entrance into adulthood. In North America, however, there is no specific time or ceremony that confers adult status. Legal ages also differ with regard to marriage, drinking, voting, driving a car, and entering into a contract. While there is confusion about legal ages, there may be excessive pressure to adopt an early or premature identity. Social pressure from peers to go steady or even to marry makes it difficult for the adolescent to experiment with different roles.

Moral Development

In terms of moral development, the adolescent individual begins to reason according to the expectations which others hold for him as he moves toward conventional moral thinking. The individual perceives the maintenance of the expectations of the family, group, or nation as valuable in their own right. The attitude is one of conformity to social order, and moral judgments are now based on role taking and legitimately perceived expectations. Most adults reason at the conventional level.

Stage three is the first stage of conventional moral thinking. Here an individual is concerned about other people and their feelings and is motivated by what others expect of him or her. Thus praise and blame are important to individuals at this stage. For example, the individual is concerned about being a good boy or a nice girl and maintaining mutual relations. The person is also aware of shared feelings and agreements in these relations, and mutual expectations become the reference point for moral decision making. The value of human life is based on empathy and feelings toward others: "Andy, age sixteen: (Should the doctor 'mercy kill' a fatally ill woman requesting death because of her pain?) No, he shouldn't. The husband loves her and wants to see her. He wouldn't want her to die sooner, he loves her too much."[15] Stage three reasoning may begin around age 10 but is more likely to occur around 11 or 12. This is the dominant stage in high school students and is often observable in the peer group, that is, being one of the boys.

At the next level of development the individual is concerned with maintenance of the social order and with rules that support that order. The central issue for stage four orientation is that he or she sees society prior to the individual. In short, the individual exists to serve society, as there is no conception of individual rights prior to society. Life is conceived as sacred in terms of its place in a categorical moral or religious order of rights and duties. In response to the query, "Should the doctor 'mercy kill' the woman," a stage four response is: "The doctor wouldn't have the right to take a life, no human has the right. He can't create life, he shouldn't destroy it."[16]

At this stage the individual has moved beyond an interpersonal orientation to a societal perspective that usually does not fully manifest itself until ages 16 to 18. Therefore grades 10, 11, and 12 should contain some students at this stage.

Adulthood

Early Adulthood

Erikson suggests that after the person has gained a sense of identity he can enter into intimate relationships. Following the period of identity versus identity diffusion is the stage of intimacy versus isolation. The individual now has enough security within himself or herself to become involved in a close interpersonal relationship, usually in the form of marriage. In an intimate relationship there is respect for each person's identity so that there is mutual awareness of individual development and the other person's needs. Healthy adulthood is sometimes characterized by engagement in love and work so that this stage of development can establish the beginning of a meaningful adult life.

If the person cannot establish these beginnings, then isolation can result. The individual will feel alone and cut off from satisfying interpersonal relationships. The person may also sense an alienation from society if he cannot experience a satisfying relationship with society through work.

During this third decade the individual can fully integrate postconventional moral reasoning. At stage five—the social-contract legalistic orientation—right action tends to be defined in terms of individual, inalienable rights and standards that have been critically examined and agreed upon by the whole society. The individual recognizes that rules can be changed and negotiated through the democratic process, and the "official" morality of most democratic governments is at this stage. There is also a theoretical and abstract view of society as existing for and organized to serve people, as well as the general welfare. At stage four society was seen prior to the individual; at stage five the individual is seen prior to society. Life is valued in terms of its relation to human welfare and in terms of being a universal human right.

Middle Adulthood

After establishing a shared intimacy and mutuality, the individual is ready to turn his concern toward the next generation. This concern may take the form of care for growing children or the transmission of ideas, values, and wisdom. This stage has been named by Erikson as generativity versus self-absorption. If the individual does not care about his or her children or the future of other children, he or she can become lost in self-absorption. The self-absorbed individual cuts himself or herself off from communal goals and concerns.

During the early part of this period (early thirties) the individual can fully incorporate the final stage of moral reasoning. Only a small percentage (e.g., 5 percent) of the population attain this stage of moral development. At this stage "right" is defined by applying self-chosen ethical principles that appeal to universality and consistency. These principles are abstract and ethical (e.g., the Golden Rule) and are not concrete rules like the Ten Commandments. Basically these are principles of justice that focus on equality of human rights and respect for the dignity of human beings as individual persons. Not only is life seen as a basic right, an obligation is felt toward the lives of all other human beings.

Late Adulthood

As adults reflect on their own lives they gain a fuller perspective on their own life cycles and thus develop a sense of *integrity*. Integrity also rests on acceptance of mankind's collective and individual cycle, according to Erikson, as "something that has to be and that, by necessity, permitted no substitutions: It thus means a new, different love of one's parents. It is a comradeship with the ordering ways of distant times and different pursuits." If the individual is overwhelmed by death, he or she can succumb to a sense of despair. However, if the individual does not give in to despair but retains his or her integrity, "healthy children will not fear life, if the parents have integrity enough not to fear death."[17]

The Practical

The developmentalists present a vision of the person who moves toward intellectual and moral autonomy through interaction with the environment. Piaget suggests that development occurs through maturation, physical interaction, social interaction, and equilibration. Equilibration occurs when the individual restructures his or her thinking to accommodate new problems.

Development takes place when the individual builds new structures of thought as a result of interaction with the physical and social environment. Kohlberg suggests that moral development occurs through social interaction when the person grapples with a moral dilemma and is exposed to higher levels of moral reasoning.

Central to this orientation is the idea that the student has the opportunity to inquire about the physical, moral, and social world. The learning environment, then, although structured, should be rich in materials and ideas and allow for open inquiry into various problems. Application of the developmental orientation to the classroom generally involves the following steps: (1) sensitivity to developmental differences; (2) presentation of a task or dilemma; and (3) student interaction with the task or dilemma and teacher follow-up.

Sensitivity to Developmental Differences

The first step for the teacher is to be aware of the child's stage of development. The psychologists themselves are empathetic to the child's view of the world. As an example, for Piaget the child can be considered a *cognitive alien*, since the child has cognitive styles which differ from adult thought. The preoperational child, for instance, believes that nature is conscious and is endowed with purpose like himself or herself. Piaget calls this characteristic "animism." An example of animism is when the children say the sun follows them to "show them the way."

In order to be "effective" the teacher or adult responding to the child must be careful not to impose an adult vision on the child's perspective. In responding to children's questions, it is important that the teacher listen and answer within the cognitive framework of the child in a manner that can also stimulate further development.

Erikson has also referred to teacher responses that are conducive to psychosocial growth. There is a danger that an adolescent may adopt a negative identity, and if teachers accept a negative self-concept the "young person may well put his energy into becoming exactly what the careless and fearful community expects him to be—and make a total job of it."[18] From his background of clinical experience Erikson states that if the negative identity of the adolescent is understood and properly handled, the identity does not necessarily have to become a final one.

Erikson's concept of mutuality is also relevant here. In brief, mutuality is a relationship where partners depend on each other for the development of their respective strengths. To facilitate growth, it is important that schools provide encounters and settings where the generative needs of the teacher can interact with the competence and identity needs of the child. Some of Piaget's concerns are related to Erikson's concept of mutuality. In communicating with children it is important that teachers respect the children's right to say what they think. If there is not an atmosphere of mutuality and teacher empathy, the child will not have sufficient confidence to explore, or "to be wrong," in the adult sense. If, for example, children think that six coins spread out in a top row are "more" than six coins clustered together in a bottom row, they should be able to say so with confidence. If they are afraid, then they will not want to explore and may be retarded.

Kohlberg also recognizes the importance of teacher awareness of developmental stages. The teacher should be a good listener so that he or she can identify the various levels of moral reasoning in the classroom. After identifying the level, the teacher can then establish student groupings for moral discussions. This is important, because the individual tends toward the next stage of reasoning and will eventually adopt the next stage under appropriate conditions. The person, however, cannot understand reasoning that is two stages above his or her own (i.e., stage four reasoning cannot be understood by a stage two person). The teacher should identify the approximate levels of reasoning in the classroom and then try to match the stages in student groupings so that students are exposed to one level higher than their own.

Task Presentation and Cognitive Conflict

After identifying the approximate level of development, the teacher should present the student with a task or problem that stimulates cognitive conflict. For Piaget conflict occurs when the child's thinking is thrown into a state of disequilibrium through exposure to some problem. Smedslund, for example, has done research on the effect of conservation problems on nonconservers to induce cognitive conflict. In his experiments Smedslund presented the child with two pieces of clay equal in size and shape. When the child agreed that they were equal, he would change the form of one of the pieces and ask the child whether the deformed piece contained more or less clay. If the child said that it contained more, Smedslund added a small bit of clay to the nondeformed piece or subtracted some clay from the deformed piece and again asked for a comparison. Thus the addition–subtraction operation would conflict with the child's perceptions and the cognitive conflict would bring about an attempt at resolution. Smedslund usually found that, if approached at the appropriate point in the child's development, the child would subscribe to conservation based on the addition–subtraction operations. In sum, cognitive conflict usually facilitates cognitive growth, since the child will develop new mental processes to deal with the problem.

Kohlberg is in agreement with this perspective and has constructed a number of case studies which pose moral conflict questions. For these moral dilemmas there is no right answer, but the child's attempt to wrestle with them is generally facilitative of moral development. Kohlberg's classic dilemma is about Heinz:

In Europe, a woman was near death from a special kind of cancer. There was one drug that the doctors thought might save her. It was a form of radium that a druggist in the same town had recently discovered. The drug was expensive to make, but the druggist was charging ten times what the drug cost him to make. He paid $200.00 for the radium and charged $2000.00 for a small dose of the drug. The sick woman's husband, Heinz, went to everyone he knew to borrow the money, but he could only get together about $1000.00 which is half of what it cost. He told the druggist that his wife was dying and asked him to sell it cheaper or let him pay later. But the druggist said: "No, I discovered the drug and I'm going to make money from it." So Heinz got desperate and broke into the man's store to steal the drug for his wife. Should the husband have done that?[19]

It should be noted that the intent of the developmental framework is not to present children with excessive cognitive conflict that creates too much tension. The cognitive conflict should induce the children to examine their reasons but not immobilize them with excessive anxiety. Although cognitive conflict should be introduced, the type of conflict differs with each aspect of development. For cognitive development the materials and type of problem are crucial. For example, materials relevant to conservation problems are most appropriate for children at the end of early childhood. With regard to moral development, Kohlberg has asserted that the content of a dilemma is not crucial. Most dilemmas can be presented at many stages of development, as the more important factor is exposure to a higher level of reasoning in discussing the dilemma. For emotional development Erikson suggests that conflict is more often an internal state, and the adult's task is to help prevent the negative tension from becoming predominant.

Interaction with the Task or Dilemma

The opportunity to act on the task or dilemma is important for dealing with the cognitive conflict. For example, as Piaget discovered in his conservation experiments, cognitive growth is more likely to occur if the child has the opportunity actively to manipulate the beakers and water or the clay. Piaget stated the case for activity when he said:

As far as education is concerned, the chief outcome of this theory of intellectual development is a plea that children be allowed to do their own learning. . . . You cannot further understanding in a child simply by talking to him. Good pedagogy must involve presenting the child with situations in which he himself experiments, in the broadest sense of the term—trying things out to see what happens, manipulating symbols, posing questions and seeking his own answers, reconciling what he finds one time with what he finds at another comparing his findings with those of other children . . .[20]

The key to this process is not movement or activity per se but an environment where the child can introduce relations or transformations between objects and find out the effects of such transformations. The active process may not necessarily involve external actions of the learner. Piaget said that Socrates used an active method with language which allowed the learner to actively construct his or her own knowledge and beliefs.

During early and middle childhood, concrete materials can facilitate the active process. For example, in gaining an understanding of conservation, rows of coins or a piece of clay are valuable aids to the process. It is important that the materials be developmentally matched to facilitate growth. As an example, for the child about 6 or 7 years old, the materials should be chosen to generate cognitive conflict with respect to conservation problems.

It is not an easy task for the teacher to develop situations that assist the active process. One project based on Piaget's work found that it was very easy to fall into the trap of expecting the "right answer." Kits were developed for preschoolers to sort materials, but when they did not sort in ways the kit was intended, the teachers said, "That's nice; but ... can you think of another way?" (i.e., the teachers' way).[21] In this setting the children became insecure and lacked initiative. Only when the teachers provided situations where the students got direct feedback from the materials did they approach learning with confidence and initiative. As an example, if the child thought that a wooden block would sink when put into water, and carried out the experiment, the block's own reaction led the student to understand the object's movement as being a natural reaction rather than a teacher expectation.

Erikson has also found concrete materials valuable in reading and understanding the child's emotional concerns. When a child is given a set of toys to play with, Erikson suggests that the child will not only express mastery but also indicate areas that he or she has not mastered entirely. For example, toys spread over a whole table indicate balance to Erikson, while examples of construction which are built against the wall or in one corner can indicate that a particular strain exists within the child.

As the student interacts with the problem or dilemma, Kohlberg suggests that the teacher should ask questions which help the student to clarify his or her thinking and which stimulate development. With regard to moral development, the teacher can stimulate dilemma discussions with a variety of questions or probes. Some of these probes include:

- Clarifying probe (asks the student to explain his or her position further)
- Universal consequences probe (asks the student to consider what

would happen if everyone reasoned or acted in a particular manner)
- Role switch probe (asks the student to assume the perspective of another person in the dilemma)
- Issue-specific probe (asks the student to explore a particular moral issue, e.g., justice, authority, etc., that is central to the dilemma).[22]

By following up with probes the teacher lets the student reflect on his or her position. The teacher in the developmental orientation does not work, then, in a laissez-faire manner but stimulates further interaction.

Play

One aspect of the active process during early childhood is play. Piaget and Erikson, in particular, emphasize the importance of play in relation to the development of ego strength. Piaget, for example, has worked out the concept of symbolic play, where the child acts out unpleasant scenes or actions. As an example, consider the following instance described by Piaget, as cited by Pulaski:

At 4:6, I knocked against J's hands with a rake and made her cry. I said how sorry I was, and blamed my clumsiness. At first she didn't believe me, and went on being angry as though I had done it deliberately. Then she suddenly said, half appeased: "You're Jacqueline and I'm daddy. There! (She hit my fingers.) Now say: 'You've hurt me! (I said it.) I'm sorry, darling. I didn't do it on purpose. You know how clumsy I am," etc. In short, she merely reversed the parts and repeated my exact words.[23]

Children are able to turn passivity into activity at this stage while they play at something that was in reality done to them. Play also allows the child to reduce the unpleasantness of existence and in the process gain ego strength. Erikson holds a similar view when he states the "small world of manageable toys is a harbor which the child establishes, to return to when he needs to overhaul his ego."

Gradually, play becomes the ability to engage in creative activity. Piaget recorded this transition in his own son Laurent.[24] At 7 he created a village by making maps of the country where the village was and by imagining all the sorts of people who lived there. After age 8 the imaginary characters disappeared but more detailed maps were developed. At 9 his interests changed to real maps of all parts of Europe and at age 10 the maps led to a study of history related to the geographical areas. Laurent reconstructed the costumes, furniture, and architecture of various periods and was concerned about the quality of the reproductions. Here play has developed toward intellectual and artistic creativity.

During late childhood and early adolescence, play becomes creative imagination and is gradually integrated with intelligence and identity. Erikson argues that as children grow older they must be given the opportunity to test their creative notions in real social contexts, otherwise:

No wonder, then, that some of our troubled children constantly break out of their play into some damaging activity in which they seem to us to "interfere" with our world, while analysis reveals that they only wish to demonstrate their right to find an identity in it. They refuse to become a speciality called "child," who must play at being big because he is not given an opportunity to be a small partner in a big world.[25]

In sum, early childhood education should provide opportunities for play, while educational environments during later stages of development should allow the testing of ideas and ideals in community contexts. Piaget and Erikson are in basic agreement on the fundamental importance of play in relation to the child's ego development. Although Kohlberg has not stressed play per se, he has referred to the importance of peer interaction and participation in assisting moral development. This is related to another aspect of interaction—role taking.

Role Taking

Related to play is the importance of role taking. Piaget has suggested that through interaction with their peers, children begin to see the other child's viewpoint. In general, this process facilitates the child's comprehension of rules, justice, and reciprocity. By seeing the role of the other child, the student perceives the needs of the other children and the importance of rules and reciprocity in reconciling those needs. Kohlberg has conducted research which indicates that role taking also helps facilitate moral development.[26]

Erikson has emphasized the importance of *role experimentation* in the context of adolescent identity development. Erikson's concept of psychosocial moratoria, for example, suggests a variety of institutions and opportunities for role experimentation. Work in community settings can be one form of moratorium. For example, Erikson refers to one of his patients whose work in a steel mill helped him through an acute identity crisis:

When my patient, for the first time, really enjoyed his work in a steel mill, he said aloud to himself, 'My God, this is as good as studying Chinese!' This is a strange statement, but maybe you will understand that to me, it was a good sign, for he had realized that any number of work methods carry their own satisfaction within them, and while at this moment he would not have wanted to go back to Chinese, at any rate he had accepted work as such as an important part of himself.[27]

Piaget has also made similar references to the importance of adolescent work in the community as a facilitator of human growth. He states that work helps the adolescent meet the storm and stress of that period: "True adaptation to society comes automatically when the adolescent reformer attempts to put his ideas to work."[28] In general, Piaget seems to support Erikson's concern that individuals have the opportunity to work and to temporarily commit themselves to community contexts.

Some schools have developed individual courses that offer opportunities for direct contact with areas of community concern and, as a result, contribute to the growth of identity. The Community Involvement Program used in Ontario is an example. In this secondary school program the student receives credits for work in a community service agency (e.g., old age home, day care center, etc.). The student spends part of the day in the community agency and the rest of the day at school. In school there is an opportunity to examine issues related to the work experience and to carry out independent study. In general the program allows for role experimentation and identity formation in a variety of community contexts.

Developmental Programs

There have been several other educational programs designed around the developmental orientation. At the elementary level, many programs have been developed in accordance with Piaget's thinking. One program for children 4 to 7 years old has been developed by Celia Lavatelle. This curriculum consists of several activities to be conducted within 10-minute time periods with small groups of children. Lavatelle also outlines activities that allow for self-directed play. The objective is to develop basic skills (e.g., classification and measurement skills).[29] While Lavatelle's curriculum is highly structured, David Weikart's program is less structured.[30] The objective of his program is to facilitate cognitive skill development through physical activity and language development. Sociodramatic play and field trips are also included in the curriculum along with classification, seriation, and spatial arrangement activities. Finally, Kamii and DeVries emphasize play as important to the preschool curriculum and have developed games that are designed to develop physical-social and logico-mathematical knowledge.[31] All these programs emphasize the importance of self-directed learning, play, and thinking skills and deemphasize direct instruction.

Many curriculum materials have also been developed to stimulate moral development. These programs involve moral dilemmas presented in a variety of formats (e.g., print, filmstrips, film) which can be used for discussion and role playing. Kohlberg has also emphasized the importance of the school environment. Kohlberg has argued that the school should be a "just community" where teachers and students collaborate and make decisions, particularly decisions that relate to discipline and rule making. In small secondary schools this takes the form of town meetings to discuss and decide how certain programs should be settled. In these meetings the student's vote counts equally with the vote of a staff member.

Summary and Appraisal

Educational Aims.   Gradual movement to higher stages of development; avoidance of stage retardation and integration of various aspects of development, for example, cognitive, moral, and ego.

Conception of Learning.   Learning is related to development. Cognitive and moral development occur when the individual restructures his or her thought patterns to deal with cognitive conflicts and moral dilemmas. Learning takes place when task and/or problems which stimulate new patterns of thought are presented to the student. Learning involves an interactive process between the learner and the environment.

Conception of the Learner.   The learner is seen as an active agent who is constantly structuring and restructuring his or her thinking.

Conception of the Instructional Process

1. Teacher awareness and understanding of student's developmental level
2. Presentation of task or dilemma to the student
3. Student interaction with the task or dilemma with teacher assistance.

Learning Environment.   The learning environment should be geared to the student's stage of development. Materials should be related to the appropriate developmental tasks.

Teacher's Role.   The teacher structures the overall learning environment and then acts as a guide within that environment. The teacher should gather the learning materials appropriate for his or her students. Within the overall environment the teacher questions and probes to stimulate thinking. The teacher is not passive but is actively involved with the child's learning.

Evaluation.   Learning and development should be evaluated in a formative and summative manner. In a formative manner, the teacher observes how children are dealing with various tasks and dilemmas.

The teacher will then follow up with probing if he or she feels the child's response needs further clarification. In a summative manner, the overall environment should be assessed to see if development is occurring. Since stage change is gradual, it is only appropriate to make this type of assessment once a year or once every two years. Standardized tests are not appropriate, so tasks and dilemmas that allow the child to express his or her own reasoning should be used.

This orientation has struck a positive chord with some educators because it offers an overall vision of human development. The vision of growth portrayed by Piaget, Kohlberg, and Erikson appeals to many because it offers a positive view of the developing person that is also congruent with democratic theory. In general, the orientation encourages schools to assist the development of children so that they have the cognitive skills, the moral reasoning, and the ego strength to participate in the democratic process. There is also a significant amount of research to support the theory and the effects of certain programs on development.[32]

A criticism of the developmental approach is that it is culturally tied to western industrialized countries and thus the claims of universality are unfounded. Some critics suggest that the higher stages of moral development in particular reflect this bias. Carol Gilligan, an associate of Kohlberg, also suggests that the moral development continuum is biased in favor of males and needs to be reexamined in terms of female development.

Another criticism is that since stage development is natural and universal, why bother with educational programs? The response of the developmentalists is that half of the population does not reach the formal operations stage and that only 20 percent reach postconventional moral reasoning. Thus they argue that programs should be developed to facilitate intellectual and moral autonomy.

Notes

1. R. A. Sprinthall and N. A. Sprinthall, *Educational Psychology: A Developmental Approach* (Reading, Mass.: Addison Wesley, 1974), p. 148.

2. L. Kohlberg and C. Gilligan, "The Adolescent as a Philosopher: The Discovery of the Self in a Post-Conventional World," *Daedalus*, 100 (1971), 1077–78.

3. Mary A. Pulaski, *Understanding Piaget* (New York: Harper and Row, 1971), p. 20.

4. Sprinthall and Sprinthall, *Educational Psychology*, pp. 133–34.

5. Erik H. Erikson, *Childhood and Society* (New York: W. W. Norton, 1963), pp. 209–12.

6. Sprinthall and Sprinthall, *Educational Psychology*, p. 111.

7. Ibid., p. 112.
8. Ibid., p. 139.
9. Lawrence Kohlberg, "Moral Education in the School," *School Review* 74 (1966), 9.
10. Kohlberg and Gilligan, "The Adolescent as a Philosopher," pp. 1061–62.
11. Pulaski, *Understanding Piaget*, p. 68.
12. Ibid., p. 69
13. Kohlberg and Gilligan, "The Adolescent as a Philosopher," p. 1063.
14. Erik Erikson, "Identity and the Life Cycle," *Psychological Issues* (1959), pp. 90–91.
15. Kohlberg, "Moral Education in the School," p. 9.
16. Ibid.
17. Ibid., p. 73
18. Erik Erikson, *Identity: Youth and Crisis* (New York: W. W. Norton, 1968), p. 192.
19. Nancy Porter and Nancy Taylor, *How to Assess the Moral Reasoning of Students* (Toronto: Ontario Institute for Studies in Education, 1972), p. 11–12.
20. Quoted by C. Kamii, "Pedagogical Principles Derived from Piaget's Theory: Relevance for Educational Practice," in M. Schwebel and J. Raph, eds., *Piaget in the Classroom* (New York: Basic Books, 1973), pp. 199–200.
21. Ibid., p. 209.
22. Richard Hersh et al., *Models of Moral Education* (New York: Longman, 1980), pp. 137–47.
23. Pulaski, *Understanding Piaget*, p. 109.
24. Ibid., p. 112.
25. Erikson, *Childhood and Society*, p. 238
26. L. Kohlberg and E. Turiel, "Moral Development and Moral Education," in G. Lesser, ed., *Psychology and Educational Practice* (Glenview, Ill.: Scott Foresman, 1971), p. 449.
27. J. M. Tanner and B. Inhelder, eds., *Discussion on Child Development*, Vol. 3 (London: Tavistock, 1959).
28. Pulaski, *Understanding Piaget*, p. 167.
29. Celia Lavatelle, *Piaget's Theory Applied to an Early Childhood Curriculum* (Boston: American Service and Engineering, 1970).
30. David Weikart et al., *The Cognitively Oriented Curriculum for Preschool Teachers* (Washington, D.C.: National Association of Young Children, 1971).
31. Constance Kamii and R. DeVries, "Piaget—Basic Curricula for Early Childhood Education," in Ron Parker, ed., *The Preschool in Action*, rev. ed. (Boston: Allyn & Bacon, 1974).
32. Bruce Joyce and Marsha Weil, *Models of Teaching* (Englewood Cliffs, N.J.: Prentice-Hall, 1980), pp. 127–28. There, the reader is referred to: Myron Rosskopf et al., *Piagetian Cognitive Development Research in Mathematical Education* (Washington, D.C.: National Council of Teachers in Mathematics, 1971); a review by Herbert J. Klausmier and Frank H. Hooper, "Conceptual Development in Instruction," in Fred N. Kerlinger and John B. Carroll, eds., *Review of Research in Education* (Itasca, Ill.: Peacock, 1974), pp. 3–54; a very thorough review by F. H. Hooper, "An Evaluation of Logical Operations in Instruction in the Preschool," in R. K. Parker, ed., *The Preschool in Action: Exploring Early Childhood Education Programs*, rev. ed. (Boston: Allyn & Bacon, 1974), pp 134–86; and Lawrence Kohlberg, ed., *Recent Research in Moral Development* (New York: Holt, Rinehart & Winston, 1977).

Cognitive Process Orientation

Individuals working within the cognitive process orientation study how people think and develop programs which stimulate various modes of reasoning. Some individuals within this orientation suggest that such programs should be the central focus of schooling. For example, Carl Bereiter has argued that schools should only concentrate on the three Rs and thinking skills. In the first section of this chapter, Bereiter's general position is presented along with his most recent work in developing thinking games and writing skills. Several other approaches are also outlined in this chapter. For example, David Ausubel has developed a model within the cognitive process orientation identified as the advance organizer model. This is an approach to deductive thinking that is based on powerful explanatory concepts, or advance organizers, that help teachers present new information to students.

Floyd Robinson and his associates at the Ontario Institute for Studies in Education have originated a major project to develop thinking skills in elementary school. In particular, Robinson has developed programs that facilitate inquiry and problem-solving skills.

The late Hilda Taba was noted for her work in curriculum as well as for developing an elementary school social studies program that centered on thinking skills. Her approach stimulates inductive thinking so that students can manipulate data and draw generalizations from those data.

Finally, Edward de Bono has worked with what he calls lateral thinking. Lateral thinking is an approach to creativity and differs from vertical thinking (e.g., inductive and deductive thinking).

Although all these approaches differ in emphasis, there is commonality in the approaches in that they are concerned with how thinking occurs and the development of programs designed to stimulate cognitive processes.

108

Schools Without Education

Carl Bereiter has been one of the leading spokespersons for the cognitive process orientation. Not only has he articulated what is involved in teaching thinking skills, but he has argued that these skills should be the focus of schooling. In Bereiter's view, efforts to influence the student's personal development should be left to the parents. In other words, schools should not educate.[1] Instead, Bereiter feels that schools should stress training and child care. Training does not attempt to develop the whole child but instead to produce certain skills. In Bereiter's words, "What the child does with the acquired skill, how it is integrated into his personality is a concern that lies beyond training."[2]

Child care is characterized by its neutrality. In child care resources, activities, and love are provided for children but there is no effort to shape the child's development in any way. In Bereiter's view only parents have the right to influence the child's development in a particular direction.

Skill training can be justified because the competencies which are developed can help free the student from the teacher and thus increase his or her options. The three Rs along with certain thinking skills should be the main focus of a skill-training program. Bereiter argues that training programs have been successfully developed that achieve the intended goals. Most recently, Bereiter himself has been involved in programs that develop writing skills. The thinking skills that Bereiter suggests should be taught include "reasoning, idea production, inquiry, and problem solving."[3]

Bereiter argues that other types of learning should not be included in schools. Specifically he refers to direct application learning, learning of background knowledge, and personal learning. Direct application learning occurs when the person can see the immediate use of learning something. Examples include learning to drive or learning a trade. In Bereiter's view the school is not a good place for direct application learning. "In the world at large you learn a job on the job, you learn to ski at a ski resort, you learn to paint in a painter's studio."[4] When schools become involved in direct application learning, the results are disastrous:

Another problem with centering direct-application learning in schools is that it becomes more remote from practice and begins to drift into the learning of basic skills and background knowledge. A school course in electricity, which may attract students who are eager to build radio sets or tricky photocell gadgets, drifts into a course of elementary knowledge about electricity and ends by boring students. The tendency for formal instruction to drift in the direction of teaching background knowledge is probably inevitable and is, I think, the basis of pedantry.[5]

Background knowledge is also inappropriate to schools. Learning history in schools, for example, is difficult for several reasons. One difficulty is deciding what history is appropriate for the classroom. In Bereiter's view, it is difficult to predict what background knowledge will be useful to students in the future. Other problems involve motivation, retention, and retrieval. When a student asks, "Why do we have to learn this stuff?" the teacher often responds with coercion. Retention is another problem. Bereiter cites studies which suggest that students forget about 80 percent of factual material within a year. Finally, the problem of retrieval is also significant. The only time that the student is usually required to retrieve information is when he or she is being tested. The result is what Bereiter calls inert knowledge which cannot be applied to other contexts.[6]

In general, Bereiter makes a strong argument against the subject/ disciplines orientation. He suggests that the disciplines movement of the sixties was unsuccessful because the material was too abstract and beyond the reach of almost all elementary school students and most secondary school students. Bereiter summarizes his position: "If we were starting elementary schools now for the first time, it is doubtful that anyone knowledgeable about children would support the unpromising notion of teaching children subjects like science, history, and geography."[7]

Personal learning attempts to develop values and personality, and for Bereiter, it has no place in schools. First, it contradicts the mandate of the home, and second, he suggests schools are very ineffective in this area. In Bereiter's view, personal learning should be voluntary.

The only general provisions for personal learning that I find morally acceptable are provisions for what might be broadly characterized as self-improvement. These would include counseling and psychotherapy—offered on a voluntary basis, of course. But they could also include forms of help for people who wanted to improve their physical fitness, their intellectual abilities, their tastes, or their habits in such matters as orderliness or inquisitiveness. I would think, however, that these should generally be provisions for adolescents and adults. For children there should be no formal provisions for personal learning except for children in serious need of therapy.[8]

As mentioned previously, schools should focus on training and child care, and these two functions should be clearly separated. Bereiter states that training is characterized by three elements: (1) it is done as a means of access to a desired activity; (2) it is removed from the rest of life and it has its own distinct criteria; (3) training is conducted by an individual whose responsibility is narrowly conceived around a particular skill such as writing. Thus training differs from education in three key respects. In education, learning is carried out for its own sake; it is connected to the overall development of the child; and is guided by a teacher whose concern is beyond special skills.[9] In most schools Bereiter states that training and other types of learning (e.g., personal, learning of background knowledge, etc.) become intertwined and confused.

But then, just as meaningful learning becomes contaminated with performance learning, so does skill training get muddled up with the effort to promote understanding, creativity, and the like. A reading lesson and a science lesson thus come to have much the same ingredients—a mish-mash of memorization, drill, procedure learning, inquiry, question-and-answer recitation, factual exposition, craft projects, and free-floating discussion.[10]

In practice Bereiter suggests that schools be divided into an area for child care and a separate area for skill training.

Take an ordinary old elementary school. Announce to the teachers that they can have their choice between being child care workers and scholastic skill trainers. Put the child care workers on the ground floor and tell them that their job is not to educate children but simply to provide them with an abundance of things to do in and out of school that will make for a good life. Put the trainers upstairs or in the basement, assign them either language arts or arithmetic as their subject, and tell them to find a way to teach it successfully to any child who walks in the door, using no more than three hours of his time per week. Give the child care workers an ample equipment and field-trip budget and give the trainers some time off to be trained themselves in any teaching method of their choice.[11]

Training and child care do not have much in common. Training is highly structured and authoritarian, while child care allows a reasonable amount of freedom. Training has definite goals, while child care is goal free. Training is focused, while child care is concerned with the whole child. Since training and child care are so different, they should be separated and conducted by people with different competencies.[12]

Bereiter is concerned that schools strive for goals which can be realistically achieved. He feels the calls for greatness that teachers hear so frequently should be minimized and instead schools should concentrate on simple, attainable ends. Although few schools have been designed specifically on the Bereiter model, there is a vocal minority that continues to echo the Bereiter argument. Some parents strongly object to schools attempting to teach values, as they feel schools should stick to teaching basic skills. A minority of parents, like Bereiter, feel schools should train children in certain skills and stay away from personal and social education.

More recently, Bereiter has been involved in curriculum work that reflects his interest in training students in thinking skills and writing skills. To develop thinking skills, Bereiter and Anderson have written a set of materials entitled *Thinking Games*.[13] These books include games intended to develop problem-solving skills in a manner that children can enjoy. The games are designed for use at school and at home, as in either setting they involve a minimum of supervision. The games focus on the following skills:

Pattern detection
Foreseeing consequences
Educated guessing
Interpolative thinking (figuring out the missing link)
Extrapolative thinking (figuring out what will come next)
Identifying needed information
Formulating questions
Inferring rules
Seeing something from several points of view
Defining
Identifying truth, falsity, and uncertainty
Inferring possible causes
Testing hypotheses
Thinking of possibilities
Detecting irregularities
Proving
Determining relevance
Persuading and resisting persuasion
Planning
Formulating problems
Using analogies
Using maps
Using logical representations
Using negative information
Checking for errors and omissions
Anticipating actions of others
Inferring motives
Thinking of examples
Recognizing progress toward a solution
Identifying contradictions
Categorizing
Applying rules
Explaining
Reducing conclusions.[14]

An example of a thinking game is "Read-Around."

Name: Read-Around.
Players: Any number, 3 to 6 makes for the liveliest game.
Level: Any age, but all players must be able to read.

Equipment: A book that is easy reading for the players, but not one they know by heart.
Object of game: To win a turn as leader by guessing the next word in the sentence.
Procedure: Players sit in circle. Leader holds book, selects any sentence, reads first word. Player to left tries to guess second word. If he fails, leader reads first two words, and turn passes to second player to left, who tries to guess third word. Play continues until a player guesses word, then *he* becomes leader.
Example: Leader: "After . . ." Player 1: "the." L: "After lunch . . ." Player 2: "was." L: "After lunch, Tom . . ." Player 3: "and." L: That's right. "After lunch Tom and Linda went to the park." Player 3 takes book and becomes new leader.[15]

Thinking skills in this game involve educated guessing and extrapolative thinking.

Thinking games, according to Bereiter, mainly require figuring something out rather than relying on "luck, memory, speed, strength, and so on."

Most recently Bereiter has been a principal investigator in a project to improve students' writing skills. He is a coauthor of a book entitled *Writing for Results*, and the orientation is reflected in the introduction: "The main thrust of this program has been toward understanding the cognitive processes of writing and how these develop in school-age children."[16] The book consists of consequential tasks or short writing exercises where the objectives are clearly stated.

Deductive Thinking

David Ausubel is recognized as one of the leading theorists in cognitive psychology. He has studied how the mind processes new information and how teachers can apply these findings to instructional activities. Ausubel is concerned with assisting teachers to present information, new material in particular, in a meaningful and efficient manner. Specifically, Ausubel has developed the advance organizer concept, which helps the teacher prepare students to assimilate information. He has been concerned also with developing students' cognitive structures, which organize information.[17] Ausubel suggests that cognitive structures help determine whether we see new material in a meaningful manner. If we can strengthen students' cognitive structures, we can assist them in learning and retaining new information. Ausubel rejects the notion that expository learning leads to passivity and rote learning.[18]

Ausubel states that meaningful learning is related to what we have learned previously. If learning is meaningful, we are able to transform it and apply it to new situations. However, rote learning does not develop the cognitive structures we need to apply our learning to new situations. In rote learning we also tend to forget material quickly, while in meaningful learning we retain detail in relation to key concepts, or organizers.

Ausubel suggests that whether learning is meaningful depends in part on the learning set of the student and the nature of the material. When the student has the appropriate learning set, then learning will be enhanced. The teacher must be able to relate new material to the present learning set of the student. Ausubel's advance organizer technique facilitates acquiring the appropriate learning set. In dealing with new information, the mind of the learner can be quite active. Even during a lecture, Ausubel suggests the learner will be analyzing the information in relation to his or her cognitive structures. The person will be examining new information in relation to concepts which are already understood. Ausubel's approach is designed to assist what he calls "active reception learning."[19] He sees the mind processing information much as an academic discipline processes data. In an academic discipline there is a network of interrelated concepts. For example, in sociology such concepts as class structure, role, and norm form a network. As we learn some of these concepts, they explain other concepts. For instance, after we learn about class structure, we are ready to learn about the different classes in a society. If concepts are presented that are too remote from concepts that have already been presented, they are not integrated into the student's cognitive structure. Thus the teacher must present the key concepts in sequence so that the student can assimilate new ideas.

Ausubel's approach to teaching tends to be deductive, that is, he recommends proceeding from general ideas to specific information. He calls this process "progressive differentiation." He also develops the idea of "integrative reconciliation," which means that the teacher should develop new concepts that are closely related to the ideas that have been presented previously. Progressive differentiation and integrative reconciliation provide the principles for organizing curriculum and instruction. Thus textbooks and learning materials should be organized according to these principles (e.g., progressive differentiation) rather than presenting information at the same level of abstraction. Texts should proceed from general organizing concepts to more specific information.[20]

Advance organizers facilitate progressive differentiation and integrative reconciliation. Advance organizers are concepts that are abstract and inclusive and prepare the student to learn new information. Advance organizers should use ideas and terms that are already familiar to the learner. An example of this process comes from ecology. If students were beginning a unit on ecology, the teacher might first present the concept of interconnectedness within ecological systems (the idea that if one part of an ecological system is changed then there will be a ripple effect through the entire system). Thus, if the northern tundra is affected, the entire ecological system associated with the tundra is also affected. The concept of interconnectedness can be used, then, as one advance organizer in a unit on ecology.

The advance organizer should be carefully explained before proceeding. If students do not understand the concept of interconnectedness then the rest of the unit will be confusing to the student. Advance organizers are usually developed around generalizations, concepts, and principles. Other examples of advance organizers include:

- The law of supply and demand might be used as an advance organizer for a unit on prices.
- The concept of life cycle could be examined before looking at specific aspects of the cycle.

Ausubel describes two major types of organizers: expository and comparative. Expository organizers are used in most cases to explain new material and usually consist of general concepts, so that new subconcepts and ideas are understood. For example, the idea that norms are present in most cultures would be presented before examining specific norms within cultures.

Comparative organizers are used with more familiar material. They can be used to explore new concepts in relation to concepts that exist within present cognitive structures. For example, if the students have been studying addition they can use an understanding of number relationships in studying subtraction.

Joyce and Weil have outlined how the advance organizer can be used in the classroom.[21] The first step is to clarify the aims of the lesson so that expectations are clear. After the aims have been clarified, the advance organizer is presented. The advance organizer contains a major concept that is used to explain the remainder of the material in the lesson or unit. Advance organizers are not simple introductory material but powerful explanatory concepts. The essential features of the organizers must be carefully explained and examples provided. All language connected with the organizer must also be carefully explained to the student. The teacher should explain the main attributes of the organizer and the context in which the attributes are to be used. After the advance organizer has been presented, the teacher then moves on to present the new material. This is done through traditional vehicles such as lectures, discussion, and visual aids. However, the teacher should proceed in a logical manner relating the new information back to the advance organizer. In most cases, the teacher moves from the general to the specific. In the last phase the teacher can remind students of the main ideas and ask students to summarize the main attributes of the lesson. The teacher can also ask students to relate the material back to the advance organizer. The teacher can involve the students by:

1. Asking students to describe how the new material relates to a single aspect of their existing knowledge.
2. Asking students for additional examples of the concept or propositions in the learning material.
3. Asking students to verbalize the essence of the material, using their own terminology and frame of reference.
4. Asking students to examine the material from alternative points of view.
5. Relating the material to contradictory material, experience, or knowledge.[22]

Students can also be asked to examine assumptions and inferences in the material and thus develop a critical approach to the subject matter. During the process, the teacher can point out the relationship between new knowledge and existing knowledge so that the learning is meaningful.

An example of an advance organizer is taken from the Anthropology Curriculum Project developed at the University of Georgia. The advance organizers deal with acculturation in Kenya.

The advance organizer begins the unit:

Acculturation takes place when the people of one culture acquire the traits of another culture as a result of contact over a long period of time. The British governed Kenya for about 80 years. During this period, the direction of cultural change was largely one way . . .

The unit then proceeds:

African traits were replaced or modified by European traits. Almost all African traits have been influenced by European culture, especially in the cities. The people in the cities have been most affected by modernization in Kenya. In 1886, Kenya came under the control of the British. Kenya was ruled by the British for almost 80 years. British laws became the law of Kenya. English became the official language. The schools that were started were taught in English.

Contact with the British brought many changes to African culture. This contact with the British is an example of innovations coming from outside the culture. . . . This kind of innovation is called acculturation, because Africans and British came into direct contact. Acculturation is the change that takes place in a culture over a period of time as a result of contact between different cultures. . . .

The direction of acculturation was largely one way; European traits replaced or changed African traits, but African traits had little impact on European traits. The new traits have helped in the modernization of Kenya. Modernization in Kenya has resulted in the replacement of African traits by European traits.[23]

Ausubel's view of thinking is clearly different from Bereiter's. Ausubel suggests that cognitive structures are organized similarly to the way academic disciplines are organized, and the advance organizer model is used to teach concepts associated with the disciplines. Bereiter's concept of cognitive process is not tied to the academic disciplines. In fact, he suggests it is futile to teach science and history to elementary school students. Thus there is certainly no consensus within the cognitive process orientation about how people think. The differences in programs arise from the various theorists' views of how the mind works.

Problem Solving

Floyd Robinson has worked with both Bereiter and Ausubel. He is the coauthor of a text in educational psychology with Ausubel and has worked with Bereiter in a major project on thinking skills. For example, Bereiter's thinking games mentioned earlier in this chapter are part of the Elementary School Thinking Project at the Ontario Institute for Studies in Education. Robinson and Bereiter have been principal investigators in this project.

In an article on this project, Robinson describes a general growth scheme of children's thinking abilities. At the lowest level are the primitive intellectual abilities. These abilities appear in young children without formal instruction and include "observing, classifying, seriating and setting up correspondences." When the child begins school, the focus shifts to "finding out skills." These skills include decoding written symbols, computation, measurement, graphing, and tabulating data. Robinson suggests that these skills can be broken down to the first-level skills and that teachers should be aware of the relationship between the skill levels. "For example, although most schools treat measurement as a somewhat isolated component of the arithmetic programs, simple analysis reveals that it is built upon skills of observation and setting up correspondences."[24]

The next level of skills appears around age 11 and is called problemsolving or inquiry strategies. Here the student gains an understanding of what is involved in an experiment and how elements interact within a physical system.

For example, near the end of the junior grades, or in the early senior elementary grades, the student may learn the notion of an "experiment." This concept acts as an organizing device that informs the student what skills are to be brought into play, and in what order, when he is trying to figure out "what affects what" in a physical system. For example, as he tries to figure out what characteristics of a steel rod influence the amount it will bend, this strategy will inform the student that he should first identify the variables in the system (classification); then identify those that are potentially causal (classification); then vary one of these latter factors (measurement) while holding the others constant and observing the variation in the amount the rod bends (measurement); and finally interpret the result (numerical computation, classification).[25]

Problem-solving skills and inquiry strategies have been a major focus of Robinson's work, and he states the project has demonstrated effectiveness of programs focusing on problem-solving skills. These inquiry skills include: (1) logical/quantitative thinking; (2) causal thinking, which includes experimentation and randomization, correlational analysis, and case study analysis; and (3) decision making.

Robinson argues that problem solving should be a "subject of study by the student in its own right."[26] Thus problem solving and thinking are not necessarily tied to academic disciplines in the Robinson approach. However, the skills can be applied to such disciplines as science, math, history, and geography.

In its most general form, the problem-solving model proceeds by the following steps, pictured in Figure 2:

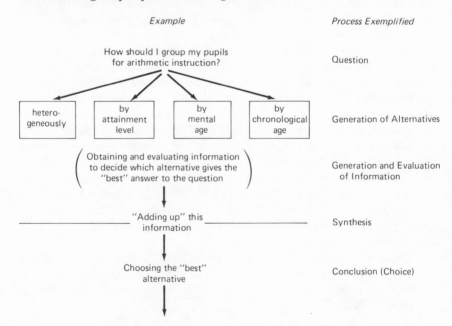

Figure 2. Visual Presentation of Problem Solving.

SOURCE: Floyd G. Robinson, John Tickle, and David W. Brison, *Inquiry Training: Fusing Theory and Practice* (Toronto: Ontario Institute for Studies in Education, 1972), p. 5.

1. Identifying a question
2. Identifying possible alternative answers or avenues of inquiry that will produce an answer
3. Finding information about the alternatives
4. Adding up or synthesizing this information in some way
5. Choosing an alternative.[27]

Two examples of this model are now presented. First, let us examine a historical case study. This case is drawn from Canadian history and deals with the question, Why did Champlain locate his Habitation (Colony) in Québec?[28]

Identifying the Question

The student formulates a specific question or set of questions around the topic of concern. The student should also identify criteria that make for an inquiry-oriented question. For example, questions should be open ended, demand use of facts, and be manageable in terms of time and resources.

Identifying Alternatives

Students generate a reasonable number of alternative solutions to the question. During this process the student learns to identify cause-and-effect relationships, to tolerate criticism, to challenge other viewpoints constructively, and to risk an unpopular or untried solution. The student should also be aware that additional alternatives may arise during the data-collection stage. Referring to our example, alternatives for why Champlain settled in Québec include defense, food, transportation, climate, fuel, and water.

Data Collection

During this step, students should learn to recognize how the question can guide the collection of information. Data collection allows the student to employ a wide range of skills in the collection of data such as

1. The ability to locate the desired information
2. The ability to collect information
3. Library skills
4. Interviewing skills
5. Data interpretation skills.

The student also learns to evaluate the information critically in relation to the original problem and to draw tentative conclusions based on the data collection. In the example the data collected in relation to each alternative included:

Defense: cliff, narrows

Food: forest, river, plains

Transportation: fur trade, supplies

Climate: winter

Fuel: forest

Water: river.

Synthesis

The student arrives at a conclusion based on an examination of the data. This means selecting the alternative which is best supported by the data and applying criteria to evaluate the data. Once he or she has evaluated the data, the student will then draw a conclusion indicating the relative importance of the various factors and outlining any limitations to the conclusion. In the Champlain example, the conclusion could be (1) there were many natural advantages to the site and (2) the harsh winter climate was a major drawback.

Assessing the Conclusion

The student assesses whether the conclusion adequately deals with the original problem. In the Champlain example, the assessment is that the data were adequate; however, Champlain's personal reasons were unknown.

Expressing the Conclusion

In this step the student presents the conclusion. Here the student examines how to present the problem and the conclusion and considers what materials (e.g., graphs, charts, audiovisual aids) are appropriate for the presentation. For instance, the student can dramatize how Champlain and his advisers discussed the various locations for the Habitation. The dramatization can bring forth the data as researched by the students.

Evaluation

In evaluation the student assesses the conclusion and the presentation in relation to the original question. Here the student looks at the conclusion in relation to the comprehensiveness of the data, the possible biases in the data collection, the applicability of the conclusion to other contexts, and the appropriateness of the inferences made from the data. Again the student also examines the suitability of the presentation in relation to its purpose, the nature of the data, and the audience and the time available for research.

A shorter example of problem solving is taken from science:

An example of the sort of analysis we expect (in experimentation) is illustrated in figure 2 [Fig. 3, this volume], a locally produced variant of one of our causal models. To illustrate how this works, we might imagine that a grade 7 science student, in the normal course of his work on magnetism, has formed the notion (hypothesis/idea) that "the number of turns of wire makes a difference to the magnet's strength" (to use the sort of language that a grade 7 student might come forth with). He has, then, arrived at the starting point for a problem-solving episode, and we would expect him to do the following things in line with the model outline:

1. State the problem as a question, using whatever language he finds appropriate: "Does the number of turns make any difference to the strength of the magnet?"

2. Clarify this question by identifying the hypothesized effect (the strength of the magnet), the means by which this variable will be measured (e.g., by the number of nails that the magnet will lift), and the supposed causal factor (the number of turns) and how this will be measured, progressing in this manner to a clarified question: "Does the number of turns affect the strength of the magnet, measured by the number of one-ounce nails it will lift?"

3. Make a plan for answering that question, which involves identifying the factor to be changed, the variables to be held constant, and the means by which some estimate of the error can be obtained (essentially by replication).

4. Record the data in a manner that lends itself to analysis, as indicated in figure 2 [3].

5. Compare the effect of varying the experimental factor to the error obtained when it was not varied.

6. Judge whether the change that occurred when the experimental factor was varied was beyond the range of variation that could be attributed to error.

We do not, of course, simply lay this model on students. Rather, our approach has been to get students to muddle their way through a problem of this type in their normal fashion, reflect on the adequacy of their approach, make suggestions for improvements into a model that becomes the basis for further independent experimentation.[29]

Robinson refers to several studies to support his claim that these approaches to problem solving have led to significant increases in student thinking skills. A recent report by two of his coworkers corroborates the claim of significant effects with an updated version of the model designated "the interdisciplinary skills list."[30] Robinson also suggests that "we attribute whatever success we have obtained in our thinking program to the opportunity team members had of spending many hours studying the thinking performance of individual children."[31] This is a classic statement of the cognitive process position as Robinson acknowledges how the project has focused on how chil-

State the problem as a question	Clarify and reword the question	Make a plan for answering the revised question	Carry out the plan	Record the data obtained to show relationships	State relationships observed	Interpret the relationships
'Does the number of turns make any difference to the strength of the magnet?'	Name the factor you are trying to influence (D.V.)* Say how you will measure this factor (D.V.) Name the factor(s) that is supposed to influence the D.V.(E) Say how you will measure that factor (E) Reword the question if necessary. 'Does the number of turns affect the strength of the magnet, measured by the number of one-ounce nails it will lift?'	Make a list of the factors that could affect the D.V. If E is not named in the question, select it from this list. Say how you will change E and hold the other factors as constant as possible. Say how you will obtain an estimate of the affect of not holding other factors constant.		Make a graph table of the form: |	E1	E2
---	---	---
	—	—
	—	—
	—	—	 		n1 10 turns	n2 20 turns
---	---	---
	23	32
	21	36
	24	35		Calculate the *average* value of D.V. for each value of E. Calculate the *variation* in the D.V. for constant values of E. Say how much the D.V. changed when E changed (difference in averages). Say how much the D.V. changed when E was constant (variation).	By comparing the difference in averages with the variation, judge whether E affected the D.V.

Figure 3. Experimental Problem Solving

SOURCE: Floyd Robinson, "The Major Thrust Project in Elementary School Thinking," *Orbit* (Ontario Institute for Studies in Education) 7(2) (1976), 8.

* D.V. = Dependent Variable

dren think and then developed programs to stimulate more complex thinking skills.

Robinson suggests that, whenever possible, teachers should also work with children in a one-to-one situation. "It is no secret that many of the significant cognitive leaps occur in the same one-to-one situation, where the teacher can judge the precise moment to force such a leap and can devise a teaching vehicle that is particularly right for this individual child."[32] The teacher who works from a cognitive process orientation should closely observe how children think and then intervene to stimulate cognitive growth. This intervention, in Robinson's view, must be based on a sound understanding of how children think and how cognitive processes develop, and of programs which have proven effective in stimulating cognitive growth.

Inductive Thinking

Hilda Taba saw thinking as an active transaction between the individual and information. As the student interacts with information, he or she will develop conclusions, generalizations, and concepts. According to Taba, cognitive processes cannot be taught directly. Instead, the teacher can assist the student in examining data and making inferences from the data. Taba argues that thinking processes develop according to "lawful" processes, and teaching strategies must be in accordance with these processes.

Taba directed the Contra Costa School District Social Studies Project, which focused on developing thinking skills for elementary school students. Taba's programs were developed around concept formation, interpreting data, and applying principles.

Concept Formation

According to Taba, students develop concepts when they respond to questions that require them "(1) to enumerate items; (2) to find a basis for grouping items that are similar in some respect; (3) to identify the common characteristics of items in a group; (4) to label the groups; and (5) to subsume items that they enumerated under those labels."[33] Taba suggests that these skills develop in a definite hierarchy.

The teacher can facilitate the development of skills with certain questions. For example, enumeration and differentiation can be elicited by the question "What do you see, or note?" At the sixth-grade level the student might ask: What differences in living would you expect to find if you moved to South America?

The next step in concept formation is to group and identify common properties. To elicit grouping, the teacher can use questions such as "What belongs together?" and "What criteria did you use to group things?" At the sixth-grade level students will list the differences between living in South America and living in the United States. Taba states that students should do the operations on their own without referring to the teacher.

The final step in concept formation is to label and categorize. Here the student determines the hierarchical order of items. The teacher can facilitate this last step of concept formation with questions like "What would you call these groups?" and "What belongs under that?" The process of categorizing information is outlined below.

Discussion Excerpt: Categorizing (Grade 6)

Sequence of remarks	Speaker	
1.	Teacher	Can you give us a heading for these words?
2.	Jan	"Facilities and conditions."
3./4.	Teacher	That's good. "Facilities and conditions," you say? Now, let's get these so we don't have too many, because I'm going to run out of room. So let's get them very concise.
5.	Kim	"Education."
6./7.	Teacher	That's fine. What could education come under also?
8.	Joe	"Schools."
9./10.	Teacher	"Schools" can come under "education," but I mean one more heading.
11.	Joan	Well, they have different ways.
12.	Max	"Customs."
13./15.	Teacher	That's it—customs is a word we use to say different ways. That's good—we've got it into one word. Now let's take a quick look at this and see if we have missed anything that should be here. What do you say, Sam?
16.	Sam	"Natural resources."
17.	Ted	"Physical features."
18.	Teacher	That's good—begin with this right here and let's go right down the list and say where we would put them. Which category would we put them, Sara?
19.	Sara	Electricity under "facilities and conditions."
20.	Teacher	Let's look at these. Where would poor pavement go? Do you have any idea?
21.	Sara	Under the "conditions."
22.	Teacher	That would be good. We could put it under "facilities and conditions." Where would you say to put it?

23.	Rex	"Transportation."
24.	Teacher	Without good pavement transportation wouldn't be as good, would it? Let's decide on that. How many think poor pavement would be under "transportation" or under "conditions"? How many say "conditions"? Now don't look around. Let's everyone think for ourselves. All right now, "transportation" wins. We'll put it under "transportation."[34]

Interpreting, Inferring, and Generalizing about Data

These operations require three steps.

1. Looking at similar aspects of selected samples with the same questions in mind. (For example, What are the educational patterns in Brazil, Mexico, and Bolivia?)
2. Explaining what is seen, such as comparing and contrasting the different literacy levels in two countries and explaining the difference.
3. Arriving at generalizations by inferring what the common features and differences are (in the case of the above example, regarding the educational patterns).[35]

At the first step, the student differentiates by identifying key points. The teacher can elicit this operation by asking a question such as "What did you notice?" At the second step, the student relates points to one another and determines cause-and-effect relationships. He or she accomplishes this cognitive operation through explaining items that have been identified. The teacher can facilitate this process by asking, "Why did so-and-so happen?" At the final step, the student draws inferences and then goes beyond what is given. The teacher might facilitate the last step by asking, "What does this mean?" and "What would you conclude?" An example of this process is given below. In this example, students have been working in three committees to study education in Brazil, Mexico, or Bolivia. The discussion is designed to integrate the findings of the committees.

Discussion Excerpt: Interpreting Data (Grade 6)

Sequence of Remarks	*Speaker*	
1.	Teacher	All right, how about education? You remember in Mexico we had what kind of an educational system?
2.	Phil	Well, Mexico is improving its education and the children go to school and come home and teach

		their parents what they learned, because when their parents were young they didn't have the chance to go to school.
3.	Teacher	Why didn't they?
4.	Phil	Because there weren't enough schools and teachers, and there weren't enough people that knew how to read and write.
5.	Teacher	You mean there weren't enough teachers that could possibly have taught those people to read and write?
6.	Phil	Yes.
7.	Judy	Well, in Mexico they have a motto for education. "Each one teach one." So that when the children come home from school they teach their parents or maybe their sisters or brothers who can't go to school, and their relatives.
8.	Teacher	Does this help the education standard in that country?
9.	Dan	Well, each person could teach another person and then the person that was taught could go on and teach someone else and it spreads the education. Some people have never even gone to school; they get educated by someone they know.[36]

Application of Principles

Applying principles is the highest level of thinking in the Taba approach. This usually occurs at the end of the unit. For example, if sixth graders understand the concept of a one-crop economy, they can hypothesize what will happen if the crop fails.[37]

Applying principles is a three-step process. The first step is to predict consequences, or to hypothesize. Here the student analyzes the nature of the problem and retrieves relevant knowledge. The teacher can elicit hypotheses with questions like "What would happen if . . . ?" An example given by Taba includes "What would happen to the way of life in the desert if there was sufficient water?"

At the second step, the student explains and supports the hypothesis. Students determine the causal links leading to the predictions. Teachers can facilitate this process by asking questions such as "Why do you think this would happen?" For example, if the students predict that cities will eventually be built, they need to establish links between water in the desert and the building of cities. The students might reason that the availability of water would lead to growing crops. Nomadic life would then end and trade centers be established.

At the last step, students verify the prediction by using logic or facts to assess the validity of their prediction. The teacher can elicit verification by asking the question, "What would it take for the generalization to be generally true or probably true?" For example, one can establish whether or not the desert soil in question contains salt and then deduce whether or not the availability of water would make any difference for plant life.

Taba suggests that different student thinking styles can complement each other in the classroom. The predictions of the less verbal student tend to be more concrete and can complement the more abstract reasoning of the more verbal students. Thus the class can produce a more complete and varied set of predictions than could be generated by one student.

In Taba's approach, the teacher needs to listen to children's thinking. Taba has developed cognitive maps of student thinking to help the teacher understand how children deal with problems. Taba also suggests that teachers focus on only one thinking task at a time. In her view, difficulties can occur when students are asked to perform more than one skill at a time. Instead, the teacher should ask questions that let students probe or develop their thinking in one skill (e.g., grouping, discrimination, etc.). Thus each step of the teaching strategy is pursued in depth so that all students have had a chance to respond and that a variety of models are represented. This process is repeated with each step of concept formation, interpreting data, and applying principles.

Lateral Thinking

Edward de Bono has done extensive research on creative thought. Specifically, he has studied lateral thinking, which he distinguishes from vertical thinking. In de Bono's view, lateral thinking is similar to insight, creativity, and humor but is a more deliberate process. Lateral thinking generates new ideas. It is concerned with "breaking out of the concept prison of old ideas" and looking at things in a new way.[38]

De Bono states that lateral thinking and vertical thinking (i.e., inductive and deductive thinking) are complementary. However, de Bono is concerned that too much of education has focused on vertical thinking. In de Bono's view, education has stressed the development of concept patterns. There has been little emphasis on "restructuring these patterns (insight) and provoking new ones (creativity)."[39]

Like other cognitive psychologists, de Bono has a conception of how the mind works. In de Bono's view, the mind is a pattern-making system. The mind is constantly creating and recognizing patterns. These patterns of information facilitate memory. Patterns that are recalled frequently form a "stock of preset patterns that are the basis of communication."[40]

De Bono argues that communication is based on the mind's working with preset patterns. Sequential use of these patterns is vertical thinking, while a leap or sudden switch of patterns leads to humor or insight. If the switch into another pattern is temporary, it is humor. If the switch is permanent it gives rise to insight. De Bono cites an example of humor: "Mr. Churchill sat down next to Lady Astor at dinner one day. She turned to him and said, 'Mr. Churchill, if I was married to you I should put poison in your coffee.' Mr. Churchill turned to her and said, 'Madam, if I was married to you . . . I should drink the coffee.'"[41] Here Churchill's answer thwarts our expectations (or pattern of thought) and humor is the result.

Although patterns facilitate communication, there are disadvantages to patterns. Some of these disadvantages are that patterns tend to become established and rigid. Thus it is difficult to change patterns, once they have been established. Similarly, when patterns become established, information tends to be used only within that pattern. Thus the mind gets into a rut. In de Bono's words, "the mind is a cliché-making and a cliché-using system."[42]

Vertical Thinking and Lateral Thinking

Vertical thinking is convergent. It is concerned with selecting the one right path to the correct answer. On the other hand, lateral thinking is characterized by diversity and richness. Instead of seeking one path, several alternatives are sought even after one path in particular has been identified as the most promising.

In vertical thinking, the person knows where he or she is going. In lateral thinking, there is no step-by-step sequence so the individual does not know the specific direction. Instead, the individual may play around with experiments, models, and ideas without a definite sense of direction. Vertical thinking is analytical, lateral thinking is provocative. Below is an example outlining the difference in the two modes of thought:

One may consider three different attitudes to the remark of a student who had come to the conclusion: "Ulysses was a hypocrite."
1. "You are wrong, Ulysses was not a hypocrite."
2. "How very interesting, tell me how you reached that conclusion."
3. "Very well. What happens next? How are you going to go forward from that idea?"[43]

The second response is an example of vertical thinking, while the third response encourages lateral thinking.

Vertical thinking is sequential while lateral thinking can make jumps. Most of the cognitive process approaches described in this chapter are examples of vertical thinking. In lateral thinking the person jumps around and then fills in the gaps afterwards. In vertical thinking one closely follows every step or chaos can result. In lateral thinking the individual does not have to be correct at every step. In vertical thinking one concentrates and excludes what is irrelevant. In lateral thinking one welcomes chance intrusion. In vertical-thinking categories, classifications, and labels are fixed, but in lateral thinking they are not. Categories are essential to most systems of vertical thinking, while a sudden change of meaning is useful to lateral thinking.

De Bono acknowledges that vertical thinking will usually yield some sort of solution. In lateral thinking there is the risk that there may be no solution, although there is the possibility that a more comprehensive solution will be reached.

Lateral thinking is both an attitude and a method of using information. Lateral thinking means one is open to new patterns. In other words, there is a readiness to explore alternatives in a nonjudgmental manner. In lateral thinking there is more interest in future effects than in past reasons.

Lateral thinking is used in a variety of ways. For example, it is used in problem solving, particularly problems where there is a need to rearrange information into new structures. Lateral thinking is also useful in examining assumptions and making overall reassessments. As an attitude, de Bono suggests that lateral thinking can be used to prevent polarization. Sometimes in vertical thinking we can fall into rigid patterns of thought. Lateral thinking can help us to see new patterns and thus "counter arrogance and rigidity."

Techniques

De Bono outlines a number of specific methods that employ lateral thinking and suggests they can be used in the classroom. One of these techniques is the generation of alternatives. De Bono states, "The most basic principle of lateral thinking is that any particular way of looking at things is only from among many other possible ways."[44]

In lateral thinking the search is for as many alternatives as possible. The person does not look for the best choice but for as many different alternative choices as possible. Often, the lateral search will explore alternatives that at first do not seem reasonable; but when reexamined, they may partially assist in the solution of the problem.

To assist lateral thinking, de Bono suggests that quotas and geometric figures be used. With quotas we identify a definite number of alternatives to generate. Thus we make an effort to generate alternatives rather than jumping to one conclusion. De Bono suggests suitable quotas might be three, four, or five alternatives.

De Bono also believes that geometric figures are helpful. In using figures in the classroom the teacher might proceed in the following manner.

1. The teacher draws the figure on the board or hands copies of the figure to the students on separate pieces of paper.
2. The teacher then asks the students to generate different ways of describing the figure.
3. The teacher can then ask for volunteers to outline their descriptions.
4. The teacher can list these descriptions on the board. However, initially there is no judgment of the alternatives. Instead, each student should have the opportunity to explain his or her figure.

Lateral thinking can also involve creating designs. Here students are asked to make visual designs. The purpose is to show that there are different ways of doing things. Here are some sample design tasks.[45]

Design:
An apple-picking machine.
A potato-peeling machine.
A cart to go over rough ground.
A cup that cannot spill.
A machine to dig tunnels.
A device to help cars to park.

Redesign:
The human body.
A new milk bottle.
A chair.
A school.
A new type of clothes.
A better umbrella.

Other techniques in lateral thinking include suspended judgment, the reversal method, brainstorming, analogies, and random stimulation. De Bono's techniques are similar to right brain thinking techniques advocated by transpersonal educators. However, de Bono is basically working from a cognitive process orientation rather than a transpersonal orientation. His program is derived from a conception of how the mind works rather than from a holistic perspective.

Summary and Appraisal

Aims. Development of thinking skills (e.g., making inferences, critical thinking, hypothesizing, lateral thinking).

Conception of Learning. Most of the cognitive process approaches are based on a conception of how children think. The theorists' views of the thinking process shape their conception of learning and curriculum. The theorists, then, are oriented to different styles of thinking (e.g., deductive, inductive, and lateral thinking).

Conception of the Learner. Almost all the theorists working from this orientation conceive the learner as actively manipulating information. The learner is someone who seeks to make meaning with the information that he or she encounters.

Conception of the Instructional Process. The conception varies with the different approach.

Deductive thinking (Ausubel)
1. Present and explain advance organizer
2. Present and explain new information with reference to advance organizer
3. Critically examine information and clarify relationships between information and advance organizer.

Problem solving (Robinson)
1. Identify problem
2. Identify alternatives
3. Seek information in relation to alternatives and criteria
4. Examine information and synthesize data
5. Draw conclusion
6. Assess conclusion.

Inductive thinking (Taba) (Concept formation)
1. Enumerate items
2. Identify common characteristics of items in a group
3. Label the groups
4. Subsume items under the labels.

Lateral thinking (de Bono)
1. Identify problem
2. Generate a variety of alternatives using various techniques (e.g., brainstorming, use of geometric figures)
3. Choose a solution.

Learning Environment. The environment contains learning materials that encourage various cognitive processes.

Teacher's Role.   Teachers should be keen observers of children's thinking. If possible, the teacher should work one-to-one with children or in small groups. The teacher is generally a facilitator who challenges, probes, and stimulates thinking with questions, problems, and analogies.

Evaluation.   Evaluation should focus on cognitive processes and skills. Thus the test would involve problems so that students can apply various thinking skills.

It is clear that the cognitive process approach will vary with how children think. Bereiter suggests that schools should focus only on the three Rs and various thinking skills. However, Ausubel's view of thinking is allied to thinking in academic disciplines, and his advance organizer is designed to facilitate the retention of concepts and information in various subject fields. Taba's approach is designed to let the student develop concepts and generalizations from information. Robinson and de Bono focus on problem-solving skills, although each offers a different approach.

Despite these differences the theorists are concerned with how children think and how the curriculum can be organized to stimulate various thinking skills.

There is little question that this orientation offers a rich source of inquiry for curriculum theorists and teachers. There is also an ample amount of empirical evidence to support the effectiveness of programs designed to stimulate thinking. At the same time, there are problems with implementing the approach. For example, consider Robinson's comments:

There are some very significant ways in which school climates must change if they are to foster the development of thinking skills. At a fairly superficial level of analysis, it seems obvious that the school that wants to teach thinking must be prepared to abide by the troublesome implications of student thought. At a certain phase the student will sharpen his newly acquired thinking skills on whatever material comes to hand, and the decisions and judgments of teachers and principals may become favorite targets for this expertise. We have seen inquiry-trained students, for example, openly challenge the decisions of a principal on the grounds that his solution was based on an inadequate conceptualization of the problem and was inferior to theirs. Such intellectual muscle-flexing could be disturbing to the teacher or principal who plays the omniscient role.[46]

There is also need for extensive teacher training in order to implement these approaches. If teachers are to teach thinking, then they need extensive training in observing children's thinking, developing programs based on cognitive processes, and implementing these programs in the classroom. Training teachers would require a major shift in emphasis from the traditional focus on traditional subject areas.

The narrowness of Bereiter's position is also open to question. To focus programs narrowly on the three Rs and thinking skills as articulated in his book, *Must We Educate*, is not supported by the large majority of parents and educators. As indicated in recent Gallup polls, about 75 percent of the public supports values-education programs. Most parents want their child treated as a whole child in schools, where there is as much a concern for the development of a positive self-concept as there is for training in the three Rs. (It should be noted that other theorists in this orientation do not share the limited vision of Bereiter. Robinson, for example, has developed programs in values education.)

Still, some educators working from this perspective can become so involved in defining cognitive processes that they lose perspective on how these processes can be applied to human problems. There is a danger that skill development can become the sole focus rather than the application of these skills to resolving social, economic, and moral dilemmas.

David Brison has dealt with this issue.[47] Brison, who has worked with Ausubel and Robinson, has developed the Community Involvement Program. In this program, which could also be classified under the social and even developmental orientations, the student applies decision-making skills to work in the community. Thus problem solving does not become an isolated activity but is integrated into the student's work in various community service agencies. This program, based on more than one orientation, integrates different perspectives into an approach that is cognitively sound and socially relevant.

Notes

1. Carl Bereiter, "Schools Without Education," *Harvard Educational Review* 42 (3) (August 1972).
2. Ibid.
3. Carl Bereiter, "Elementary School: Necessity or Convenience," in Elliot W. Eisner and Elizabeth Vallance, eds., *Conflicting Conceptions of Curriculum* (Berkeley, Calif.: McCutchan, 1974), p. 26.
4. Ibid., p. 23.
5. Ibid.
6. Ibid., pp. 28–29.
7. Ibid., p. 32.
8. Ibid., p. 34.
9. Bereiter, "Schools Without Education," p. 405.
10. Ibid.
11. Ibid., p. 407.
12. Ibid., p. 406.
13. Carl Bereiter and Valerie Anderson, *Thinking Games*, Books 1 and 2 (Toronto: Ontario Institute for Studies in Education, 1975).

14. Carl Bereiter, "Games to Teach Thinking," *Orbit* (Ontario Institute for Studies in Education) 3 (1) (1972), 10–19.

15. Ibid., p. 18.

16. Marlene Scardamalia, Carl Bereiter, and Bryant Fillion, *Writing for Results* (Toronto: Ontario Institute for Studies in Education, 1981), p. x.

17. David Ausubel, *The Psychology of Meaningful Verbal Learning* (New York: Grune & Stratton, 1963), p. 27.

18. Bruce Joyce and Marsha Weil, *Models of Teaching* (Englewood Cliffs, N.J.: Prentice-Hall, 1980), p. 77.

19. Ibid., p. 78.

20. David Ausubel, *Educational Psychology: A Cognitive View* (New York: Holt, Rinehart & Winston, 1968), p. 153.

21. Joyce and Weil, *Models of Teaching*, pp. 84–87.

22. Ibid., p. 86.

23. Elmer V. Clauson and Marion G. Rice, *The Changing World Today*, Anthropology Curriculum Project, Publication 72-1 (Athens: University of Georgia, 1972), p. 56.

24. Floyd Robinson, "To Create a Thinking Program for the Elementary School," *Orbit* (Ontario Institute for Studies in Education) 5 (4) (1974) 14.

25. Ibid.

26. Floyd G. Robinson, John Tickle, and David W. Brison, *Inquiry Training: Fusing Theory and Practice* (Toronto: Ontario Institute for Studies in Education, 1972), p. 7.

27. Ibid., p. 13.

28. Ontario Ministry of Education, *Research Study Skills* (Toronto: Author, 1979).

29. Floyd Robinson, "The Major Thrust Project in Elementary School Thinking," *Orbit* (Ontario Institute for Studies in Education) 7 (2) (1976), 5–6.

30. John A. Ross and Florence J. Maynes, *Teaching Problem Solving* (Toronto: Ontario Institute for Studies in Education, 1982).

31. Robinson, "To Create a Thinking Program," p. 15.

32. Ibid.

33. Hilda Taba, *Teacher's Handbook for Elementary Social Studies* (Reading, Mass.: Addison-Wesley, 1967), p. 92.

34. Ibid., pp. 98–99.

35. Ibid., p. 100.

36. Ibid., p. 103.

37. Ibid., pp. 108–15.

38. Edward de Bono, *Lateral Thinking: A Textbook of Creativity* (London: Ward Lock Educational, 1970), p. 11.

39. Ibid., p. 14.

40. Ibid., p. 28.

41. Ibid., p. 36.

42. Ibid., p. 40.

43. Ibid., p. 63.

44. Ibid.

45. Ibid., p. 115.

46. Robinson, "To Create a Thinking Program," p. 15.

47. David Brison, "Restructuring the School System," *Interchange* 3 (1) (1972), 63–74.

7

Humanistic Orientation

The humanistic orientation became prominent in the sixties. In part, humanistic education was a response to the excesses of the disciplines orientation as humanistic programs attempted to relate curriculum to personal meaning. Humanistic education, which has also been referred to as "affective education" and "psychological education," has focused on two major themes. One has been the enhancement of the student's self-concept. Humanistic educators refer to the research that links a positive self-concept with school achievement and have designed programs to facilitate a positive student self-image. The other major theme has been the development of interpersonal skills. Approaches such as Teacher Effectiveness Training have centered on improving the teacher's communication skills.

Humanistic education has its roots in the humanities and psychology. Certainly, the most influential force has been humanistic psychology. For example, Abraham Maslow exerted an influence on humanistic education with his concept of self-actualization. His work on self-actualization provided part of the theoretical support for the humanistic programs that deal with self-concept. Another humanistic psychologist, Carl Rogers, has influenced the thrust on interpersonal skills and group development. Rogers's concepts of empathy, genuineness, and regard have been applied to education by individuals such as Gazda and Aspy.

This chapter begins with a discussion of the work of Maslow and Rogers and then outlines different humanistic curricula.

Psychological Humanism

Humanistic psychology is closely linked with humanistic education. Sometimes referred to as the third force in psychology, humanistic

135

psychology provides an alternative to Freudian and behavioristic psychology by stressing human health rather than neurosis or mechanistic responses. During the fifties and early sixties two psychologists were instrumental in outlining a vision of human fulfillment. Maslow and Rogers inspired many educators to develop programs that facilitate student self-esteem and interpersonal skills.

Self-Actualization

In 1954 Maslow's book *Motivation and Personality* was published. In this book, Maslow discussed human health and the concept of self-actualization. Maslow, like other humanistic psychologists, argued that psychology focused too much on neurosis and pathology. In Maslow's view, there was very little research on how humans move to higher levels of functioning. In the preface to the revised edition Maslow states the main theme of *Motivation and Personality*:

> If I had had to condense the thesis of this book into a single sentence, I would have said that, in *addition* to what the psychologies of the time had to say about human nature, man also had a higher nature and that this was instinctoid, i.e., part of his essence. And if I could have had a second sentence, I would have stressed the profoundly holistic nature of human nature in contradiction to the analytic-dissecting-atomistic-Newtonian approach of the behaviorisms and of Freudian psychoanalysis.[1]

One important aspect of Maslow's theory is his view of human motivation. Maslow believed that human needs could be placed within a hierarchy. Within this hierarchy are a range of needs so that lower needs that must be satisfied before going to higher needs.

The first level includes physiological needs. The person's needs for food, water, warmth, and sex must first be met, then another set of needs arises. According to Maslow, the next level of needs includes safety needs. Safety needs include "security, stability, dependency, protection, freedom from fear, from anxiety and chaos."[2] Unless the individual feels safe and secure, the person's higher needs will not arise. In some sectors of society (e.g., the inner city) safety needs are not met and thus there is little opportunity to move to needs on a higher level.

The next level of needs centers on belongingness and love. If physiological and safety needs are met, the person will feel the need for affection and love. The person "will hunger for affectionate relations with people in general, namely for a place in his group or family. . . . Now he will feel sharply the pangs of loneliness; of ostracism, of rejection, of friendlessness, of rootlessness."[3] If the belongingness needs have been met, the person will begin to focus on the need for esteem. The need for esteem involves the desire for achievement, mastery, and competency as well as the need for recognition, appreciation, and status. If these needs are not met, the person will not become self-confident but can be overcome by feelings of inferiority.

At the top of the Maslow hierarchy is the need for self-actualization. At this level the person seeks the actualization of his or her deepest potentials. "What a man can be, he must be. He must be true to his own nature. This need we call self-actualization."[4]

Although Kurt Goldstein coined the term "self-actualization," the concept was fully developed by Maslow. He studied adults who were self-actualized and developed a list of characteristics that are associated with self-actualization.[5] These individuals are characterized by:

- More efficient perception of reality and more comfortable relations with it
- Acceptance of self, others, and nature
- Spontaneity, simplicity, naturalness
- Problem centered (that is, these individuals customarily have some mission in life, some task to fulfill)
- Quality of detachment, the need for privacy
- Autonomy, independent of culture and environment; active agents
- Continued freshness of appreciation
- Openness to mystic experience and the peak experience
- Identification and sympathy with other human beings and the human race in general
- Deeper and more profound interpersonal relations
- Democratic character structure
- Ability to discriminate between means and ends
- Philosophical sense of humor
- Creativeness
- Resistance to enculturation (the transcendence of any particular culture).

Maslow suggests that self-actualization is not usually attained in young adulthood. Instead, it arrives after age 35 or 40. However, the other needs have been applied to teaching and learning, and it has been argued that students progress through the hierarchy. Thus it is important that the student's physiological, safety, and belongingness needs be met if the student is to master much of the work that is expected in the classroom.

Toward the latter part of his life Maslow wrote about transcendence as a stage beyond self-actualization. Transcendence "refers to the very highest and most inclusive or holistic levels of human consciousness, behaving and relating, as ends rather than as means, to oneself, to significant others, to human beings in general, to other species, to nature, and to the cosmos."[6] This concern of Maslow's was part of a thrust toward transpersonal psychology and education that appeared in the late sixties and early seventies.

Empathy, Genuineness, and Respect

Carl Rogers is another figure who has had a major impact on humanistic education. Although Rogers's work has been wide ranging, one important area of activity has been his description of facilitative conditions that are crucial to a helping or teaching relationship.

Rogers in particular has mentioned qualities in teachers and counselors that generally facilitate healthy human relations, notably genuineness, regard, and empathy. Genuineness is the capacity to be in tune with or congruent with one's own feelings and concerns. It means not putting on a facade but accepting feelings and dealing with them at a conscious level. An example of this is the behavior of a teacher who made art materials available to her students for creative work but was bothered by the chaos of the room:

I find it maddening to live with the mess—with a capital M! No one seems to care except me. Finally, one day, I told the children ... that I am a neat, orderly person by nature and that the mess was driving me to distraction. Did they have a solution? It was suggested there were some volunteers who could clean up.... I said it didn't seem fair to me to have the same people clean up all the time for others—but it would solve it for me. "Well, some people like to clean up," they replied. So that's the way it is.[7]

Regard describes the teacher's ability to convey respect for the individual student and his potential for growth. It also involves the teacher's respect for the student's right to make decisions affecting his growth. Regard does not involve relinquishing authority but means that the teacher conveys his sense of respect for the student's concerns, feelings, and values.

Empathy describes the teacher's ability to understand the student's perceptions and to convey that understanding. It means trying to put oneself in the student's shoes. If the teacher is not aware of the child's perspective, the child's growth may be thwarted.

Rogers has also developed the concept of self-directed learning. In 1958 he stated his "Personal Thoughts on Teaching and Learning." These thoughts form a number of assumptions often associated with the humanistic orientation.

It seems to me that anything that can be taught to another is relatively inconsequential, and has little or no significant influence on behavior....

I realize increasingly that I am only interested in learning which significantly influences behavior....

I have come to feel that the only learning which significantly influences behavior is self-discovered, self-appropriated learning.

Such self-discovered learning, truth that has been personally appropriated and assimilated in experience, cannot be directly communicated to another. . . .

As a consequence of the above, I realize that I have lost interest in being a teacher.

I realize that I am only interested in being a learner, preferably learning things that matter, that have some significant influence on my own behavior.[8]

Self-directed learning is based on the hypothesis that "individuals have within themselves vast resources for self-understanding and for altering their self-concepts, basic attitudes, and self-directed behavior; these resources can be tapped if a definable climate of facilitative psychological attitudes can be provided."[9] Again, these facilitative attitudes include genuineness, empathy, and respect. Rogers argues that if these attitudes are present, the individual will naturally develop toward what Rogers calls a fully functioning person. Fully functioning people are individuals

Who are able to take self-initiated actions and to be responsible for those actions
Who are capable of intelligent choice and self-direction
Who are critical learners, able to evaluate the contributions made by others
Who have acquired knowledge relevant to the solution of problems
Who, even more importantly, are able to adapt flexibly and intelligently to new problem situations
Who have internalized an adaptive mode of approach to problems, utilizing all pertinent experience freely and creatively
Who are able to cooperate effectively with others in these various activities
Who work, not for the approval of others, but in terms of their own socialized purposes.

The fully functioning person also is in touch with his feelings and inner being in an immediate and open way.

Such a person experiences in the present with immediacy. He is able to live in his feelings and reactions of the moment. He is not bound by the structure of his past learnings but these are a present resource for him insofar as they relate to the experience of the moment. He lives freely, subjectively, in an existential confrontation with this moment of life.[10]

Rogers believes that group experiences facilitate the development of fully functioning people. During the sixties and seventies Rogers was involved in the encounter-group movement. Encounter groups are small groups (10 to 12 people) where people are encouraged to drop their "role behavior" and share their inner feelings. The facilitator sets the tone for the group by conveying genuineness, respect, and empathy. However, the group is nondirective in that there is no prescribed agenda. Instead, group members attempt to get in touch with their inner feelings and express them in an uninhibited manner. Rogers has advocated that encounter groups be used for staff development in school systems. Rogers suggests that encounter groups can improve leadership and communication skills as well as bring about change in organizational climate. In his book *Freedom to Learn*, Rogers explains how the encounter group can be used with administrators, teachers, and parents. Rogers argues that these groups can reduce defensiveness, promote feedback so that each individual learns how he or she appears to others, improve group cohesiveness within the organization, and facilitate the use of innovations.[11]

In recent years, Rogers has continued to work with groups but he has teamed with other facilitators to work with large groups in a variety of settings. For example, in Brazil he worked with a group of 800 people. Like the smaller groups, however, these large groups follow a similar pattern of development. They usually begin chaotically as people demand some structure and leadership. However, eventually the group members begin to share their thoughts and feelings and accept the feelings of other group members. Even though only a small minority can speak in a large group, Rogers suggests that others find "comfort and help in discovering that their own problems are being voiced by the speaker."[12]

At the end of the group experience, there is usually a sense that the group is together and individuals begin to talk about their "back-home" situation. Rogers says "a majority of the crowd of eight hundred has jelled into a cooperative community, although some are skeptical.... They feel together."[13]

Although Rogers has continued to advocate use of the nondirective group experience, the research on the effects of these groups has been mixed. Indeed, the encounter group has become less popular and has given way to other personal and organizational growth techniques.

Social Humanism

A second source of the humanistic orientation has come from the humanities. Although less influential than psychology, educators have argued that philosophy, history, the arts, and literature can encourage creativity and exploration of human meaning. Elizabeth Simpson has stated that humanistic education is bound to the traditional humanities by the concern for man's highest values and the respect for those values that are the "product of passion as well as intellect, of emotion as well as reason." The humanities have also confronted questions that are common to humanistic education: What is life? What are humanness, justice, love, faith, community, and awe? However, within the humanities these questions have sometimes been approached in a sterile manner.

Left to its classical proponents, until recently education in the humanities had diminished, becoming each year more of an evaporating lake, inaccessible, cold, and threatening, with a scabrous overlay of intellectuality and elitism. Are the humanities for all who are human or for the few? Are they—as content —to be the humanistic studies of today or the ornamentation of a small "cultured" class? Those are the questions that educators, not scholars, will decide. Either these studies will be adaptive in process and content, like self-renewing institutions, or the hide binding their scholarly traditions will serve as shroud.

Further, a humanistic education based on the humanities cannot remain solely in the private places of personal experience and reflection. It moves out, into public places, into the streets and structures where action—social, political, and economic—is carried out.[14]

Simpson's statement leads to a third source of humanistic education: social humanism. Social humanists do not accept self-realization as the main goal; instead, social change is their principal aim. Educators such as Alfred Alschuler and Fred Newmann are social humanists, and their work is discussed in Chapter 4, "Social Orientation." Social humanism is meta-orientation based, a connection between the social and humanistic orientations.

Humanistic Programs

Below are some key assumptions and criteria of humanistic programs:

- Humans have a tendency to realize their positive inner potential. Students are capable of a range of behaviors, and if the right conditions are provided they will move toward higher levels of functioning.
- Individuals have the capacity to direct their own behavior. Although young children need the teacher's assistance, as they mature they are increasingly able to carry out their own learning.
- Values play an essential role in the learning process. It is important that students understand and develop a coherent value system that gives meaning to their lives and provides inner direction to their actions.
- Self-concept is integral to how a student learns and develops. Humanists cite evidence correlating positive self-concept with student learning and achievement. Thus they try to develop a classroom climate and curricula that are conducive to developing a positive self-concept.
- Cognitive, affective, and psychomotor learning are interrelated. Humanistic educators see these aspects of learning as interconnected, and thus cognitive learning is viewed in relation to affective and psychomotor development.
- Teachers should be facilitators of learning. Although at times the teacher may be directive, the main task is to develop a trusting and

open classroom climate and then help students achieve their learning goals.

- In the humanistic classroom the students' concerns are accepted as valid content. Although the teacher may not be able to respond to all the concerns, at least he or she can create a climate so that the concerns can be acknowledged.[15]
- Self-evaluation is central to humanistic education. Kirschenbaum states, "Humanistic education tends to move away from teacher controlled evaluation and shift to the student as he learns to evaluate his own progress toward his goals."[16]

Many programs in humanistic education can be grouped under two major areas of emphasis. The first has its roots in Maslow's work and focuses on the development of positive self-concept. The second focuses on building interpersonal skills and is related to Rogers's theory.

Self-Concept

Central to the humanistic orientation has been the importance of a positive self-concept. A person who has done a significant amount of work in this area has been William Purkey. He has written two books, *Self-Concept and School Achievement* and *Inviting School Success: A Self-Concept Approach to Teaching and Learning*.

In the latter book, Purkey summarizes recent research on self-concept. A positive self-concept is correlated with successful behavior and negative self-concept is correlated with anxiety, aggressive behavior, and psychosomatic symptoms. Research on classroom discipline, for example, reveals a relationship between low self-concept as a learner and student misbehavior in the classroom. The theoretical implication of this strand of research is that "negative feelings about oneself as a learner may be a contributing factor in student disruption."[17] Research has also linked negative self-concept and delinquent behavior.[18] Finally, there is research linking self-concept and achievement in school. It should be noted, however, that almost all of this research is correlational. In other words, we do not know whether self-concept is causally linked with achievement and behavior. More logically, there is probably an interactive relationship. Thus, if someone experiences achievement in school, this will enhance self-concept. Similarly a positive self-concept helps develop positive expectations about how one will achieve.

Purkey states, "A student's self-concept ... does not cause the student to misbehave in the classroom. A better explanation is that the disruptive student has learned to see himself or herself as a trouble maker and behaves accordingly."[19] Purkey argues that, outside of the family, the school probably contributes most to how students see themselves. He cites research which indicates that decrease in self-regard and attitudes toward school occur as students progress through school.[20]

To counter this trend, Purkey has developed the concept of the invitational teacher and the invitational school. The invitational teacher invites the student to learn. This is done by first viewing the student as able, valuable, and responsible. The invitational teacher can also encourage student learning through certain skills. These skills include: (1) reaching each student, (2) listening with care, (3) being real with the student, (4) being real with oneself, (5) inviting good discipline, (6) handling rejection, and (7) inviting oneself.[21]

In inviting good discipline the teacher communicates positive but realistic expectations to each student. Sometimes the teacher's invitations will be rejected and Purkey suggests teachers must learn to handle such rejections. Sometimes students are not accustomed to the invitational approach and thus may reject the teacher's initial invitations. According to Purkey initial rejections can turn to acceptance.

An apparent rejection of an invitation is often just the opposite. For example, one beginning teacher invited a student to help her move some supplies after class. "Are you jiving?" the student responded. "I got more important things to do." The teacher was resentful because she assumed that her invitation had been rudely rejected. Later she was startled when the student showed up to help. Minority-group members, especially, will accept or reject invitations in their own ways and on their own terms. It is important to understand that acceptances come in many forms. Just as the person who extends an invitation determines the "rules" under which it is extended, the person receiving the invitation determines how it will be acted upon.[22]

Purkey suggests teachers must also be prepared to invite themselves. "If we believe that invitations are important, then we begin with self-invitations; to stand tall, dress better, eat less, take exercise, become involved, join groups, and find ways to be present in this world."[23]

Purkey suggests some specific techniques to invite student investment in learning. Some of them are:

1. Arrange a pleasant classroom atmosphere.
2. Find the person in the student, or find from each student what they are interested in.
3. Have students share their names, and find out what they like to be called.
4. Encourage students to tell something about themselves so their uniqueness comes through.

5. Maintain an expendable library—keep books on hand that students can use and on occasion give books to students.
6. Let students know they are missed. If a student is absent, send him or her a note.
7. Send double-strength invitations—praise students in front of other teachers and parents.
8. Maintain a mail service—set up a mailbox where students can send notes to each other or to the teacher.
9. Use student experts—teachers can use student expertise where possible.[24]

Purkey also believes the school can be organized in an invitational manner. In particular, he supports the idea of the "family school." In the family school there is mutual support and concern with the welfare of other group members. All people involved in the life of the school should feel part of the school community. These individuals include custodians, bus drivers, cafeteria staff, office personnel, counselors, librarians, administrators, volunteers, aides, and teachers. Purkey states that a warm psychological climate, a cooperative spirit, and positive expectations can help create a family school.

While Purkey has focused on student self-concept, Arthur Combs has developed a teacher-training program at the University of Florida that facilitates the self-concept of the teacher. Combs believes that behavior is a function of perception, particularly self-perception. The task of teacher training, then, is helping students see that the personal meaning they impose on the world is as important as events themselves. The future behavior of the teacher is then dependent on the teacher's view of himself or herself. Thus the teacher must:

1. Be well informed about his subject matter
2. Have "accurate perceptions" and beliefs about people and broad identification with them (the capacity for empathy)
3. Have a positive perception of his self, "leading to accuracy"
4. Have accurate perceptions about the purpose and process of learning
5. Have personal perceptions about appropriate methods to carry out his purposes.[25]

At the University of Florida the focus is on the teacher's search for personal meaning and the facilitation of self-esteem. Thus there is little comparison between students. Instead the program advocates guidance and counseling with faculty advisors. The program itself consists of three components of experience: work with children through field experience, exposure to ideas, and discovery of personal meaning through seminar discussions.

This last component is the unique feature of this program, as Combs is concerned with how student-teachers see themselves. The basic principle behind the seminar discussions is "any information will affect a person's behavior only insofar as he or she has discovered the personal meaning of that information."[26]

Related to this concept is Combs's focus on the self as instrument. In Combs's view it is not enough to focus on methodology and techniques; teacher education must also concern itself with persons rather than competencies.

The good teacher is no carbon copy but stands out as a unique and effective personality, sometimes for one reason, sometimes for another, but always for something intensely and personally his own. He has found ways of using himself, his talents, and his environment in a fashion that aids both his students and himself to achieve satisfaction—their own and society's too. Artists sometimes refer to "the discovery of one's personal idiom," and the expression seems very apt applied to teaching as well. We may define the effective teacher *as a unique human being who has learned to use his self effectively and efficiently for carrying out his own and society's purposes.*[27]

Thus the seminar attempts to let teachers discover themselves. One of the objectives of the seminar is for the teachers to discover their own uniqueness as it relates to teaching. According to Combs, the more the teachers can discover themselves as persons, the more effective they will be as teachers.

Values Clarification

Values clarification attempts to develop a positive self-concept through a specific valuing process. In the view of educators such as Simon, Raths, and Kirschenbaum students can often be apathetic, flighty, uncertain, inconsistent, drifting, and conforming. Values clarification attempts to develop positive, purposeful, consistent behavior and attitudes. Values clarification has four key elements:

1. *A focus on life.* Values clarification focuses on relevant life issues. It asks students to focus on their life style and how their personal priorities reflect a hierarchy of values.
2. *Acceptance of what is.* It is important to indicate to students a nonjudgmental acceptance of their value position. This does not necessarily mean that we communicate approval of what someone says or does. This acceptance is meant to assist students in accepting themselves as individuals and in being honest with themselves.
3. *An invitation to reflect further.* Values clarification calls not only for acceptance but also for reflection on values. This is done through "(a) more informed choices, (b) more awareness of what it is a person prizes and cherishes, and (c) better integration of choices and prizings into day-to-day behavior."[28]

4. *A nourishment of personal powers.* Proponents of values clarification hold that as individuals engage in values clarification, they can gain a sense of personal direction and fulfillment.

Central to values clarification is valuing process that consists of choosing, prizing, and acting. The overall process is divided into seven subprocesses.

1. *Choosing freely.* There is little likelihood that an individual who is forced to adopt a particular value will integrate that value into his or her value structure.
2. *Choosing from alternatives.* This is closely related to the first subprocess. Making a number of choices available to the individual increases the chance that the individual can choose freely.
3. *Choosing after considering the consequences.* Valuing is a thoughtful process in which the individual attempts consciously to reflect on what will happen if he or she chooses a particular value. Choosing impulsively will not lead to an intelligent value system.
4. *Prizing and cherishing.* We should prize and cherish our values and consider them an integral aspect of our existence. We should be proud of our values.
5. *Affirming.* If we have chosen our values freely after considering the consequences, then we should be willing to affirm these values. We should not be ashamed of our values but should be willing to share them when the occasion arises.
6. *Acting upon choices.* The values we hold should be apparent from our actions. In fact, our activities should reflect the values we cherish.
7. *Repeating.* If we act on our values, we should do so in a consistent and repetitive pattern. If our actions are inconsistent with our values, then we should examine more closely the relationship between our values and actions.[29]

In the classroom, teachers use clarifying responses and specific strategies. Clarifying responses are used in one-to-one discussions between teacher and student. They are used to stimulate each one of the various subprocesses of valuing. Below is an example of a clarifying response that focuses on the acting subprocess.

T.: What exactly do you like about science?
S.: Specifically? Let me see. Gosh, I'm not sure. I guess I just like it in general.
T.: Do you do anything outside of school to have fun with science?
S.: No, not really.
T.: Thank you, Lise. I must get back to work now.[30]

The clarifying response is used as the situation arises. However, values clarification is most popular with teachers because of the large number of classroom strategies developed by Simon, Harmin, and others. These include activities such as values voting, rank ordering, forced choice, and unfinished sentences.

Next is an example of a ranking activity. The following strategy focuses on *choosing* among competing alternative values. This is the *forced-choice ladder*. Here the teacher asks the students to construct a choice ladder with eight steps. The teacher then presents a series of alternatives which represent certain values. Using a key word, a student ranks each alternative depending on how strongly he or she feels about a specific value, or on the basis of whether he or she is for or against the value. As an example of the latter, the student would rank eight items ranging from "the person I'd least like to be like" at the bottom of the ladder, to "the person I'd most like to be like" at the top.

A set of choices that could be used in this ladder is as follows:

1. A rich person who gives very generously to charities. (*Philanthropist*)
2. A person whose prime concern is conserving the environment so that he becomes involved in various conservation projects. (*Ecologist*)
3. An individual whose main concern in life is integrating herself through self-help techniques, such as meditation and yoga. (*Meditator*)
4. An individual whose main focus in life is getting involved with and helping other people through the Salvation Army. (*Helper*)
5. An individual whose main value is serving his country through the armed forces. (*Patriot*)
6. A person whose primary focus in life is his small business. He devotes most of his energy toward running an efficient and profitable business. (*Business person*)
7. An individual whose primary concern is taking care of and spending time with her family. (*Family head*)
8. A person who feels that the only hope for humanity is through world organizations and who commits her life to working for the World Federalists. (*Internationalist*)

Values clarification has come under sharp attack in recent years. For example, the book *Values Clarification* by Sidney Simon et al. has been publicly burned by religious fundamentalists. Even more moderate educators have objected to the relativism associated with the approach. Some critics have pointed out that values clarification is process oriented and a values framework has not been clearly articulated.

Self-Science Education

Gerald Weinstein has developed an approach within humanistic education that facilitates self-analysis. He first presented this approach in
Toward Humanistic Education (coauthor, Mario Fantini). *Toward Humanistic Education* was published in 1970 and along with George Brown's
Human Teaching for Human Learning outlined the principal thrust of
humanistic education in the early seventies.

Self-science education applies the inquiry method to self-
examination. Weinstein suggests that one's self-concept is in part a
cluster of hypotheses about oneself. "Self-science" consists of examining these hypotheses to see how accurate they are. Sometimes we hold
beliefs about ourselves that we have never checked out. Self-science
education lets individuals see their own unique style of relating to the
world. Weinstein hypothesizes that more accurate perceptions can
have a positive impact on self-concept.

The central tool in self-science education is the "trumpet." The
trumpet applies problem-solving skills to self-inquiry. The term "trumpet" is used because the shape of the trumpet is such that something
goes in the narrow end and becomes expanded when it comes out.
According to Weinstein, this should also occur with self-knowledge.
The trumpet employs the following steps for examining individual
concerns:

1. *Confrontation.* The individual confronts a situation that elicits some
   sort of response. In the classroom structured activities can be used
   to initiate such a confrontation.
2. *Inventorying.* In this step the person lists his or her responses and
   takes inventory of thoughts, feelings, and behaviors. Here the individual responds to questions such as, How did you respond? What
   is unique and what is common to your response?
3. *Recognizing patterns.* Here the individual examines any consistent
   patterns to the response. An example of such a pattern occurs as
   an individual examines her response when the teacher asks for an
   opinion in class. For example, someone might say, "Whenever I'm
   in one of my academic classes and there is a discussion which calls
   for our opinions, I begin to experience feelings of nervousness,
   fright. My heart begins to pound. I say to myself, 'Don't be a fool.
   Don't take any chances. Even if you have something you'd like to
   say, cool it. Just listen and make like you understand whatever is
   happening.' And so I sit, and when I have something to say, I
   don't. I just clamp down on it and try to look my wisest."[31]
4. *Own patterns.* At this step the person examines what function the
   pattern serves. This can be done by asking, What does this pattern
   do for me? What does it protect me from or help me avoid? "By

not talking in class, it helps me avoid saying something foolish or stupid. It protects me from being put down by others. I suppose what it gets for me is the feeling that I'm not dumb."[32]

5. *Consider consequences.* Here the person examines the price or consequences of the behavior pattern. In our example, the response might be as follows: "Well, one way I pay is that by being so quiet I never get a chance to express myself in public. I'm always holding back and that's not a very satisfying feeling. I get particularly annoyed when something I was thinking of saying is mentioned by someone else, and everyone thinks it's great—and I sit there stewing over the fact that I could have said that. I guess, too, that my passivity in that situation carries over to other situations that I'm not even aware of."[33]

6. *Allow alternatives.* At this stage the individual examines alternative patterns of response. In the example we are using, the person may decide that during the coming week he or she will try to offer at least one opinion in three different classes. In order to accomplish this it may be necessary to rehearse all during those classes. Repeating the sentence, "What I say is good and intelligent so I don't have to prove my smarts to anyone" over and over before venturing the opinion is a suggested route.[34]

7. *Make evaluations.* After the new behavior, the person can ask how it worked. Was the new response satisfactory or should another response be tried?

8. *Choose.* In this last step the person decides whether he or she wants to adopt the new pattern, return to the old pattern, or try another set of responses.

The trumpet is not meant to be simply another problem-solving technique. Although it uses problem-solving skills, its broader purpose is self-examination. Ideally, the student should learn the method and apply it regularly in his or her life to gain greater self-understanding.

Communication Skills

Another major thrust in the humanistic orientation has been to develop communication skills and interpersonal skills. Among the approaches that focus on communications skills are the Aspy/Gazda models and Gordon's Teacher Effectiveness Training.

Gazda's Human Relations Model

George Gazda has built on the work of Carl Rogers and Robert Carkhuff. Specifically, he has developed a model which enhances the teacher's capacity for empathy, respect, and other communication dimensions. Gazda suggests that effective teachers need to work in three major areas. First, they must be prepared in their own subject area. Second, they must have knowledge of learning theory. Finally, they must have a set of skills which promote effective interpersonal relationships in the classroom.

Gazda refers to studies by Aspy which indicate that students of teachers with high levels of interpersonal skills achieve better than students working with teachers with low interpersonal skills. The positive relationship between teachers' interpersonal skills and student achievement and behavior has been supported by other studies.[35]

Gazda has based his model on Carkhuff's approach, which consists of a helping cycle. In this cycle, the person starts with self-exploration, then moves to better self-understanding, and finally to more appropriate action. The teacher or helper assists the student or person in moving through these phases. The process is diagrammed in Figure 4.

Self-Exploration. In this first phase, the teacher builds a positive relationship with the student. This relationship should encourage self-exploration by the student. Carkhuff and Gazda state three communication skills that are helpful in facilitating student self-exploration: empathy, respect, and warmth. Empathy is to put oneself in the shoes of the student and, according to Gazda, it is the most important dimension in the helping relationship. Here is an example of a high-level empathy response: "Male: 'I'm so fat—I know that's why I don't have many dates.' The teacher responds: 'It's depressing to see everyone around you having fun and not be part of it. *You don't know what will happen to you if you don't improve your appearance.'*"[36]

Respect means belief in the abilities of the student. It can grow as the teacher learns about the uniqueness of each student. Warmth is a third dimension and means caring for the student. Warmth is often communicated through nonverbal means.

Self-Understanding. As the students develop trust in the teacher, they learn more about themselves through a trusting classroom climate. To facilitate self-understanding three interpersonal skills are important: concreteness, genuineness, and self-disclosure. Concreteness refers to teachers being specific about their own feelings and attitudes. This skill facilitates students' being more specific about their own feelings.

Genuineness refers to the ability to be real or honest with one's feelings. This does not mean a brutal honesty but instead a genuineness that encourages self-understanding. Here is an example of a high level of genuineness: "Eighth-grader to teacher: 'I'm really upset over that F you gave me on the exam! I thought I knew the material well enough to pass it, at least.' Teacher's response: 'I know you were disappointed

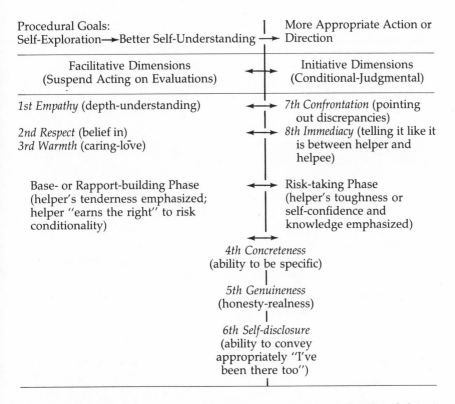

Figure 4. Outline of the Key Concepts of a "Helping" (Problem-Solving) Relationship*

* Each of the eight dimensions involves the act of perceiving (becoming aware of) and the act of responding (acting on awareness).
SOURCE: George M. Gazda, *Human Relations Development* (Boston: Allyn and Bacon, 1973), p. 24.

with your score and feel for some reason it's my fault. It upsets me to be seen by you as punishing.' "[37]

Self-disclosure can facilitate better rapport between teacher and student. However, it must be appropriate self-disclosure and related to student concerns. Below is an example of appropriate self-disclosure:

Sixth-grade student to teacher: "Whenever we pick sides at school I'm always the last one chosen. The kids all know I'm so clumsy I can't help out their team much. It's really disappointing. I like to play, but they're just too good for me. Around home I'm the biggest guy, and they all want me to play even though I'm a little clumsy, but here I don't have a chance. What do you think I should do?"

Teacher's response: "You know, when I was in the sixth grade, no one wanted me on their softball team. It took me a long time to get over that. It sounds like you're experiencing some of the same kind of disappointment I experienced at your age. Maybe we can work this out together."[38]

The Action Phase.   In the final phase of the helping process the teacher assists the student in actually dealing with a problem. Two skills are used in this phase of the helping process: confrontation and immediacy.

Confrontation consists of pointing out discrepancies between the person's actions and words. It assumes a high level of trust has developed between student and teacher. It also assumes that the teacher is able to convey high levels of respect, empathy, and warmth. Below is an example of confrontation:

Student to teacher: "I'm about ready to give up. I just don't see how I can succeed. I've tried as hard as I possibly can, yet I don't do as well as I'd like to in class. It's not enough for me to get A's; I want to feel I'm really learning something useful to me."

Teacher's response: "While you are succeeding by external standards, your own deepest feelings tell you that you are failing."[39]

The immediacy dimension means that the teacher and student are able to discuss their relationship. At the highest levels of immediacy, teacher and student discuss their interpersonal relationship as it exists at that moment.

Building on Carkhuff's work, Gazda has developed a training program for teachers. The program first develops skills in perceiving so that the teacher can identify appropriate levels of communication. For example, the teacher learns to discriminate between high-level and low-level empathy responses. In the second aspect of the program, the teacher learns to respond with or communicate the various skills (empathy, respect, warmth). During the training program the teacher will use scales developed by Gazda. The scales rate the communication dimensions from 1 to 4. At the lowest level the teacher is ineffective in communicating the skills and at the highest level the teacher is most effective. With the use of the scales the teacher learns to perceive low- and high-level responses. In the second part of the training the teachers learn to respond with the dimensions. Training involves trainer modeling, didactic instruction, and experiences in responding. It is important that the training be conducted by a person who is functioning at high levels. The training sessions ask the teacher to respond to printed statements, role-played situations, and other group member statements. The final phase of training should include teachers' working with students under the supervision of the trainer.

The model employed by Gazda, Carkhuff, and Aspy has been extensively researched. There is evidence supporting effectiveness of training programs designed to improve skills in discrimination and responding.[40]

Teacher Effectiveness Training

Thomas Gordon studied with Carl Rogers and has developed a communications approach that reflects a Rogerian emphasis on empathy and congruence. Teacher Effectiveness Training (T.E.T.) was designed in 1966 and evolved from Gordon's earlier work in Parent Effectiveness Training.

Gordon states that the relationship between a teacher and a student is good when it has

1. *Openness or transparency,* so each is able to risk directness and honesty with the other
2. *Caring,* when each knows that he is valued by the other
3. *Interdependence* (as opposed to dependency) of one on the other
4. *Separateness,* to allow each to grow and to develop his uniqueness, creativity, and individuality
5. *Mutual needs meeting,* so that neither's needs are met at the expense of the other's.[41]

In order to move toward this type of relationship, Gordon describes three key elements of T.E.T.: problem ownership, active listening, and I-messages.

Problem Ownership, Active Listening, and I-messages

Gordon states that each teacher decides what is acceptable and unacceptable student behavior. If student behavior falls into the unacceptable area, the teacher experiences a problem. For example, if the student carves initials on the top of his desk and the teacher finds this unacceptable, it becomes a problem for the teacher. In Gordon's terms, the teacher owns the problem. Problem ownership is a central concept to T.E.T. "It is absolutely imperative that teachers be able to distinguish between those problems students have in their lives that cause them a problem but not the teacher, and those that have a tangible and concrete effect on the teacher by interfering with the teacher's needs."[42] If student behavior is interfering with the teacher's needs, then he or she needs to respond in some way. If the student behavior does not interfere, then it is either a problem owned by the student or not a problem for anybody. A large portion of behavior is not a problem for the teacher or the student. This is the ideal situation, which Gordon calls the Teaching-Learning area. The goal of T.E.T. is to help the teachers increase the time spent in the Teaching-Learning area.

However, teachers often use roadblocks to effective communication and this reduces teaching/learning time. These roadblocks include:

1. Ordering, directing
2. Warning, threatening
3. Moralizing, preaching
4. Advising, offering solutions
5. Teaching, lecturing, giving logical arguments
6. Judging, criticizing
7. Name calling, stereotyping
8. Interpreting, analyzing, diagnosing
9. Praising, agreeing
10. Reassuring, sympathizing
11. Questioning, probing
12. Withdrawing, being sarcastic.[43]

These are roadblocks when the student owns a problem. If a student has a problem, any of the above responses tends to cut off communication between teacher and student. The most effective response by the teacher when the student owns a problem is active listening. According to Gordon, active listening consists of feeding back to the student what we hear. Active listening is related to Rogers's notion of empathy. Here is an example of active listening: Student: "This school sure isn't as good as my last one. The kids there were friendly." Teacher: "You feel pretty left out here." Student: "I sure do."[44]

Active listening means to focus on student feelings. The teacher must also trust the students' ability to solve their own problems, since active listening encourages students to reflect more deeply on their problems.

Gordon argues that active listening produces a number of positive results. According to Gordon, it facilitates problem solving, keeps responsibility focused on the student, helps students defuse strong feelings, and promotes a closer relationship between teacher and student.

Gordon advocates active listening when the student owns the problem. When the teacher owns the problem, Gordon believes that I-messages are most effective. I-messages are related to the Rogerian concept of congruence or genuineness. The I-message allows teachers to express their feelings without putting down the student. Here are some I-messages expressed by teachers: "*I can't work* when I have to first clean up a lot of materials that have been left around." "*I'm frustrated* by this noise." "*I'm really annoyed* when people get pushed around in this room."[45]

I-messages place responsibility on the teacher for his or her feelings. Yet they also open the door for students to assess their own behavior. According to Gordon, I-messages are conducive to change in student behavior, contain little negative evaluation of the student, and do not injure the relationship.

The I-message contains three components. First, it refers to conditions resulting from student behavior. Second, it points out the concrete effect on the teacher. Finally, the I-message contains feelings generated within the teacher because he or she is tangibly affected.

Gordon has also discussed how teachers can resolve conflicts in the classroom. Gordon discusses conflicts that arise when the behavior of the student and teacher interferes with one another's needs. Conflicts involve the needs of both student and teacher so that both own the problem. When both student and teacher own a problem, a six-step problem-solving process can be used:

1. Defining the problem
2. Generating possible solutions
3. Evaluating the solutions
4. Deciding which solution is best
5. Determining how to complement the decision
6. Assessing how well the solution solved the problem.[46]

Gordon suggests that this method has a number of positive benefits. It leads to no resentment by student or teacher; it increases motivation to implement the solution; it uses thinking of two parties; no power is required, it helps uncover real problems; and students become more responsible. However, it should be noted that Gordon does not cite any research or studies to support his claims for T.E.T.

Summary and Appraisal

Educational Aims. Development of positive self-concept and interpersonal skills.

Conception of Learning. Learning is self-appropriated; that is, learning should be related to personal meaning. Thus, in many situations, learning is self-directed.

Conception of the Learner. The students are viewed as capable and trustworthy. If the appropriate facilitative conditions are provided, the students will be able to develop their potential as learners and as persons.

Conception of the Instructional Process. This can vary with different approaches. Some approaches such as values clarification are structured with specific strategies. Other approaches such as a Rogerian group experience are nondirected. The common theme, however, is that students should have some choice in what is happening in the classroom. Also, the felt concerns of the students should be shared in the classroom.

Learning Environment.   The teacher should create a caring and trusting classroom atmosphere. The student should feel nonthreatened and be able to share his or her feelings in the classroom.

Teacher's Role.   The teacher helps set the tone of the classroom. Through active listening and use of I-messages the teacher models appropriate communication skills. The teacher should be a learner in that he or she is open to new ideas.

Evaluation.   Evaluation involves honest and helpful feedback to students. Teachers and students can mutually participate in the process.

Humanistic education developed as a distinct orientation during the sixties. Rooted in humanistic psychology, it attempted to reorient curriculum from excessive abstraction to curriculum based on the needs and interests of the learners.

One of the strengths of the orientation was the attempt to ground curriculum in terms that were personally meaningful to the student. Thus the humanistic orientation is designed to encourage a high degree of motivation in the learner—motivation that is intrinsic rather than extrinsic. However, some humanistic curricula have been developed around techniques and strategies which may or may not be related to the concerns of the learner. Thus the teacher must carefully examine the relevance of these strategies and techniques to his or her classroom.

The humanistic orientation is rooted in a vision of personhood, autonomy, and a democratic society. The orientation encourages the individual to exercise his or her own decision-making capacities and actively participate in community. The orientation has been part of a general cultural movement that has encouraged different groups to assert their personhood. These groups include women, ethnic minorities, students, and the handicapped. For example, the handicapped are demanding to be treated as part of society, not as a remote and separate element. Special education programs have attempted to respond to this need. Thus the humanistic orientation has been most powerful and successful when viewed in this broader social context.

The humanistic orientation has also helped teachers view the learner in a broader context. Part of the humanistic orientation has been to see the students not only in terms of cognitive development but in terms of their emotional needs. One teacher's comments summarize this emphasis:

My outlook on the student who fools around in class has changed. I handle that student a lot differently than I would have the first year. I would have said, "You are bothering me. Out." I wouldn't have been as compassionate I guess as I am now. You get a whole different point of view when you get to know the kids. You get to understand them. So and so has family problems whereas before you never bothered looking into that. Otherwise I would be failing as a teacher if I didn't.[47]

As mentioned earlier, there have been problems with this orientation. It is difficult to evaluate these programs because there are very few tools that are available. Thus there is lack of empirical evidence to support the claims that are made for some of the programs. The Gazda-Carkhuff model has been extensively studied and there is evidence to support its effectiveness. There is some evidence supporting the use of values clarification; however, there is not a large body of well-controlled studies that make a strong empirical case for its effectiveness. There is little research on many other humanistic programs.

However, a more significant problem has been the gimmickry associated with some of the humanistic approaches. Some humanists have been locked into techniques and gimmicks rather than focusing on the underlying theory which recognizes the autonomy and integrity of the individual. It has been argued that in encounter groups a subtle pressure can build that forces self-disclosure. Some individuals have also criticized values clarification in that students may not feel that they can "pass" and may be manipulated into saying more than they would like. This pressure to reveal one's inner feelings may be all right in an encounter group consisting of adults who have volunteered, but it is unacceptable in a public school classroom where there is a captive audience.

The humanistic orientation has also been criticized for excessive narcissism or preoccupation with self. Even people within the orientation have made this criticism. Consider Richard Farson's comments:

To my mind one of our gravest errors in all this has been our preoccupation with *self*. For many humanistic psychologists therapy is a program to create an autonomous self, a person set free from dependence upon others, an individual who feels responsible only for his or her own experience. Others of us believe that personal development comes from a sense of connectedness, a recognition of interdependence, a moral consciousness of the predicaments of others and the effect of our lives upon theirs. . . . We have a long way to go before our therapies will be able to help us position ourselves morally and politically, so that therapy does not actually increase our isolation.[48]

Humanists have responded to this type of criticism in two different ways. One response, discussed in Chapter 4, is social humanism, which relates humanistic theory to social change. This can be seen in the work of Freire, Alschuler, and Newmann, discussed there. Another response has been the transpersonal orientation, which focuses on the individual's spirituality and connectedness to the environment. This orientation is discussed in the next chapter.

The eighties appear to be a difficult time for educators working within a humanistic orientation. With the back-to-basics movement and a conservative political climate in the ascendant, humanistic educators have to be concerned about their place in the educational system. Despite this overall climate, however, the focus on the right to personhood continues to exert a strong influence. Viewed as part of this thrust, humanistic education should continue to be a viable orientation within the educational spectrum.

Notes

1. Abraham Maslow, *Motivation and Personality* (New York: Harper and Row, 1970), p. ix.
2. Ibid., p. 39.
3. Ibid., p. 43.
4. Ibid., p. 46.
5. Ibid., pp. 149–80.
6. A. H. Maslow, *The Farther Reaches of Human Nature* (New York: Viking, 1971), p. 279.
7. Carl Rogers, *Freedom to Learn* (Columbus, Ohio: Charles Merrill, 1969), p. 108.
8. Carl Rogers, *On Becoming a Person* (Boston: Houghton Mifflin, 1961), p. 276.
9. Carl Rogers, *A Way of Being* (Boston: Houghton Mifflin, 1980), p. 115.
10. Carl Rogers, *Client Centered Therapy* (Boston: Houghton Mifflin, 1951), pp. 397–98, and "Toward Becoming a Fully Functioning Person," in *Perceiving, Behaving, Becoming*, Association for Supervision and Curriculum Development Yearbook (Washington, D.C.: National Education Association, 1962), p. 31.
11. Rogers, *Freedom to Learn*, pp. 306–307.
12. Rogers, *A Way of Being*, p. 322.
13. Ibid., p. 323.
14. Elizabeth Leonie Simpson, *Humanistic Education: An Interpretation* (Cambridge, Mass.: Ballinger, 1976), p. 7.
15. Howard Kirschenbaum, "What's Humanistic Education?" in Thomas B. Roberts, ed., *Four Psychologies Applied to Education* (Cambridge, Mass.: Schenkman, 1975), p. 329.
16. Ibid.
17. William Watson Purkey, *Inviting School Success: A Self-Concept Approach to Teaching and Learning* (Belmont, Calif.: Wadsworth, 1978), p. 25.
18. Ibid.
19. Ibid., p. 30.
20. Ibid., p. 38.
21. Ibid., pp. 44–63.
22. Ibid., p. 60.
23. Ibid., p. 62.
24. Ibid., pp. 74–77.
25. Simpson, *Humanistic Education*, p. 43.
26. Arthur Combs, "Humanistic Education, Too Tender for a Tough World?" *The Phi Delta Kappan* 62 (February 1981), 447.
27. Arthur Combs, "The Personal Approach to Good Teaching," in

Donald A. Read and Sidney B. Simon, eds., *Humanistic Education Sourcebook* (Englewood Cliffs, N.J.: Prentice-Hall, 1975).

28. Louis Raths, Merrill Harmin, and Sidney Simon, *Values and Teaching* (Columbus, Ohio: Charles Merrill, 1978), p. 10.

29. Ibid., pp. 27–28.

30. Ibid., p. 57.

31. Gerald Weinstein, Joy Hardin, and Matt Weinstein, *Education of the Self* (Amherst, Mass.: Mandala, 1976), p. 30.

32. Ibid., p. 31.

33. Ibid., pp. 31–32.

34. Ibid., p. 33.

35. George M. Gazda et al., *Human Relations Development: A Manual for Educators* (Boston: Allyn and Bacon, 1973), p. 15.

36. Ibid., p. 72.

37. Ibid., pp. 129–30.

38. Ibid., pp. 134–35.

39. Ibid., p. 141.

40. Ibid., pp. 15–16.

41. Thomas Gordon, *T.E.T., Teacher Effectiveness Training* (New York: Peter Wyden, 1974), p. 24.

42. Ibid., p. 39.

43. Ibid., pp. 48–50.

44. Ibid., p. 70.

45. Ibid., p. 137.

46. Ibid., p. 128.

47. John P. Miller, Gilbert Taylor, and Karen Walker, *Teachers in Transition: Study of an Aging Teaching Force* (Toronto: Ontario Institute for Studies in Education, 1982), p. 49.

48. Richard Farson, "The Technology of Humanism," *Journal of Humanistic Psychology* 18 (2) (Spring 1978), 24.

8

Transpersonal Orientation

Abraham Maslow, one of the pioneers in humanistic psychology, toward the end of his life focused on transcendence. In 1968 he stated, "I consider Humanistic, Third Force Psychology, to be transitional, a preparation for a still 'higher' Fourth Psychology, transpersonal, transhuman, centered in the cosmos rather than in human needs and interest, going beyond humanness, identity, self-actualization and the like."[1]

While the humanistic orientation stresses the development of a positive self-concept and interpersonal skills, the transpersonal emphasizes intuition and transcendence. Through intuition the person has access to creative thinking and holistic perception. Transcendence connects the inner self and the environment. Thus inner and outer worlds become one.

Intuition and transcendence are discussed in the first part of this chapter. Following that, several transpersonal programs are also discussed. One example is Rudolph Steiner's Waldorf education. This approach to schooling, which has become somewhat popular in North America, stresses the arts as an integral part of the curriculum. Another comprehensive approach is confluent education. Developed in the late sixties, this approach uses a variety of awareness and visualization techniques to facilitate student growth and integration.

Finally, two approaches more limited in focus are also discussed. One approach is synectics, which develops creative thinking skills. A second approach is suggestology, which uses visualization and breathing techniques in learning large amounts of factual information.

Transpersonal Theory

Intuition

Transpersonal educators seek to establish an appropriate balance between rational thinking and intuitive thought. Transpersonal educators

160

argue that schools have traditionally emphasized rational thinking at the expense of intuition. Split-brain research provides, in part, the argument that transpersonal educators make about a synthesis between analytic and intuitive thinking.

This split-brain research was initially conducted by Roger Sperry and Joseph Bogen. The research was conducted on epileptic patients whose corpus callosum (the bundle of fibers that joins the two hemispheres of the brain) was severed. Tests were conducted with these patients to see how the two hemispheres functioned. As a result of these tests, we know that the left hemisphere is specialized for analytic thinking. It operates in a linear mode and processes information sequentially. The left hemisphere is responsible for language and mathematical functions. Although the left hemisphere is dominant for speaking and reading, the right brain is not completely nonverbal. Functions can dominate in one hemisphere but each hemisphere has some capacity for the various functions.

The right brain integrates information simultaneously. It is responsible for orientation to space, artistic endeavor, crafts, body image, and recognition of faces. The right hemisphere is also superior to the left hemisphere with regard to kinesthetic and auditory capabilities. Physical activity and musical sensibilities seem to rely, then, on this hemisphere.

Transpersonal educators argue that educational programs should seek a balance between right brain–intuitive thinking and left brain–analytic thought. Based on studies he conducted, Robert Samples suggests that when programs are designed to facilitate this type of integration the following results occur:

1. Student's self-esteem increases.
2. The performance of skills associated with the left hemisphere (e.g., language and mathematics) increases at the same time.
3. Students choose to explore a greater number of content areas in greater depth in the five arts, sciences, and the humanities.[2]

The use of imagery is often integral to intuitive thinking. For example, in creative thinking imagery is often associated with intuitive insight. According to Wallas, the creative process proceeds by the following steps: The first element is *preparation*, where the individual gathers information relevant to the problem or project. At the second stage, *incubation*, the individual relaxes and does not make an effort to work consciously on the problem. Instead, it is suggested that the images realign themselves in the individual as he or she consciously attends to something else. In the *illumination* stage the solution will occur, often spontaneously and unexpectedly. The final stage is *verifica-*

tion, or revision, where the individual puts the idea into use and consciously works with the idea in a more detailed manner.[3]

Incubation apparently occurs in the right hemisphere and imagery is a necessary ingredient to the process. For example, many artists and scientists have reported how imagery is central to the creative process. Hunt and Draper describe an experience of the young scientist Nikola Tesla quoting poetry to a friend:

As he was walking toward the sunset quoting these words, the idea came like a flash of lightning and the solution to the problem of alternating current motors appeared before him as revelation. He stood as a man in a trance, trying to explain his vision to his friend. . . . The images which appeared before Tesla seemed as sharp and clear and as solid as metal or stone. The principle of the rotating magnetic field was clear to him. In that moment a world revolution in electrical science was born.[4]

Einstein also acknowledged the importance of intuition in his work. He stated that the discovery of the theory of relativity was based on picturing himself on a ray of light. Einstein said, "The psychical entities which seem to serve as elements in thought are certain signs and more or less clear images which can be voluntarily reproduced and combined."[5]

Transpersonal educators suggest that imagery and intuition may be related to student behavior. Jerome Singer has done research which suggests that an undeveloped imagination can be a source of "delinquency, violence, overeating and the use of dangerous drugs."[6] This trend appears early, as children who are impulsive and who are excessively dependent lack a developed inner life. Children who can use their imagination tend to be more relaxed and independent in their behavior. In another study, it was found that imaginative children were less likely to be violent. Like other children in a child guidance clinic, the imaginative children experienced emotional difficulties but were not as aggressive as these other children.

To enhance right brain thinking, transpersonal educators advocate more extensive use of imagery in the classroom. For example, in one class students studying electronics used imagery to visualize the magnetic field surrounding a transformer. After darkening the room, the teacher asked the students to relax and empty their minds. Then they were told to imagine themselves as incredibly small pieces of magnetically charged matter—electrons. They saw themselves as electrons entering a force field surrounding two large coils of wire. The students were told to enter the wire of the coil and experience the movement generated by the rapidly changing force field. The two fields surrounding the coils were interacting and coming closer together, causing the electrons to move faster and faster. After the fantasy the teacher discussed the experience with the students.[7]

Below are some imagery exercises that Frances Vaughn suggests can be used in the classroom.

1. Imagine yourself as a seed in the earth which begins to germinate and grow. What kind of plant are you? How do you experience each of the seasons as the growth process continues? How do you experience being the roots of this plant? The stem? The flower or the leaves? What does the sunlight feel like? The rain? The wind? Imagine that as this plant you are sensitive to everything in your environment.
2. You are standing before a closed door. Over the door is written a word. (The guide may suggest a specific word or let the subject imagine his own.) Someone you know brings you a key. You open the door and go in.
3. You are at the foot of a mountain which you are prepared to climb. The ascent is difficult but you are able to overcome the various obstacles which you encounter on the way. Take your time and keep going until you reach the top of the mountain.
4. You are walking up a mountain path and you see a cave. You enter the cave and see a fire glowing deep within. As you approach the fire, you see a very old person seated by the fire. This person is very wise and will answer any question you ask, and will give you a significant object to bring back with you.
5. You are standing at a crossroads. There is a sign at the crossroads. You read the sign and choose to follow one of the roads. Notice what you are taking with you on this journey. Follow the road of your choice and see where it leads.[8]

Intuition and imagery are central to a transpersonal perspective because of the tendency of intuition to perceive similarities between phenomena rather than differences. In short, intuition allows the person to see connections between phenomena rather than differences. When left brain thinking is predominant, we tend to focus on differences and single out specific events; when intuition is predominant there is a tendency to see things as part of a whole. Intuition, according to transpersonal educators, allows us to see the oneness behind all phenomena. Theilhard de Chardin has commented on this aspect of intuition:

The farther and more deeply we penetrate into matter, by means of increasingly powerful methods, the more we are confounded by the interdependence of its parts. Each element of the cosmos is positively woven from all the others. . . . *It is impossible to cut into this network, to isolate a portion without it becoming frayed and unravelled at all its edges.* All around us, as far as the eye can see, the universe holds together, and only one way of considering it is really possible, that is, to take it is as a whole, in one piece.[9]

This sense of connectedness between inner and outer worlds is a central element of a transpersonal perspective.

Transcendence and Spirituality

The transpersonal orientation is also characterized by transcendence. Transcendence involves openness to Being. Through transcendence emerges a dynamic relationship between the person and the universe. To open to the infinite is to also open to human spirituality. Spirituality connotes a link between a person's inner life and the infinite. Transpersonal education attempts to develop the link between a person's inner and outer worlds. This is done through such techniques as visualization, meditation, and dreamwork. Transpersonal education is distinguished from other orientations by its emphasis on inner work and spiritual awareness.

Transcendence and spirituality are experienced through relationships—relationships which form a whole. According to Phillip Phenix, "Reality is a single interconnected whole, such that a complete description of any entity would require the comprehension of every other entity."[10] Fritjof Capra has commented on this aspect of transcendence in his writing. He argues that modern physics through quantum theory and the theory of relativity has demonstrated this connectedness. He suggests quantum theory has demonstrated that the notion of fundamentally separate objects is false and indicates that the universe is an interrelated web of relations. Relativity theory, on the other hand, shows the intrinsically dynamic nature of the universe and the intimate relationship between matter and energy.

Subatomic particles, then, are not "things" but are interconnections between "things," and these "things," in turn, are interconnections between other "things," and so on. In quantum theory you never end up with "things"; you always deal with interconnections.

This is how modern physics reveals the basic oneness of the universe. It shows that we cannot decompose the world into independently existing smallest units. As we penetrate into matter, nature does not show us any isolated basic building blocks, but rather appears as a complicated web of relations between the various parts of a unified whole.[11]

Capra has linked modern physics to various mystical traditions. Eastern and western mysticism have also asserted that the individual participates in a universal ground of being that links all beings in a unified totality.

Transcendence like intuition is a source of creativity. Since transcendence is characterized by openness to the infinite, it encourages a creative encounter with life. If educators become too rigid or entrapped in convention, it provides little opportunity for creativity. The transpersonal orientation with its stress on transcendence also affirms creativity. Approaches which focus on the development of creativity such as synectics can be seen as a part of the transpersonal orientation.

This openness to the unknown which is part of transcendence is also a source of empathy and compassion. Robert Griffin has called the state of being where teachers truly open to their students the compassionate service level of consciousness. According to Griffin, the compassionate teacher accepts his or her students.

You do not feel set off against them or competitive with them. You see yourself in students and them in you. You move easily, are more relaxed, and seem less threatening to students. You are less compulsive, less rigid in your thoughts and actions. You are not so tense. You do not seem to be in a grim win-or-lose contest when teaching.[12]

Because compassionate teachers do not want something from the students in relation to their ego needs, they do not feel alienated from them. Because of their openness, compassionate teachers recognize the fluidity of the classroom situation and are able to move with different student needs. Since transcendence is characterized by an openness to Being there is no attempt to control events. As soon as there is an attempt to control or manipulate the environment according to the needs of the ego, there is a movement away from openness, transcendence, and compassion.

At the heart of transpersonal perspective is the concern for wholeness. Thus the transpersonal curriculum explores relationships between disciplines and subject matter. According to Phenix, "Transcendence leads to the acknowledgment that the truth of any discipline mode is never the whole truth. . . . In this sense, the curriculum in the light of transcendence is interdisciplinary as well as multidisciplinary."[13] The concern for wholeness is also rooted in a holistic view of the child. The child is seen as not only capable of cognitive development, but a person whose emotional, aesthetic, physical, and spiritual needs are also important.

Transpersonal Programs

Waldorf Education

Waldorf education was founded by Rudolph Steiner. Steiner founded the first Waldorf school in Germany in 1919. Steiner also developed Anthroposophy, which studies human nature, particularly the inner life of the individual. Steiner said he was concerned with "reconnecting the inwardness of man with the universe or seeing how man and the universe are part of the common physical spiritual linkage."[14] Thus Steiner was concerned with the person's inner development. Steiner said, "The outer world with all its phenomena is filled with divine splendor, but we must have experienced the divine within ourselves before we can hope to discover it in our environment."[15] Steiner outlines his approach to education in *Education of the Child in the Light of Anthroposophy*. He starts this book with a description of how the nature of the child forms the basis of Waldorf education: "In the following pages we shall endeavour to prove this for one particular question—the question of Education. We shall not set up demands nor programmes, but simply describe the child-nature. From the nature of the growing and evolving human being, the proper point of view for Education will, as it were, spontaneously result."[16]

Steiner states that child development occurs in seven-year cycles. At each stage, or seven-year period, there is a different organization or "body." Steiner calls the first body the physical body which lasts to about age 7. During this period it is important that the physical environment be appropriate so that the body can develop. Steiner suggests that toys and games allow for fantasy and imagination. According to Steiner, the children should not be given commercial toys but those they can work with. He recommends the use of homemade dolls and picture books with movable figures. Steiner also believes songs, music, and dance are important to the child's development at this age. Songs and clapping hands are used in association with learning letters and words. Songs and music also provide part of the ritual of each day at school. Sometimes in kindergarten the day is started with the children and teacher sitting in a circle. At the end of the day the teacher may stand at the door and say goodby to each child as they leave.

Education in the elementary years is not based on the intellect but imagination and inner images. The elementary years are associated with what Steiner calls the development of the etheric body, which begins around age 7 with the growth of new teeth. Steiner says, "The formation and growth of the etheric body means the moulding and developing of the inclinations and habits, of the conscience, the character, the memory, and temperament. The etheric body is worked upon through pictures and examples, i.e., by carefully guiding the imagination of the child."[17]

Another characteristic of children during this age (7–14) is their desire to love and respect their teachers. According to Steiner, this need is met in the Waldorf school by having the same teacher work with a child through eight years of elementary school. Although other teachers work with the children in special subject areas, the principal teacher works with the child over a long period and thus can clearly identify a child's strengths and needs. M. C. Richards believes this allows the teachers to be more than information machines or policemen. According to Richards, the teachers "give themselves as human beings to the children. The children are affected by the inner being of their teachers. This makes the process of education a mutual adventure all the way through. The teachers are assured that their own inner growth serves others."[18]

Steiner also feels that elementary students can benefit from the study of history and biographies of great men and women. Thus he suggests young children can study fairy tales, legends, and myths, and in the late elementary years biography and history. Steiner also advocates the use of pictures and parables. The use of pictures and images can attune the inner life of the student to what is to be learned. Like Bruno Bettelheim, Steiner also believes that fairy tales, myths, and parables can reach the inner child. Steiner believes that we should not overconceptualize or intellectualize material during the elementary school years. This can come during adolescence.

With regard to reading and writing, Steiner suggests that children should write to explain their drawings. Colored pencils and crayons can be used. After these experiences, Steiner suggests that reading can begin.

Feeling is developed by exposure to the arts. In fact, artistic activity is central to Waldorf education. The method focuses on how form, color, and rhythm are part of the wholeness of experience and how art and feeling are related to learning. Movement experiences are also important when seen in this light. Steiner says:

> To think out gymnastic exercises from this point of view requires more than an intellectual knowledge of human anatomy and physiology. It requires an intimate intuitive knowledge of the connection of the sense of happiness and ease with the positions and movements of the human body—a knowledge that is not merely intellectual, but permeated with feeling. Whoever arranges such exercises must be able to experience in himself how one movement and position of the limbs produces an easy feeling of strength, and another, an inner loss of strength.[19]

Richards suggests that at the heart of Waldorf education is developing a sense of connectedness between oneself and the universe. This connection is also at the center of a transpersonal orientation. Richards says:

> I believe the tone of his [Steiner's] meaning is this: in every individual there is an instinctive sense of connection between oneself and the universe. There is a built-in sense of meaning and of identity. There is an inner world of spiritual being and of spiritual beings in which mankind, nature, and universe participate. A sense of connection with this inner spirit is what is ordinarily called religion. It is as natural to people as a sense of self and a feeling for nature. It is a crossing point between inside and outside.[20]

There is no formal religious instruction in Waldorf schools. Instead, simple rituals are performed such as sitting in a circle and singing. The focus on artistic experience attempts to let children and teachers have access to their inner life. Holidays, however, are celebrated. At Christmas the teachers might put on a folk drama of the Nativity. Advent might be celebrated by what is called the Advent Garden. A spiral path is laid out in the classroom with wood. At the center of the spiral is a lighted candle. The children walk toward the candle with smaller candles. They light their candle and on returning on the path they set down their own candles. Thus at the end of this exercise the path has turned into a garden of lights.

Language arts are also developed around feeling and artistic experience. According to Steiner, "Speech is rooted in human feeling. In feelings you are linked to the whole world and give whole world sounds that in some way express these links of feeling."[21] Thus language education should be grounded in meaning. Words, according to Steiner, must make a connection with the inner life of the student. His comments on the use of nouns and adjectives are interesting:

By learning to name things with nouns we distinguish ourselves from the world around us. By calling a thing a table or a chair, we separate ourselves from the table or chair; we are here, the table or chair is there. It is quite another matter to describe things with adjectives. When I say: the chair is blue — I am expressing something that unites me with the chair. The characteristic I perceive unites me with the chair. By naming something with a noun I dissociate myself from it; when I describe it with an adjective I become one with it again. Thus the development of our consciousness takes place in our relationship to things when we address them; we must certainly become conscious of the way we address them.[22]

For Steiner, education is an art. The teacher like the artist should be in touch with one's inner resources and with creative imagination. To educate means to provide a form for expression of the inner life so that it becomes perceptible. In elementary school, the Main Lesson is taught in the morning. The Main Lesson focuses on language development or mathematics; however, these subjects are integrated with art. Thus in geometry the children make colored figures and string constructions.

Each Main Lesson will call upon the child's powers of listening, of body movement, of thinking, and of feeling. Artistic activity is particularly related to the will: it is an experience of doing, of making. Artwork also invites the child's feeling for expressiveness and encourages a kind of intuitive thinking about how to get things done. In the early grades, some teachers allow the children to copy what has been drawn on the board so that they may learn to draw in ways they would not otherwise know. Other times the children draw freely. Variety exists, according to teacher and grade.[23]

In the afternoon the children learn other subjects such as foreign languages, music, handwork, eurhythmy (a form of movement education), gardening, and physical education. Eurhythmy is usually performed to spoken poetry and attempts to put words into motion.

In high school the student moves to the next stage in Steiner's cycle (ages 14–21). This is called the astral period, characterized by independent judgment, abstract thinking, and critical assessment. In high school the student works with various teachers. However, the student will often study with the same math teacher over four years. Other subjects include chemistry, physics, botany, biology, zoology, and geometry. Art continues to be integrated into these subjects as it was in elementary school. "Mathematics and geometry lead not only to capacities for thinking, but to surveyor's maps and projections of planetary orbits and artistic modeling. Connections between projective geometry and plant growth are rendered in drawings and in watercolor plates."[24]

Other subjects include foreign languages, handicrafts, eurhythmy, music, and painting. Mythology is still part of the curriculum as it is linked with history. High school students also share in running the school. They raise money for field trips by putting on dinners, bazaars, and plays. The culminating event is a play put on by the seniors. According to Richards, "The production makes use of their talents and skills—which are considerable by this time—in painting, arts, singing, acting, playing instruments, doing eurythmy, and bringing into their characterizations a depth of human understanding."[25]

Throughout the Waldorf schooling the teacher attempts to focus on the inner life of the child. After school in the evening, the teacher may try to visualize or develop an inner picture of each child. By concentrating on the image of the child the teacher attempts to perceive the needs of the children. According to Richards, teachers see their work with children as a vehicle for growth.

> Growth may be felt as pain. Pain may alert us to something that needs understanding or correcting. Teachers particularly take on the fact of pain, as every day they experience themselves in human relationships where they always have so much to learn. The children are like Zen counsellors: rapping their teachers over the head when they fall asleep, that is, when they fall into unawareness or, because of their own suffering, are not able to respond generously to another person's need.[26]

Confluent Education

Confluent education attempts to facilitate self-integration and personal wholeness. Confluent education began as a project in the sixties. The project was directed by George Brown, who summarized the results in *Human Teaching for Human Learning*. In the early stages of the project teachers met one weekend a month and experienced various exercises such as sensory awareness, improvisational theatre, and a variety of group processes. The teachers also were exposed to Gestalt therapy. The teachers then applied some of these techniques to their own classrooms.

Confluent education first focused on the integration of the cognitive and affective. The affective domain encompasses feelings, emotions, attitudes, values, intuition, and creativity. The cognitive domain includes intellectual functioning. However, confluent education has moved beyond this limited definition. For example, confluent also refers to the integration of the intrapersonal, interpersonal, extrapersonal, and transpersonal. Intrapersonal refers to the person's internal space-feelings, and self-perceptions. The intrapersonal also refers to each person's subpersonalities such as aggressive or passive, masculine and feminine, as well as other subselves. Confluent education attempts to facilitate awareness of the different subselves and eventually bring them into harmony.

The interpersonal dimension consists of relations with others, how students perceive other people, and how they communicate with them. The next dimension, extrapersonal, refers to the context or social structures that encompass the experiences of the student. These include the structure of the school, the community, and the society.

Tom Yeomans, who developed these dimensions as part of confluent education, argues that they are interrelated. The most desirable education is where all three are integrated:

For example, if a curriculum is designed to teach democratic processes, and individual students share in decisions affecting them, work in small groups in a decision-making process, and participate with the teacher in setting classroom rules, a confluence exists among intrapersonal needs, interpersonal relations, and the extrapersonal setting. If the teacher governs the class autocratically, however, the situation is not confluent.[27]

It can also be argued that a fourth dimension, the transpersonal, surrounds the first three. This refers to the cosmic, or spiritual, dimension of the student's experience. The transpersonal provides the universal context for examining basic questions of meaning and spirituality.

Confluent education has developed techniques which can be used in the classroom to facilitate development in the four areas: intrapersonal, interpersonal, extrapersonal, and transpersonal. However, confluent education begins with the awareness of the teacher. Teachers first become aware of themselves and how they respond to students. This self-awareness is critical. Next the teacher must extend the awareness to the students. The teacher should of course be sensitive to the internal life of the student in order to use confluent approaches. Finally, the teacher applies the awareness to methodologies and curriculum to attempt to relate the course content to the student's experience.

Confluent education has three broad goal categories: "to achieve traditional subject matter goals, to achieve nontraditional goals of personal and interpersonal or social development, and to learn process skills that will help students to attain their own goals."[28]

Confluent education has focused on the first goal by using such techniques as guided fantasies and nonverbal awareness exercises to enhance traditional learning experiences. For example, in working with the book *Lord of the Flies* one teacher asked students to imagine themselves as animals in the forest encountering other animals. This exercise is related to animal imagery in the book, where the boys visualize themselves as animals. Another example comes from a class where students role played words and their opposites. A college instructor used this approach to examine word meanings. These exercises attempt to link the internal world of the student with the external world of subject matter. At the same time there is an attempt to motivate students toward traditional learning goals.

A second goal concerns personal development and interpersonal skills. These include activities that develop creativity, imagination, and the ability to create and use internal images. One book that has been used in this way is *Put Your Mother on the Ceiling*, by Richard DeMille. This book is designed to allow elementary school students to gain greater awareness and control over their own imaginations. Below is an example of one imagery activity called Home:

This game is called HOME.
Do you know just how Home looks? / Do you know how all the rooms look? / Do you know where all the things are in all the rooms? / Let us play a game of changing everything around. Let us take the stove out of the kitchen and put it in some other room. What room would you like to put it in? / All right, now take the kitchen sink and put it with the stove. / How do they look together there? / Take something else out of the kitchen and put it with the stove and sink. / Take all the things that are left in the kitchen and pile them on the ceiling of the kitchen. / Turn the kitchen floor into glass. / Have some fish swimming under the floor. / Is there anything else you would like to do to the kitchen? / All right, do it.[29]

Confluent education has also used techniques associated with humanistic education such as developing interpersonal skills. Thus confluent education uses both humanistic and transpersonal techniques in the classroom. For example, in a unit on racism students fantasize that they are entering a room full of persons of a race different from their own and then share what they have experienced. In another exercise on sex-role stereotyping, the boys sit in the center of a circle with the girls on the outside. Both groups then share their perceptions of sex-stereotyped behavior that they associate with each sex.

Finally, confluent education focuses on process, or learning, skills that help students attain their own goals. Confluent education uses Weinstein's self-science education as one example of how students can learn about themselves and examine alternatives to their own behavior. Sometimes all three types of learning goals can be integrated. "For example, students may do exercises such as guided fantasies to reach a traditional objective (become more aware of the characterizations in *Lord of the Flies*), to reach a nontraditional objective (increased self-awareness), and to learn a process (internal visualization)."[30]

Gloria Castillo has also done work in confluent education. In her book *Left Handed Teaching* she has developed a number of activities that achieve traditional and nontraditional goals. Below is one example from a unit on science.

Lesson 14. Solar System Conversations

Be the sun. Talk as if you are the sun. Example: "I am the sun. I am a very large star. I have a great deal of heat. My heat gives energy to the earth."

Now, be the earth. Talk as if you are the earth. Example: "I am the earth. I have air, water, plants, and animals."

One person be the sun and another be the earth. Create a conversation between the sun and the earth. What do you have to say to one another?

Let this be an activity in improvisational theatre as well as in science. Do not correct the students if they should offer incorrect statements. After the "play," you can clarify points, give additional information, or assign further readings. Use this activity to assess what the students do and do not know about the sun and the earth.

With advanced students, add other planets of our solar system to the "play."

Dance around as if you are the earth. Circle the room once to represent one day. Choose a partner. One be the earth, the other the moon. Earth and moon dance together, in time to one another. Now both join another partnership. Two of you become the sun. All of you dance together as if you are the sun (two students), moon, and earth dancing together.

Depending on the ability of the class to do this, continue to add students to represent other solar bodies. Create a solar system dance.[31]

Evaluating confluent education demands alternative models of assessment. Since confluent education functions on a number of dimensions—intrapersonal, interpersonal, extrapersonal, and transpersonal—linear modes of "traditional, summative achievement-based evaluation could be inappropriate." Instead, Brown et al. state, "The search for new concepts of evaluation—formative, illuminative, and more holistic—is part of the process of developing confluent education beyond the preliminary models of combined cognition and affect."[32]

Initial studies, however, have indicated some positive benefits of confluent education training for teachers. One study found the teachers experiencing Gestalt training were more informal, flexible, and had an increased sense of personal contact in the classroom. "Another study of confluent teacher trainees supported these findings and also showed increase in affective expression, empathy, compassion, and openness to others."[33]

In studies on the effects of confluent education on students, it was found that confluent education led to significant increases in the self-concept of students. According to Brown and his associates, confluent education seems to have a positive impact on self-concept and personal growth of students and teachers. Furthermore, confluent education seems to also improve classroom climate, interpersonal relations, and attitudes toward learning. In some cases, it has had a positive impact on academic achievement.

Synectics and Suggestology

Synectics and suggestology use transpersonal techniques, but each of these approaches is more limited in focus than Waldorf education or confluent education. They use specific techniques rather than developing a comprehensive approach to schooling. Synectics uses metaphor to develop creativity skills in students. Because of its emphasis on right brain thinking process, however, synectics can be viewed within the transpersonal orientation: initially synectics was used in industry, but in recent years, William J. J. Gordon has developed a number of synectics materials for classroom use.

Synectics.   Gordon argues that imagination and creativity can be dealt with consciously. Synectics assumes that the creative process is not a mysterious activity but can be observed and analyzed. Further, the creative process is the same whether applied to the arts or to science. Creativity and imagination always involve similar intellectual processes.

Another assumption is that creativity and imagination can be developed in a group setting. The group can stimulate the individual's imagination and creative capacities by providing emotional and intellectual diversity.

An important element in the creative process is the nonrational or emotional element. Gordon argues that the emotional is in fact more important than the rational in the creative process. Although the solutions to problems may be logical, the process of arriving at those solutions is not. However, the nonrational is also subject to analysis. It can be observed and understood and eventually integrated into conscious action.

The key to synectics training is the use of metaphor, which allows the student to *make the familiar strange* and to *make the strange familiar*.

William Harvey's discovery of circulation is an example of making the familiar strange.

In the sixteenth century, people thought that blood flowed from the heart to the body, surging in and out like the tides of the sea. Harvey was *familiar* with this view and believed it till he closely observed a fish's heart that was still beating after the fish had been opened up. He expected a tidal flow of blood, but he was reminded of a pump. The idea of the heart acting like a pump was most *strange* to him and he had to break his ebb-and-flow connection to make room for his new pump connection. *He made the familiar strange.*[34]

This is also a good example of how the creative process is applicable to science as well as the arts. Today, however, the student observing the fish's heart is involved in a different process. If the concept of the heart as a pump has just been explained to the student and thus is relatively strange, he needs to make the concept more familiar. "Where Harvey had to break his conception of the ebb-and-flow mechanism, the student has to only make a learning connection."[35] This connection might be made through the analogy of a swimming pool, where "dirty water is pumped through the filter and back to the pool."[36] The student can easily make the link between the heart and the water pump. He can also see how "the lungs and liver act as 'filters' when they cleanse the blood."[37] In brief, he makes the strange familiar through an analogy.

Gordon asserts that there are three types of analogies useful in synectics: direct analogy, personal analogy, and compressed conflict.

A *direct analogy* is a simple comparison of two objects or concepts. The analogy of the heart and water pump is a direct one. Another example is "A crab walks sideways like a sneaky burglar."[38] Direct analogies can be very close or they can be distant and somewhat strained.

In general, five levels of strain can separate an inorganic:inorganic comparison from an inorganic:organic one. For instance, a wheel of a car can be compared to the following objects that rotate as they move:

1. the cutter on a can opener;
2. the rotor of a helicopter;
3. the orbit of Mars;
4. a spinning seed pod;
5. a hoop snake.[39]

The first analogy is a close parallel since both objects are rotating, circular, metallic, and man-made. The last analogy is the most strained because a snake is a consciously moving animal rather than a man-made, inanimate object. Not everyone will agree with these conclusions, but the discussion and exploration of analogies are part of the creative process. Metaphors are not meant to represent substantive knowledge. But they can enliven one's relationship with knowledge in a more direct and personal way.

Personal analogies require identification with inanimate or animate objects. Here there is more immediate and personal involvement with the object than in the direct analogy. Gordon asserts that there are four levels of personal analogy. At the first level there is merely a description of facts. For example, if asked to imagine himself as a fiddler crab, a student responding at the first level might say, "I would be hard on the outside because of my shell, and soft on the inside. I would have special little creases on my claws to grip and tear things, and one of my claws is twice as big as the other."[40]

Here the individual does not identify with the object but merely describes the object. Students often state a personal analogy in this way when starting synectics.

The second level of personal analogy is first-person descriptions of emotions. Responding to the same question about the crab, the student at this level might say: "I would be pretty busy getting food for myself, but I've got to be careful not to be food for a big fish. I've got to be careful not to get caught, but I must take some chances or the other crabs will beat me to it and I'll starve."[41]

Here the student begins to identify with the object, but in a minimal way.

The third level involves empathic identification with a living thing. Responding to the question about the crab at this level, the student might answer:

"O.K. I'm a fiddler crab. I've got armor all around me—my tough shell. You'd think I could take it easy, but I can't. And that big claw of mine! Big deal! It looks like a great weapon, but it's a nuisance. I wave it around to scare everyone, but I can hardly carry it. Why can't I be big and fast and normal like other crabs? No Kidding! That claw doesn't even scare anyone!"[42]

This student is becoming more involved with the object. He is not just describing the object; he now identifies in an original way with the crab.

The fourth level of personal analogy involves empathic identification with a nonliving object. This requires the most imagination and empathy. An example of this type of identification occurs as follows:

Teacher: Harold, imagine that you are the mud in which the fiddler crab makes his home.
Student: I have the feeling that no one cares if I'm here or not. I'm full of holes into which the crabs crawl at night. They never thank me. I'm mud; that's all. I'd like to do something to make the crabs thank me. After all, if it were not for me, those crabs would get eaten up in one night.[43]

Compressed conflict, the third form of analogy, contains two words that don't seem to go together. For instance, "imprisoned freedom" is a compressed-conflict description of cellophane tape. This developed from personal analogies in which students developed the following thoughts:

"I feel as though I'm in prison. I am imprisoned glue, imprisoned potential. My glue is imprisoned inside me." "I feel that potentially I am very useful, but when I'm free for use—pulled out in a strip and free, that is—then I feel that I offer only one level of freedom. If I am glue, then I'm so free to use that it takes real art to know how to use me, because I'm so free that I flow all over, and I am uncontrollable except by an expert."[44]

Scientists have used compressed conflict in developing their hypotheses. Before he discovered antitoxin, Louis Pasteur began to talk of "safe attack." Because of the surprise factor, compressed conflict can be the most powerful of the three metaphors.

Suggestology. One approach that also warrants discussion is suggestology, or Suggestopedia, developed by a Bulgarian psychologist, Georgi Lozanov.[45] Suggestology attempts to integrate the body with both left and right brain thinking abilities. Suggestology uses relaxation exercises, music, visualization, and breathing exercises to assist the learning process. In particular, the approach has led to astounding results with regard to information recall. Suggestology has been particularly successful in facilitating language learning. For example, it is not uncommon to learn one thousand words of a new language in a day. The retention rate is also high. Six months later, retention is 88 percent. In 22 months, without any use of the new language, retention is 57 percent.

A suggestology learning session begins with some relaxation exercises in which the body is made tense, then relaxed. Relaxation is then followed by positive affirmations in which the individual repeats certain statements that help create a positive atmosphere for learning.

Visualization can also be used at this stage. For example, learners imagine being at some calm place on the beach. They can also visualize some past learning experience that was successful. Individuals return to a time when they felt good about a particular learning experience. Details are recalled about the experience to re-create the overall feeling of the situation.

After relaxation and visualization exercises, the students breathe to a definite rhythm. The material that is to be learned is spoken by the teacher or presented from material that has been recorded on tape. During the time when the material is spoken, individuals hold their breath. Then there is a 4-second pause in which they breathe in and out again and become ready for the next material. All the material spoken is on an 8-second cycle. The breathing falls into a rhythmic pattern of: hold 4, out 2, in 2. The learning sessions are in two parts. First, students silently read along with the material as it is recited to them. Next, the material is repeated but this time with music. As the material is repeated they coordinate the breathing to the beat.

They can then take a quiz on the material. This allows feedback on how the process is working. Learners should also use the material after the session so that it is retained.

Suggestology is an unusual approach that is just being tested and evaluated in some schools. In Iowa Dr. Don Schuster is conducting studies of suggestology through the Society for Suggestive-Accelerative Learning and Teaching, or SALT. He has conducted studies on the achievement of 1,200 students in different public schools in Iowa. When compared with controlled groups, results showed that the performance of most students was significantly better. Junior high and high school students seemed to benefit in particular.

Summary and Appraisal

Aims.   Self-transcendence, development of intuition and creative thinking skills.

Conception of Learning.   Learning is related to awareness, particularly self-awareness. As people become more conscious of their inner life and their relationship to the world around them, other learning is subsumed within this context. In general, transpersonal education attempts to awaken the person to how he or she views the world.

Conception of the Learner.   Learning is viewed holistically. First, the learner is seen as having a number of interrelated needs (physical, cognitive, emotional, spiritual, and so on). The transpersonal orientation avoids reducing these aspects into isolated compartments but attempts to view them as part of a larger whole. The learner is also seen as part of the larger environment within which he or she interacts.

Conception of the Instructional Process.   There is no particular model and the instructional process can vary with different approaches. Generally, however, various techniques such as visualization, centering techniques, and movement activities are used to assist in encouraging the students to work with their inner selves.

Learning Environment.   The environment supports the development of intuition in relation to intellectual abilities. Thus many transpersonal environments use the various arts in an integrative manner.

Teacher's Role. The teachers work on their inner life so that students will be more open to the transpersonal dimension. Thus the teacher will probably use one or more techniques such as visualization or some other centering technique. The teacher would also try to develop a warm and caring classroom atmosphere.

Evaluation. Evaluation tends to be formative, open-ended, and holistic. Informal and innovative techniques may be used to assess how students are performing in the arts and other areas which are difficult to assess by standard means.

Transpersonal education is allied with an emerging world view that sometimes is referred to as the Aquarian Conspiracy or a New Age perspective. Marilyn Ferguson has defined the focus of the Aquarian Conspiracy in her book by the same name. At the center of this movement is a paradigm shift. A paradigm is a scheme for understanding and explaining certain aspects of reality. Thus, a paradigm shift involves a new way of thinking about things:

The paradigm of the Aquarian Conspiracy sees humankind embedded in nature. It promotes the autonomous individual in a decentralized society. It sees us as stewards of all our resources, inner and outer. It says that we are *not* victims, not pawns, not limited by conditions or conditioning. Heirs to evolutionary riches, we are capable of imagination, invention, and experiences we have only glimpsed.

Human nature is neither good nor bad but open to continuous transformation and transcendence. It has only to discover itself. The new perspective respects the ecology of everything: birth, death, learning, health, family, work, science, spirituality, the arts, the community, relationships, politics.[46]

In her book Ferguson sees education as part of this shift. Thus, she argues that education will change to fit this new paradigm with some different assumptions. Some of these assumptions include:

1. Inner experience is seen as a context for learning with the use of imagery, storytelling, dream journals, and centering exercises.
2. Divergent thinking is encouraged as part of the creative process.
3. Whole brain education is encouraged with a confluence of left brain rationality and holistic, nonlinear intuition.
4. Education is seen as a lifelong process.
5. The teacher is also viewed as a learner who is open to growth.
6. Students are grouped in different types of age groupings so there is flexibility and integration of various groups.[47]

Similarly Fritjof Capra has also discussed this paradigm shift in a book entitled *The Turning Point*. He argues that traditional assumptions in education, science, and the social sciences are no longer credible. This is due to three changes in society. One is the decline of male-dominated society; the second is the decline of the fossil fuel age, and third is the appeal of a new world view. Capra calls this world view the systems view, an ecological perspective. The essence of this view is the universal interconnectedness and interdependence of all phenomena, and the intrinsically dynamic nature of reality.

Whether the paradigm shift that Ferguson and Capra write about will become dominant in society remains to be seen. If it does, the transpersonal orientation will be part of that paradigm shift.

However, the impact of this orientation is currently very limited. The emphasis on transcendence and spirituality is counter to the traditional thrust of public schooling. There is also the danger of transpersonal quackery where pseudo-gurus intermingle with those that are genuinely seeking spiritual meaning.

The future of the transpersonal orientation, then, is allied to a larger cultural movement. How successful this movement is, and how intelligently it responds to many of the problems that are impinging on society, will determine in large part how influential the transpersonal orientation is in the coming decades.

Notes

1. Quoted in Roger Walsh and Frances Vaughn, *Beyond Ego* (Los Angeles: J. P. Tarcher, 1980), pp. 19–20.
2. Robert Samples, "Learning with the Whole Brain," *Human Behavior* (February 1975), 19–23.
3. John Curtis Cowan, "The Production of Creativity through the Right Hemisphere," *Journal of Creative Behavior* 13 (1) (1979), 39.
4. Ibid., p. 44.
5. Quoted in B. Ghiselin, *The Creative Process* (New York: American Library, 1952), p. 43.
6. Jerome Singer, "Fantasy, the Foundation of Serenity," *Psychology Today* (July 1976), p. 32.
7. Thomas Roberts and Frances Clark, "Transpersonal Psychology in Education," in Gay Hendricks and James Fadiman, eds., *Transpersonal Education* (Englewood Cliffs, N.J.: Prentice-Hall, 1976), pp. 7–8.
8. Frances Clark, "Fantasy and Imagination," in Thomas B. Roberts, ed., *Four Psychologies Applied to Education* (Cambridge, Mass.: Schenkman, 1975), pp. 505–506.
9. Pierre Teilhard de Chardin, *The Phenomenon of Man* (New York: Harper Torchbooks, 1965) pp. 43–44.
10. Phillip Phenix, "Transcendence and the Curriculum," in Elliot W. Eisner and Elizabeth Vallance, eds., *Conflicting Conceptions of Curriculum* (Berkeley, Calif.: McCutchan, 1974), p. 120.
11. Fritjof Capra, *The Turning Point* (New York: Simon & Schuster, 1982), pp. 80–81.

12. Robert Griffin, "Discipline: What's It Taking Out of You?" *Learning* (February 1977), p. 79.

13. Phenix, "Transcendence and the Curriculum," p. 129.

14. Rudolph Steiner, *Education of the Child in the Light of Anthroposophy* (London: Anthroposophic Press, 1975), p. 6.

15. Mary Caroline Richards, *Toward Wholeness: Rudolph Steiner Education in America* (Middletown, Conn.: Wesleyan University Press, 1980), p. 10.

16. Steiner, *Education of the Child*, p. 8.

17. Ibid., p. 29.

18. Richards, *Toward Wholeness*, p. 53.

19. Steiner, *Education of the Child*, p. 44.

20. Richards, *Toward Wholeness*, p. 59.

21. Rudolph Steiner, *Practical Advice to Teachers* (London: Rudolph Steiner Press, 1976).

22. Ibid., pp. 63–65.

23. Richards, *Toward Wholeness*, p. 25.

24. Ibid., p. 39.

25. Ibid., p. 40.

26. Ibid., p. 108.

27. George Issac Brown, Mark Phillips, and Stewart Shapiro, *Getting It All Together: Confluent Education* (Bloomington, Ind.: Phi Delta Kappa Educational Foundation), pp. 11–12.

28. Ibid., p. 16.

29. Richard DeMille, *Put Your Mother on the Ceiling: Children's Imagination Games* (New York: Penguin, 1976), pp. 72–74.

30. Brown et al., *Getting It All Together*, p. 19.

31. Gloria Castillo, *Left Handed Teaching* (New York: Holt, Rinehart), pp. 194–95.

32. Brown et al., *Getting It All Together*, p. 21.

33. Ibid.

34. William J. J. Gordon, *The Metaphorical Way of Learning and Knowing* (Cambridge, Mass.: Porpoise Books, 1966), p. 5.

35. Ibid.

36. Ibid.

37. Ibid., p. 6.

38. Ibid., p. 18.

39. Ibid., pp. 19–20.

40. Ibid., pp. 22–23.

41. Ibid., p. 23.

42. Ibid., p. 24.

43. Ibid., p. 25.

44. Ibid., p. 26.

45. Sheila Ostrander and Lynn Chroeder with Nancy Ostrander, "Super-learning: The Miraculous Mind/Body Approach," *New Age* (September 1979), pp. 26–35.

46. Marilyn Ferguson, *The Aquarian Conspiracy: Personal and Social Transformation in the 1980's* (Los Angeles: J. P. Tarcher, 1980), p. 29.

47. Ibid., pp. 289–91.

Meta-orientations

Most teachers do not adhere to one orientation. In fact, many teachers whom I have worked with tell me they like to draw on several orientations. In most cases, they work from a cluster of two or three orientations. Similarly, many curriculum guidelines reflect more than one orientation. In this chapter I outline three clusters or meta-orientations as well as other possible clusters. I also describe how these orientations can be useful in examining curriculum guidelines to ascertain the philosophical base of the guideline.

Three meta-orientations are described: the traditionalist meta-orientation, the inquiry/decision-making meta-orientation, and the transformation meta-orientation.

The Traditionalist Meta-orientation

Three orientations are included in this meta-orientation: the subject orientation, the cultural transmission orientation, and the competency-based orientation. This meta-position is concerned with making sure the student acquires the basic values and skills that are necessary to function in society. The back-to-basics movement is part of the traditionalist meta-orientation. The subject orientation and the cultural transmission orientation combine to provide the core of the traditionalist meta-orientation. The student is expected to master the basic skills and absorb the central values of the society. The competency-based orientation is also associated with this traditionalist position. In order to achieve the goal of literacy, some traditionalists will turn to behavioral techniques. In other words, behaviorism provides the methodology and technology to achieve goals that are espoused by traditionalists.

Table 3. Traditionalist Meta-orientation

Orientation	Cultural Transmission	Subject Orientation	Competency-Based Orientation
Focus	Inculcation of values and mores	Mastery of basic skills (e.g., literacy and computation) as well as knowledge in other subjects	Student acquisition of specific competencies
Conception of learning	Learning is viewed as adaptation process to expectations of school and society	Learning is viewed as acquisition of knowledge and skills associated with different subjects	Learning is broken down into small, identifiable units so student attains proficiency in various skills
Instructional process	Traditional methods of instruction along with teacher modeling of appropriate behavior	Traditional methods such as lecture, recitation, and drill are employed	Teacher identifies competencies to be learned and then develops specific learning tasks
Evaluation	Tests should assess whether appropriate knowledge, skills, and values are being transmitted	Standard achievement tests are used along with teacher-developed tests	Use of criterion-referenced tests

The traditionalist position (summarized in Table 3) remains strong; some would say it is the dominant meta-orientation. It could also be linked with the larger cultural movement of political and economic conservatism. Many parent groups and religious fundamentalists are strong advocates of this position. One of the main difficulties that this orientation faces, however, is the movement toward cultural pluralism. Cultural transmission rests on the assumption that there is a clearly defined set of values or norms that can be transmitted. However, the conflicts that exist within society over such issues as abortion, busing, and tax credits for private schools suggest that there is no consensus on several key issues. Thus the traditionalist position is threatened by the trend that Alvin Toffler calls the "Third Wave." Toffler foresees a trend toward the demassification of society into smaller, pluralistic units. In education, this trend is seen in the rise of the private alternative school and the difficulties that large public school systems face in meeting the demands of various parent groups.

The Inquiry/Decision-Making Meta-orientation

This meta-orientation consists of the cognitive process, democratic citizenship, and the developmental orientations. The disciplines orientation can also be associated with this meta-orientation. The focus of this position is on process, particularly the development of inquiry and decision-making skills. Thus schools and teachers adopting this orientation have students identify problems, select alternatives, analyze data, and make decisions. If the inquiry skills are used within an academic discipline, the disciplines orientation becomes part of this overall position.

Sometimes the decision-making skills are applied to social problems so that the student can function within a democratic framework. The Community Involvement Program, mentioned in Chapter 5, is an example of a program that represents this meta-orientation. In the CIP students learn problem-solving skills in the classroom and then apply them to work in various community agencies.

The inquiry/decision-making meta-orientation (Table 4) has been the principal source of innovation in schools for the past two decades. It has attempted to reorient the curriculum to a more student-centered focus with an emphasis on the development of cognitive skills. Although this meta-orientation has been the mainstream of curriculum reform, it has come under sharp attack in the past few years. Some would suggest that it has had difficulty in maintaining momentum in the eighties. It has also been argued that many of the innovations inspired by this meta-orientation actually have never really been implemented but were nonevents that were absorbed into the culture of the school. Sarason makes this argument in *The Culture of the School and the Problem of Change*. In any case, this meta-orientation, which has its roots in the work of John Dewey, is experiencing some of the same difficulties that liberal politicians are undergoing in many western democracies. Caught between conservatism and pluralistic positions, educational and political reforms are viewed with increasing skepticism.

The Transformation Orientation

This meta-orientation (Table 5) focuses on personal and social change. It contains the humanistic, social change, and transpersonal orientations. In this meta-orientation the teacher attempts to pass on to students skills that allow for personal and social transformation. Freire's work in Brazil can be viewed in this context as well as Newmann's social action model. In this meta-orientation social change is sometimes placed within a transpersonal framework. In other words, change

Table 4. Inquiry/Decision-Making Meta-orientation

Orientation	Cognitive Process	Developmental	Democratic Citizenship	Disciplines
Focus	Development of thinking skills	Movement to higher stages of cognitive, ego, and moral development	Development of skills knowledge and values so that student can participate in democratic process	Development of inquiry skills associated with disciplines
Conception of learning	Learning is related to various conceptions of how children think	Significant learning occurs when the student deals with cognitive conflict and develops new patterns of thoughts	Immersion of students in public issues so that they develop the conceptual skills to resolve policy debates	Learning involves active inquiry within academic disciplines
Instructional process	Process will vary with different approach. Generally, there is a sequential process that students follow to master various skills	Teacher presents task or dilemma and stimulates interaction between students and materials	Dilemmas and case studies are used to develop student decision-making skills	Teacher defines initial question and provides resources to stimulate inquiry
Evaluation	Assessment usually requires student to apply thinking skills to various problems	Diagnostic evaluation is important to assess student readiness. Systemative evaluation focuses on gradual stage change	Assessment of how student can analyze and present a position	Evaluation of inquiry skills and conceptual framework

Table 5. Transformation Meta-orientation

Orientation	Social Change	Humanistic	Transpersonal
Focus	Student involvement in social change, development of social change skills	Development of positive self-concept and interpersonal skills	Self-transcendence, intuitive thinking, and creative thinking
Conception of learning	Learning is related to the development of environmental competence or ability to affect the environment	Learning is self-appropriated and is related to student self-perceptions	Learning is viewed holistically. Connections are made between one's inner life and the environment
Instructional process	Student involvement in various action projects so that much of the program occurs outside of school	Varies with approach; however, student choice is encouraged along with sharing student concerns	No particular models are used but usually centering techniques are employed to enhance awareness of inner life
Evaluation	Evaluation focuses on a number of dimensions such as group skills, presenting one's argument effectively, etc.	Evaluation involves on-going feedback to students from teachers and other students; self-assessment is also encouraged	Evaluation tends to be ongoing, open-ended. Sometimes innovative evaluation techniques are employed, e.g., use of art as an expression of evaluation or feedback

is seen as moving toward harmony with the environment rather than exerting control over it. Certainly the ecology movement can be viewed within this context. Transpersonal techniques are sometimes used to work with the inner self. Centering devices such as meditation, visualization, and movement techniques are used to enhance inner awareness. With a transpersonal orientation the environment also takes on a spiritual dimension as the ecological system is viewed with respect and reverence.

This meta-orientation has had the least impact on schools. Although it has fostered a number of interesting innovations such as Alschuler's Social Literacy training, Waldorf education, and confluent education, these programs exist on the fringe of the educational system. Their future impact will be determined, in part, by the fate of a larger social and cultural movement which has been identified by Marilyn Ferguson as the "Aquarian Conspiracy" or Alvin Toffler's "Third Wave."

The three meta-orientations just described are not the only meta-orientations. Teachers come up with their own clusters. For example, some educators have combined the developmental, cognitive-process, and humanistic orientations into a cluster that provides a framework for their work. Other educators have developed a position from combining just two orientations such as the humanistic and transpersonal. In some workshops I have run with teachers, they argue that they can take a little from each of the orientations. However, too much eclecticism can lead to confusion within the classroom. If teachers draw randomly from the orientations without thinking of the consequences, the students can become confused. Since each orientation contains a distinct view of the learner, to move randomly from one orientation to another would be confusing. The student can become uncertain about what is expected. This also applies to curriculum leadership within schools. Principals should be clear where they stand on the educational spectrum. A principal who espouses a humanistic orientation but actually works from a traditionalist meta-orientation can cause confusion and alienation in a school. (I have worked with teachers who must cope with this type of principal and they often remark that they "don't know where the principal is coming from.") Although very few people work within one orientation, it is important to be constantly examining one's position and how one's work and behavior reflect one's position. In other words, you should be reasonably consistent with the orientations or meta-position that you espouse.

Below is an exercise which can be used with a staff or group of teachers to examine their positions. It is useful for teachers to complete this exercise and then discuss how their programs reflect the orientations which they have ranked at the top end of the continuum.

Approaches to Learning and Curriculum

Instructions

Below are listed seven approaches to learning and curriculum. Begin this exercise individually by ranking the seven approaches in the order that most closely represents your thoughts and feelings about an appropriate climate for learning. After the individual rankings are completed, meet in small groups and attempt to develop a consensus on the rankings.

Approach A.   This approach stresses student mastery of basic subjects and disciplines in the curriculum. In the elementary school, the stress is placed on basic literacy and computational skills. All other aspects of the curriculum such as physical education, environmental studies, and the arts are seen as less important. In secondary school the students study various academic disciplines such as math, science, language, and history. The emphasis is on acquiring the conceptual framework and inquiry skills associated with each discipline. Knowledge is viewed as arising from the disciplines and learning not linked with an academic discipline is viewed as less valuable.

Approach B.   This approach is based on a developmental conception and reflects the assumption that all individuals proceed through definite stages of development. The stages are important because if teachers are not aware of the various levels, development can be thwarted. Teachers committed to this orientation listen closely to children's observations and reasons so that they can attain some sense of the children's developmental level. This approach also emphasizes the importance of children's interaction with a wide variety of materials and experiences, particularly experiences which cause the individual to examine his or her reasons and thoughts in approaching a problem or dilemma. It is through this interaction that development is facilitated. Finally it should be noted that the aim of this approach is not to accelerate cognitive, ego, and moral development but to remove barriers that hinder the student's natural progression to higher levels of functioning.

Approach C.   This approach to learning views the student primarily as a social being. The student is seen as part of the larger social context and thus must acquire skills to participate in that context. In a democratic society, the student acquires the values and skills that are necessary to participate in the democratic process. Thus the students learn to critically analyze information, distinguish fact from opinion, and make decisions on public policy issues. In most programs this involves classroom discussion; however, in some programs the student may be encouraged to participate actively in community activities. Thus the student might work in a community agency or observe proceedings in a local court.

Approach D.   This orientation focuses on student acquisition of specific competencies. Learning tasks are often broken into small, definable units so that students can master various skills. Programmed learning and individualized instruction are often employed in this orientation. The microcomputer and other technologies are also used within this approach. Learning is often evaluated with criterion-referenced tests to assess whether the student has achieved the desired competency. Educators working within this orientation attempt to package the curriculum in an efficient manner so that learning is maximized.

Approach E.   This approach focuses on a holistic view of the child. The teacher attempts to work with the whole child—the physical, emotional, intellectual, aesthetic, moral, and spiritual dimensions. In particular, the teacher attempts to integrate analytic and intuitive thinking or the right and left sides of the brain. This is often accomplished through an integrated approach to the arts—drawing, painting, music, dance, and drama. Other aspects of the curriculum such as reading and math are also integrated with artistic activity. The teacher may also use techniques such as movement and imagery so that the child becomes aware of his or her inner life.

Approach F.   This approach to curriculum is primarily concerned with the development of intellectual skills. It is process oriented in that it attempts to develop a number of cognitive skills (analysis, synthesis, evaluation). There is also an emphasis on problem-solving skills, and so the student gains confidence in analyzing problems and evaluating possible solutions. The curriculum contains a wide variety of activities, simulations, and games that stimulate independent thinking on the part of students. The teacher's role is to help the student deal with various problems and situations so that cognitive competencies are realized. Thus the teacher often probes student reasons to stimulate further thinking.

Approach G.   This approach to curriculum emphasizes two basic aims: the development of a positive individual self-concept and skills in communicating with others. The basic emphasis is on personal growth and personal integration. Through a variety of experiences and exercises, this approach attempts to develop a sense of emotional well-being. Techniques such as role playing, classroom meetings, and communications training are employed in the classroom. School is seen as a vital and potentially enriching experience in its own right, and the present lives of the learners are a major focus of concern.

This exercise can be used over again with a school staff or a group of teachers. This allows the teachers to see whether their positions are changing and also how they are putting their philosophy into practice. Some teachers may want to develop their own statements, which may reflect modifications of the orientations.

Analyzing Guidelines

The orientations are helpful in examining curriculum guidelines. They assist the teacher in discovering what general assumptions are made about learning in the guideline. Again, guidelines usually reflect a cluster of orientations.

Two guidelines from the Ontario Ministry of Education are discussed here, although almost any curriculum statement will do. The first is *Education in the Primary and Junior Divisions*. This guideline provides an "extensive philosophical basis and rationale for the program of these divisions." In the first part of the guideline some general assumptions are presented:

Children are curious. Their need to explore and manipulate should be fulfilled through handling real things that involve more than one sense. The more all the senses are involved, the more effective the experience.

Most human activity is a purposeful search for pattern. This includes organizing new information and relating it to previously developed concepts. Incongruity between old patterns and new experiences stimulates questioning, observation, manipulation, and application in a variety of new situations. Maintaining the right balance between novel and familiar experiences in learning situations is one of the most vital tasks in the art of teaching.

Learning experiences gain power if they are part of organized and meaningful wholes.

Children have an intrinsic need for mastery over situations, a need that they express by using their experiences to search out the significant patterns in reality and thus reduce uncertainty.

Children find self-fulfillment in successful learning, and are not motivated merely by external rewards and approval. Pupils engaged in self-rewarding activity with a sensitive, consistent teacher who makes demands appropriate to their own level are having a happy experience.

Play is an essential part of learning. It is free from the restrictions of reality, external evaluations, and judgement. Children can try out different styles of action and communication without being required to make premature decisions or being penalized for errors. Play provides a context in which the teacher can observe children's handling of materials and social situations, assess their stage of development, and encourage experiences that further their growth. The teacher should know when to intervene unobtrusively, when to add to or change a play situation, when to provide a toy telephone, a costume, a question, or a suggestion that will further the fantasy or broaden the experience.

Children learn through experience with people, symbols, and things. Things may be objects, events, processes, or relationships.

The symbolic process for children develops through a sequence of representation. Initially children must understand that a real object can be represented by such symbols as a spoken word, gesture, dramatic movement, toy, model, picture; ultimately they must understand that an object can be represented by the printed word. The development of symbolism underlies the communication, recording, and coding of experience in a condensed and systematic form. Full understanding of symbols, however, is slow to emerge.[1]

These assumptions generally reflect the humanistic, developmental, and cognitive process orientations. The humanistic orientation is reflected in a positive view of the child's potential. For example, children are seen as "curious" and capable of "self-fulfillment in learning." The cognitive process orientation is reflected in assumptions such as "old patterns and new experiences stimulate questioning, observation, manipulation, and application in a variety of situations." The developmental orientation is also reflected in statements such as "Play provides a context in which the teacher can observe children's handling of materials and social situations, assess their stage of development, and encourage experiences that further their growth."

Also published by the Ontario Ministry of Education is the Intermediate Division Science Guideline (1978). This guideline contains the following aims:

Aims

The science curriculum for the Intermediate Division will provide opportunities for students:
- to gain a breadth of experience in the fundamentals of science;
- to understand scientific facts, definitions, concepts, principles, laws, models, and theories;
- to consider interrelationships between humans and their biological and physical environments;
- to improve their techniques of inquiry and laboratory investigation with a particular emphasis on safety;
- to develop the ability to distinguish fact from opinion, to identify problems, to develop hypotheses;
- to design methods of experimentation and testing, to manipulate and control variables;
- to collect and process data, to evaluate and interpret evidence, to form valid conclusions;
- to present and assess explanations, to propose theories and models, to formulate generalizations, and to understand conceptual schemes;
- to develop clear and accurate communication skills (written, oral, and visual) and to use these skills in recording information, in listening, in reporting, in demonstrating, and in expressing ideas;
- to increase competency in observing, identifying, classifying, inferring, comparing, measuring, tabulating, graphing, illustrating, and applying;
- to learn to solve qualitative and quantitative problems in a clear and precise manner;
- to develop attitudes of curiosity and interest in natural phenomena, of care and honesty in investigation, of enjoyment and satisfaction in learning, and of co-operation and openness in human relationships;
- to appreciate the contributions made by various men and women to the scientific enterprise;
- to relate science to career opportunities in technology, industry, commerce,

business, medicine, engineering, education, research, and other areas in which science plays a role;

• to cultivate an active concern regarding such issues as the wise use of energy, the preservation of an unpolluted environment, the care of plants and animals, and the dignified application of science to societal problems.[2]

Most of these objectives reflect the disciplines orientation. For example, consider "to gain a breadth of experience in the fundamentals of science" and "to design methods of experimentation and testing, to manipulate and control variables." It could be argued that the cognitive process orientation is also included with aims such as "to collect and process data, to evaluate and interpret evidence, to form valid conclusions." A few of these aims reflect a social orientation, for example, "to cultivate an active concern regarding such issues as the wise use of energy, the preservation of an unpolluted environment." However, the major thrust of this document is clearly within a disciplines and cognitive process orientation.

It is not unusual for secondary subject guidelines to reflect the disciplines/subject orientation, as the particular educational context can often influence the orientations that may be used in the classroom.

The application of the orientations, however, remains with the teacher. A subject-oriented guideline can change in the hands of the humanist just as a transpersonal document will be filtered through the perceptions of a behaviorist. Behind the classroom door, the perspective of the teacher will often shape what happens in that classroom.

Working with curriculum orientations is a lifetime task. Our philosophies about education can change as we develop as adults, and periodically we can reexamine where we stand on the educational spectrum. Through this reexamination we can see if our behavior in the classroom reflects our orientation. It is important that our actions generally reflect our philosophy. Students can readily identify when our words and actions are not congruent. Greater congruence between our philosophy and our teaching can lead to a greater sense of integration within ourselves and with our students.

Notes

1. *Education in the Primary and Junior Divisions* (Toronto: Ministry of Education, 1975), pp. 15–16.
2. *Science: Curriculum Guideline for the Intermediate Division* (Toronto: Ministry of Education, 1978), pp. 4–5.

Bibliography

General

Eisner, Elliot, and Elizabeth Vallance, eds. *Conflicting Conceptions of Curriculum.* Berkeley, Calif.: McCutchan, 1974.

Joyce, Bruce, and Marsha Weil. *Models of Teaching.* Englewood Cliffs, N.J.: Prentice-Hall, 1980.

Orlosky, Donald E., and B. Othanel Smith, eds. *Curriculum Development Issues and Insights.* Chicago: Rand McNally, 1978.

Ornstein, Allan C. "Curriculum Contrasts: A Historical Overview." *The Phi Delta Kappan* 63(6) (February 1982), pp. 404–408.

Zais, Robert. *Curriculum Principles and Foundations.* New York: Harper and Row, 1976.

Behavioral Orientation

Evans, Christopher. *The Micro Millennium.* New York: Viking, 1979.

Lessinger, Leon. *Every Kid a Winner: Accountability in Education.* New York: Simon & Schuster, 1970.

McAshan, H. H. *Competency-Based Education and Behavioral Objectives.* Englewood Cliffs, N.J.: Educational Technology Publications, 1979.

Popham, W. James. "Crumbling Conceptions of Educational Testing." In *Educational Evaluation: Recent Progress, Future Needs.* Minneapolis: Minnesota Research and Evaluation Center, 1981.

Skinner, B. F. *Beyond Freedom and Dignity.* New York: Alfred A. Knopf, 1971.

———. *The Technology of Teaching.* New York: Appleton Century Crofts, 1968.

Subject/Disciplines Orientation

Bruner, Jerome. *The Process of Education.* Cambridge, Mass.: Harvard University, 1960.

Fenton, Edwin. *The New Social Studies.* New York: Holt, Rinehart & Winston, 1967.

Postman, Neil. *Teaching as Conserving Activity,* New York: Delacorte Press, 1979.

Schwab, Joseph. "The Practical: A Language for Curriculum." In David Purpel and Maurice Belanger, eds. *Curriculum and the Cultural Revolution.* Berkeley, Calif.: McCutchan, 1972.

Smith, B. Othanel, William O. Stanley, and J. Harlan Shores. *Fundamentals of Curriculum Development.* New York: Harcourt Brace and World, 1957.

Tanner, Daniel, and Laurel Tanner. *Curriculum Development: Theory into Practice.* New York: Macmillan, 1975.

Social Orientation

Alschuler, Alfred. *School Discipline: A Socially Literate Solution.* New York: McGraw-Hill, 1980.
Bourne, Paula, and John Eisenberg. *Social Issues in the Curriculum.* Toronto: The Ontario Institute for Studies in Education, 1978.
Counts, George. *Dare the Schools Build a New Social Order?* New York: Day, 1932.
Freire, Paulo. *The Pedagogy of the Oppressed.* New York: Herder and Herder, 1972.
Newmann, Fred W. *Education for Citizen Action: Challenge for Secondary Curriculum.* Berkeley, Calif.: McCutchan, 1975.
―――, Thomas Bertocci, and Ruthanne M. Landsness. *Skills in Citizen Action: An English–Social Studies Program for Secondary Schools.* Skokie, Ill.: National Textbook, 1977.
Shaver, James, and William Strong. *Facing Value Decisions: Rationale Building for Teachers.* Belmont, Calif.: Wadsworth, 1976.

Developmental Orientation

Erikson, Erik H. *Childhood and Society.* New York: W. W. Norton, 1963.
―――. *Identity: Youth and Crisis.* New York: W. W. Norton, 1968.
Hersh, Richard, Diana Pritchard Paolito, and Joseph Reimer. *Promoting Moral Growth.* New York: Longman, 1979.
Kohlberg, Lawrence. *Essays on Moral Development: The Philosophy of Moral Development.* New York: Harper and Row, 1981.
Pulaski, Mary. *Understanding Piaget.* New York: Harper and Row, 1971.
Weikart, David, et al. *The Cognitively Oriented Curriculum for Preschool Teachers.* Washington, D.C.: National Association of Young Children, 1971.

Cognitive-Process Orientation

Ausubel, David. *Educational Psychology: A Cognitive View.* New York: Holt, Rinehart & Winston, 1968.
―――. *The Psychology of Meaningful Verbal Learning.* New York: Grune & Stratton, 1963.
Bereiter, Carl. *Must We Educate?* Englewood Cliffs, N.J.: Prentice-Hall, 1972.
de Bono, Edward. *Lateral Thinking: A Textbook of Creativity.* London: Ward Lock Educational Limited, 1970.
Robinson, Floyd G., John Tickle, and David W. Brison. *Inquiry Training: Fusing Theory and Practice.* Toronto: The Ontario Institute for Studies in Education, 1972.
Ross, John A., and Florence Maynes. *Teaching Problem Solving.* Toronto: The Ontario Institute for Studies in Education, 1982.
Taba, Hilda, et al. *Teacher's Handbook for Elementary Social Studies.* Reading, Mass.: Addison-Wesley, 1967.

Humanistic Orientation

Gazda, George, et al. *Human Relations Development: A Manual for Educators.* Boston: Allyn and Bacon, 1973.

Gordon, Thomas. *T.E.T., Teacher Effectiveness Training.* New York: Peter Wyden, 1974.

Maslow, Abraham. *Motivation and Personality.* New York: Harper and Row, 1970.

Miller, John P. *Humanizing the Classroom.* New York: Praeger, 1976.

Purkey, William Watson. *Inviting School Success: A Self-Concept Approach to Teaching and Learning.* Belmont, Calif.: Wadsworth, 1978.

———. *Self Concept and School Achievement.* Englewood Cliffs, N.J.: Prentice-Hall, 1970.

Raths, Louis, Merrill Harmin, and Sidney Simon. *Values and Teaching.* Columbus, Ohio: Charles Merrill, 1978.

Rogers, Carl. *Freedom to Learn.* Columbus, Ohio: Charles Merrill, 1969.

———. *A Way of Being.* Boston: Houghton Mifflin, 1980.

Simpson, Elizabeth Leonie. *Humanistic Education: An Interpretation.* Cambridge, Mass.: Ballinger, 1976.

Weinstein, Gerald, Joy Hardin, and Matt Weinstein. *Education of the Self.* Amherst, Mass.: Mandala, 1976.

Transpersonal Orientation

Brown, George Isaac, Mark Phillips, and Stewart Shapiro. *Getting It All Together: Confluent Education.* Bloomington, Ind.: Phi Delta Kappa Educational Foundation, 1976.

Capra, Fritjof. *The Turning Point.* New York: Simon & Schuster, 1982.

Ferguson, Marilyn. *The Aquarian Conspiracy: Personal and Social Transformation in the 1980's.* Los Angeles: J. P. Tarcher, 1980.

Hendricks, Gay, and James Fadiman, eds. *Transpersonal Education.* Englewood Cliffs, N.J.: Prentice-Hall, 1976.

Hendricks, Gay, and Russell Wells. *The Centering Book.* Englewood Cliffs, N.J.: Prentice-Hall, 1975.

Miller, John. *The Compassionate Teacher.* Englewood Cliffs, N.J.: Prentice-Hall, 1981.

Richards, Mary Caroline. *Toward Wholeness: Rudolph Steiner Education in America.* Middletown, Conn.: Wesleyan University Press, 1980.

Index